Clipped Wings

Clipped Wings

*The Rise and Fall of the Women Airforce
Service Pilots (WASPs) of World War II*

Molly Merryman

NEW YORK UNIVERSITY PRESS

New York and London

NEW YORK UNIVERSITY PRESS
New York and London

© 1998 by New York University

Library of Congress Cataloging-in-Publication Data
Merryman, Molly.
Clipped wings : the rise and fall of the Women Airforce Service
Pilots (WASPs) of World War II / Molly Merryman.
p.   cm.
Includes bibliographical references and index.
ISBN 0-8147-5567-4 (alk. paper)
1. Women's Air Service Pilots (U.S.) 2. World War, 1939-1945—
Participation, Female. 3. Women air pilots—United States—
History. 4. World War, 1939-1945—Aerial operations, American.
I. Title.
D810.W7M44   1997
940.54'4973—dc21   97-21217
                             CIP

New York University Press books are printed on acid-free paper,
and their binding materials are chosen for strength and durability.

Manufactured in the United States of America

10 9 8 7 6 5 4 3 2 1

To the Women Airforce Service Pilots, who recognized the value of their history and worked to preserve it, and who, despite cultural denial for thirty years, maintained their worth, their history, and their identity, giving their all to us.

Contents

Illustrations

All photographs appear as a group following p. 84.

Acknowledgments

This project was made possible by the interests and efforts of many. Those who were involved with my dissertation (the first draft of this book) at Bowling Green State University deserve recognition for their guidance and support. They include my advisor, Ellen Berry, and committee members William Grant, Alberto Gonzalez, and Karen Gould. Arlene Spoores of Women's Studies, Joan Conrad of American Culture Studies, and Carol Davis of Research Services also lent their support and attention to many facets of this project. Recognition also goes to Bowling Green's Graduate College for the Dissertation Support grant and the American Culture Studies program for the non-service fellowship, both of which made research travel possible. I also extend my thanks to the staff and volunteers of the United States Air Force Museum Archives, the Eisenhower Center, the Texas Women's University Archives, and the International Women's Air and Space Museum for maintaining invaluable records on the Women Airforce Service Pilots and for capably and courteously making those records available. I also extend my sincere respect and gratitude to the many WASP veterans I have come to know. I cannot list them all, but one veteran, Marty Wyall, deserves special recognition for the tireless years she devoted to maintaining WASP history and documents. Thanks also to Tom Baumann, my documentary partner and friend, who provided good ideas and didn't mind my asking questions that were of use only for this project during the shooting sessions for *Women Who Flew.* Dave Menard of the Research Division, United States Air Force Museum, Wright-Patterson Air Force Base, deserves mention for his detailed proofreading and expert identification of airplanes and their markings. Ben Urish of Temple University offered an inspiring internet dialogue on cultural history and a thorough proofreading of the first draft. Cheryl Shaw of Kent State University offered her superb typing skills in deciphering three pads of handwritten notes. I want to thank my editors at New York University Press, beginning with associate editor Jennifer Hammer, who has believed in and supported this project since its inception; Despina Papazoglou Gimbel, managing editor; and David Updike, the copyeditor. Finally, I express my dedicated gratitude to my family, without whom none of this would have been possible: my father, Ralph Merryman, whose stories about his experiences in the Army Air Forces China-Burma-India Theater during World War II helped inspire my interest in this topic; my mother, Rose Fulop Merryman, who shared stories about the perspective of women during the war years and who accompanied me during part of my research travels, thus providing me with memories of her I shall forever treasure; and my sister, Rebecca Merryman, who offered emotional support and encouragement.

Abbreviations

AAF	Army Air Forces
ATA	Air Transport Auxiliary
ATC	Air Transport Command
CAA	Civil Aeronautics Administration
CAP	Civilian Air Patrol
VFW	Veterans of Foreign Wars
WAAC	Women's Auxiliary Army Corps
WAAF	Women's Auxiliary Air Force
WAC	Women's Army Corps
WAFS	Women's Auxiliary Ferrying Squadron
WASP	Women's Airforce Service Pilots
WAVES	Women Accepted for Volunteer Emergency Service
WFTD	Women's Flying Training Detachment
WTS	War Training Service

1

Introduction

This book examines the accomplishments and struggles of the Women Airforce Service Pilots (WASPs) of World War II—their service, their premature disbandment, and how they finally got some of the recognition they deserved. The events, perceptions, and opinions that culminated in the disbandment of the WASPs are contextualized within theories of feminist history and gender construction in order to reveal how cultural constructions of gender, specifically assumptions about the roles of women in war, impacted the fate of the 1,074 pilots who served their country as the first women to fly military planes.

The purpose of this book is to provide answers to questions that have been raised for more than fifty years: Why were the WASPs disbanded when there was still a wartime need for their services? Why did the top officials of the Army Air Forces allow the disbandment to occur? Why did Congress, which authorized militarization for the women's branches of the Army, Navy, Marines, and Coast Guard, not only refuse to do so for the WASPs, but also vote to disband the entire program, even while the United States was still fighting a world war?

In order to address these questions and reveal important details about the WASPs, military documents from four archives, many of which were not declassified until the 1980s, were examined. These documents include memorandums and proposals for the program, which began as a top secret initiative; reports from numerous bases at which WASPs served, which detailed their status in a range of missions and offered overall evaluations of the program; and legal treatises that revealed the Army Air Forces' stance on the congressional hearings regarding the militarization of the WASPs. Print media sources, including articles specific to the WASPs as well as wartime issues of popular magazines, were examined to assess how the WASPs and other women in the wartime effort were being presented to and perceived by the public. Congressional records were obtained for 1941 through 1977 to document not only how Congress voted on the WASP issue, but also how it debated and voted on other women's military auxiliaries during and after the war. Finally, women who served as WASPs during World War II were interviewed to confirm documented sources and to obtain firsthand accounts of how the program and its subsequent disbandment impacted their lives. Unfortunately, the key players involved in the development of the WASP program, as well as those behind its disbandment, were deceased before the research for this book began. However, Jacqueline Cochran, the WASP director, and General Henry H. Arnold, Commanding General of the Army Air Forces during World War II, wrote accounts about their involvement with the WASPs, and General Arnold's son, Major Bruce Arnold, provided further insight into his father's opinions about the program during the 1977 congressional hearings that revisited militarizing the WASPs.

The Importance of the WASP Program as a Subject of Historical Inquiry

The historical subject is defined through her relationship with her culture and all that inhabits and constitutes it. Indeed, history is a shifting phenomenon understood only within the contexts of its associations with the various components of its culture. History is a representation of multiple meanings, in which the subject must be assessed with the understanding that it can never truly be discovered. Just as the most detailed road map never looks like the road, the most thorough accounting of a historical subject can never exactly look and respond like the subject it intends to represent.

The study of the WASPs contributes to a gathering of evidence about notions of women and war as well as notions about gender constructions and their enforcement. The WASPs were the first American wartime service unit comprised entirely of women who performed functions traditionally associated with men. WASPs were involved in activities considered both dangerous and adventurous for the men who performed them; thus, a high level of status was associated with their roles and missions.

Although women have been active participants in all wars in which the United States has been involved,[1] and although all branches of the U.S. military had women's auxiliaries in World War II, the WASP program remained unique because all of the women who served were pilots; thus they all served in positions desired and admired by men. Within military hierarchies, the World War II pilot was constructed as the most dashing and desirable among soldiers. The "flyboys" were the elite of the U.S. military. Cinematic and literary productions from the World War II era include a number of representations of the jealousy that infantrymen felt toward military pilots. For example, in Audie Murphy's autobiography *To Hell and Back*, the highly decorated World War II soldier recounts the brawls that occurred in towns near which both infantrymen and pilots were stationed—brawls which Murphy attributed to local women being more attracted to the pilots than they were to the foot soldiers.

During their years of wartime service, the WASPs flew a terrain that was very much a proving ground of masculinity. More than the WACs (Army), WAVES (Navy), Spars (Coast Guard), or Women Marines, the WASPs directly questioned the purportedly natural and expected status of men within the military by serving in one of its most desired roles—desired both because pilots were the elite of the military and because the WASPs were assigned to domestic, noncombat positions, which were the safest flying positions in the Army Air Forces. The WASPs performed missions that were both exciting and valuable. Much of what they did was top secret, and a great deal of it involved risk, such as towing targets at which live ammunition was fired. By taking on roles and missions previously associated with the masculine, WASPs challenged assumptions of male supremacy in wartime culture.

The women in other branches of the military largely served in roles that had been culturally constructed as natural for women. This does not negate the tremendous contribution of American women in these military divisions, but it did temper the threat these female soldiers posed to male soldiers. During World War II, 350,000 women served in the U.S. military,[2] providing necessary and demanding service to their country. Many women served overseas, some of them in combat situations; many were injured; some became prisoners of war; and some were killed. Many women in other branches served in roles generally associated with men, such as truck drivers and mechanics, but the majority served in roles culturally associated with women, such as clerical workers and nurses, thus deflecting attention away from those who served in roles typically associated with men.

All WASPs were pilots or pilot trainees. Therefore, the threat that these women posed to cultural constructions of gender identity can be more clearly assessed than can the threats posed by women in other World War II military branches. Within the WASPs, there were no positions of "women's work" toward which media, congressional, and public attention could be directed. Although women in the other branches served under combat conditions, were injured, and even died in the line of duty, the standing of these female soldiers has been for the most part ignored, erased, or altered to fit the cultural assumptions of the time. The narratives of war capture cultural constructions more than facts. Therefore, more attention was focused on women's roles in the home front than on their participation in the battle front, and the stories of women soldiers were mediated to fit existing and acceptable notions of gender, despite the efforts and dangers that constituted their lives. So while the Women's Army Corps was the largest women's division and included women who went overseas, served as mechanics, and worked with weapons, Army public relations disseminated stories that focused on those WACs based in the continental United States who handled work traditionally associated with women, such as secretaries and sales clerks, and the media featured stories on the feminine touches WACs brought into their barracks, such as curtains and flowers.[3] As a result, the impact that these military women had on cultural assumptions about the constitution of the female soldier was mitigated by constructions from the War Department and the media that feminized military women, tempered the threat posed by women in uniform, and insisted that these were indeed women first and soldiers later.

The WASPs are valuable in analyzing the threat that World War II military women posed to cultural assumptions about the construction of gender because their specific, masculine-valued, and frequently dangerous roles offered no means through which the message could be mediated. Unlike the majority of women serving in the other military branches, the WASPs were not taking on jobs that men did not want to perform. Instead, they were flying the newest and best planes the U.S. military had developed, the fastest fighter planes and heaviest bombers. They test-piloted experimental models and worked in the development of weapons systems. Yet, although the missions performed by the WASPs were often dangerous, they were still safer than the combat missions that men released from domestic duties by the WASPs were sent overseas to perform. Many male pilot trainees came to resent the female pilots for this reason and, in face of being sent overseas, created a significant media and public opinion campaign against the WASP program.

The existence of a military unit populated entirely by female pilots ran counter to popular assumptions regarding the capabilities and limitations of women, and the presence of women as pilots of military planes questioned assumptions of masculinity. Because of this, efforts by the Army Air Forces to militarize the WASPs met fierce resistance. Consequently, the WASP program was the only World War II women's auxiliary that was not militarized. Instead, it was a civilian volunteer group, with members paying for their initial training, transportation, and room and board. Because they were civilian volunteers, WASPs who died in service were not recognized as wartime casualties, and their colleagues often had to raise money among themselves to send their bodies home. Lacking veterans' status after the war, WASPs were unable to participate in the GI bill and other reward programs for veterans. Besides being the only women's auxiliary to be refused militarization over the course of the war, the WASP program was the only nontraining component of the military to be fully disbanded and its personnel sent home before the war was over. The WASPs were disbanded in December 1944, eight months before the war ended.

Previous historical assessments of the WASPs have not adequately answered the question of why these pilots were removed from active service before the war's end, despite the request for their services by the leading officers of the Army Air Forces. It is no small question to ask why a unit of 1,074 women, each trained at a minimum cost of twelve thousand dollars, was demobilized before the end of the war. Previous authors have assumed that the WASPs were disbanded because they were no longer necessary to the war effort; because the WASP director ineptly bungled the program into oblivion; or because conflicts between the two subgroups that constituted the WASPs (the Women's Ferrying Squadron and the Women's Flying Training Detachment) were so strong as to destroy the foundations of the program.[4] These assumptions are not supported by the facts, but instead arise from historians' attempts at establishing a rationale for the demise of the WASPs within the program itself, when the cause is found at the intersection of various cultural constituents in the United States and its military during World War II.

2

The Development of the Women Airforce Service Pilots

From Guarded Experiment to Valuable Support Role

The Women Airforce Service Pilots (WASPs) of World War II performed an essential role in the United States' war effort. The nation's first women pilots of military planes, WASPs flew every model in the Army Air Forces' (AAF) arsenal, including multi-engine bombers, pursuit (fighter) planes, cargo planes, and even the first American military jet planes. "We did whatever we were asked to do to free men for combat—we were very short on combat pilots," recalled WASP Thelma K. Miller.[1]

WASPs flew a variety of missions, including ferrying aircraft from factories to bases; towing targets for gunnery practice; test-piloting new and refurbished planes; flying military personnel; training male pilots; and piloting bombers to train navigators, gunners, and bombardiers. WASP Ethel Finley said: "We were utility pilots. We flew every airplane that the Army Air Corps had at the time. We flew everything but combat. And we flew only in the continental United States and a little bit into Canada. . . . There were so many jobs in the United States that had to be done to release men for combat, and it was never even considered that we fly in combat, although the Russians did have three squadrons of women combat fliers."[2]

Despite the range and difficulty of the missions flown by its pilots, the WASP program maintained civilian status throughout its two-year existence. "We had no insurance. We got $250 a month to fly the most dangerous and heaviest airplanes that were deployed by the United State Air Forces. We had to pay our own board bill; we bought our own uniforms," said WASP Madge Rutherford Minton.[3]

The WASP program arose as a top secret project that was not initially publicized and was not submitted for militarization until "enough experience had been obtained to determine the usefulness of the women pilots."[4] The program had its roots in the formation of two organizations in September 1942 that would later merge to form the WASPs. The first organization was the Women's Auxiliary Ferrying Squadron (WAFS), developed on September 10 and led by pilot Nancy Harkness Love.[5] Initially comprised of ten pilots, the WAFS grew to include twenty-eight pilots by January 1943.[6] On September 12, the Women's Flying Training Detachment (WFTD) was created when AAF Commanding General Henry H. Arnold approved a memorandum from Major General H. L. George of the Air Transport Command requesting a training program for women pilots.[7] General George modeled his request on a program proposed by famous aviator Jacqueline Cochran and suggested that Cochran be named director of the program. Implementation of the training program began three weeks after approval of the memorandum.[8] The two programs consolidated in July 1943,[9] and on August 20, the War Department announced that the title for the women pilots who served with the AAF would be the WASPs or Women Airforce Service Pilots.[10]

The WASP program expanded beyond all initial proposals, both in terms of missions performed and the number of women pilots. This expansion arose from the AAF's need to place all qualified male pilots overseas or into combat positions. In the early stages of the war, the United States suffered significant losses among its air forces and ground troops. Army Air Forces Commanding General Arnold wanted all qualified male pilots released for combat duty, and he wanted to redirect male trainees to the Army's ground forces. The AAF commanders also wanted to see the extent to which women military pilots could be used in the event that the U.S. mainland came under attack. General Arnold put forth three objectives in the formation of the WASPs:

1. To see if women could serve as military pilots, and, if so, to form the nucleus of an organization which could be rapidly expanded.
2. To release male pilots for combat.
3. To decrease the Air Forces' total demands for the cream of the manpower pool.[11]

The WASPs continued to grow until December 1944, when the program was disbanded following congressional opposition. In its two-year existence, the program graduated 1,074 women from Air Forces pilot training, 916 of whom actively served the Army Air Forces.[12] This compares with a total of 190,000 male pilots who served during World War II.[13] The initial class of WASPs was trained at an airfield in Houston, Texas, but the majority of the 1,074 WASP graduates were trained at Avenger Field in Sweetwater, Texas.[14] Avenger Field continues to hold the distinction of being the only military flying school to have been specifically designated for women pilots. WASPs flew a total of 60 million miles in training and missions during the two years that they were operational.[15] They delivered 12,652 planes on domestic ferrying missions[16] and conducted a variety of operational missions at nine air forces and commands.[17] These pilots served in a civilian capacity and thus received no insurance, no military benefits, and no veterans' benefits.[18] Thirty-eight WASPs died in service, twenty-seven in active service and eleven in training.[19] Families of these thirty-eight pilots could not place military service stars in their windows, nor did the WASPs receive military burials. "If we got killed in action our friends passed the hat to get enough money to send our personal effects home to the family. We couldn't have a military internment; we didn't get a flag for the coffin; and we got no burial expenses," Madge Rutherford Minton noted.[20]

The Development of American Military Air Power

The history of the WASPs cannot be realized without understanding the role of the AAF and the struggle Air Forces commanders waged throughout the war to achieve autonomy from the Army. During World War II, the AAF went from being a small army corps with outmoded planes to a military branch so sophisticated and large that it controlled the air worldwide. The WASPs served a small but important role in this expansion, and an important and undervalued role in the Allied victory.

The U.S. Army's use of air power in World War I was extremely limited. Several hundred pilots flew what amounted to little more than observation missions.[21] Attempts at bombing and air-to-air combat were crude, with pilots sometimes employing hand-held guns and amateur explosives. In the years between the two world wars, visionaries within the Army Air Service attempted to convince the United States of the significance air power would have in future wars. These attempts culminated in the 1925 court martial of the assistant chief of the Army Air Service, William "Billy" Mitchell, for his accusations that the War and Navy departments were committing treason for neglecting air power.[22] Mitchell conducted experiments that proved the vulnerability of battleships and ground forces to bombing attacks, yet the War Department, Army, and Navy refused to act upon the results. In 1926, the Army formed the Air Corps, which replaced the Army Air Service. The Air Corps had only a few hundred planes at this time and did not have the budget to conduct research and development of new models. Significant growth and change did not come until the beginning of World War II, when Germany and Japan, future enemies of the United States, proved Mitchell's theories correct.

In September 1938, General Henry "Hap" Arnold was named chief of the Air Corps, which then consisted of 1,650 officers, 16,000 enlisted men, and less than 2,000 planes.[23] The Air Corps trained 300 pilots that year.[24] Soon afterward, President Franklin Delano Roosevelt met with General Arnold to establish plans for expanding the Army Air Corps. This was done in anticipation of the United States's becoming involved in a war with Germany, following Germany's 1938 invasion of Austria and the 1938 Munich agreement, in which European leaders allowed Germany to annex the Czech Sudetenland.[25] Germany had already publicly demonstrated its air superiority in 1937 by destroying Guernica in bombing raids. That same year, Japan had a similar demonstration when it invaded China by air.[26]

Following presidential authorization, General Arnold issued directives that expanded the Air Corps' training programs and increased the number of pilots, enlisted personnel, and planes.[27] These plans called for building 10,000 new planes in 1939 (from 2,200 in 1938) and training 1,200 new pilots (from 300 in 1938).[28] The Army Air Corps continued to expand over the next two years. In June 1941, it became a more autonomous division of the Army, and its name was changed to the Army Air Forces. Immediately before the United States formally entered World War II in December 1941, the AAF expanded to 22,000 officers, 270,000 enlisted men, 9,000 airplanes in the United States and 1,100 planes overseas, of which 3,000 were combat planes.[29]

American factories were mobilized to produce planes for the U.S. military and its allies. In 1942, 47,800 planes were produced; in 1943, 86,000 were produced.[30] To handle the substantial increase in the number of planes built by American factories, the AAF developed a specialized division of pilots and support personnel to handle deliveries of planes and related supplies from factories to bases in the United States and throughout the world. The Air Corps Ferrying Command was established in May 1941, as a result of the Lend-Lease agreement with Britain that promised delivery of thousands of planes overseas.[31] In July 1942, the greatly expanded unit changed its name to the Air Transport Command (ATC), of which the Ferrying Division was one component.[32]

The ATC alone needed more pilots than existed within the entire AAF, so it began a program of hiring civilian pilots to ferry planes. Within six months after the Japanese attack on Pearl Harbor, 3,500 civilian pilots were hired by the ATC, half of whom were later commissioned into the AAF.[33] The other half, which consisted of men who were too old to be commissioned, who did not meet the rigid AAF medical codes, or who declined commissions, remained civilians under the employ of the division but were given draft-deferred status. By the end of the war in 1945, 8,500 pilots from the Ferrying Division of the ATC had delivered 21,092 planes to foreign destinations and made 291,525 domestic deliveries.[34] This number included 141 WASPs who were assigned to the Ferrying Division from September 1942 until December 1944.[35] These women delivered 12,652 planes on domestic missions[36] and flew a total of 9,224,000 miles for the ATC.[37]

The Development of the WASPs

During World War II, many women participated in diverse roles usually reserved for men because of the labor shortages caused by increased factory production and the large deployment of men overseas.[38] Members of the U.S. War Department were also concerned that the country would not have adequate personnel resources to fight and win an extended war. Consequently, both civilian factories and military branches began active recruitment of women. The Army, Navy, Marines, and Coast Guard all recruited for women's divisions of their branches. American allies England and the Soviet Union had also incorporated women into their military, including their air forces. England's Air Transport Auxiliary (ATA) had women pilots who ferried planes under combat conditions, and the Soviet Union formed several battalions of women combat pilots, including bomber units and fighter plane squadrons. The United States, which was less affected than these countries by World War II, did not begin to use women pilots until September 1942, when personnel shortages became problematic: "We anticipated then that global war would require all our qualified men and many of our women," said General Arnold.[39]

During World War I, several female aviators volunteered their services to the Army Air Corps as military pilots but were turned down.[40] In the 1930s, before the United States entered World War II, several famous women proposed that the United States incorporate women pilots into their pilot pool; among them were famous aviator Amelia Earhart and First Lady Eleanor Roosevelt, who continued to support this suggestion in her "My Day" newspaper column until the WASPs formed in 1942. Official AAF reports also reveal that the idea of using women pilots arose within the military in the late 1930s and early 1940s, before any formal proposals were submitted by either Love or

Cochran.[41] General Arnold initially rejected the idea of using women pilots because the most significant problem affecting the AAF in the years before the war was a lack of planes, not of pilots. In a memorandum dated August 25, 1941, Arnold wrote: "The use of women pilots serves no military purpose."[42] When the United States entered the war in December 1941, there were still more pilots than planes, and there was also a great need to train all available pilots for combat. In addition to these tactical reasons, General Arnold also had significant doubts about the abilities of women to fly military planes. "Frankly, I didn't know in 1941 whether a slip of a young girl could fight the controls of a B-17 in the heavy weather they would naturally encounter in operational flying."[43]

In 1941, 2,100 American women had pilot's licenses,[44] a number that increased to 3,000 by 1943.[45] Some of these women obtained their licenses through Civilian Pilot Training Program schools, which provided affordable flight training at universities nationwide, giving middle- and lower-class people the opportunity to obtain pilot's licenses, thereby increasing the pool of available pilots in the United States.[46] Because Civilian Pilot Training Program bylaws did not specify gender, women were able to take pilot training as well as the men the program had been created to train. However, women were not always welcomed into these classes.

In 1942, two separate formal proposals regarding the use of women pilots in the military were submitted by Nancy Harkness Love and Jacqueline Cochran to the AAF. In previous accounts of the WASPs and the Ferrying Division (for example, Captain Marx's "official" WASP history and books by Byrd Howell Granger and Jean Hascall Cole), much attention has been focused on whose idea it was initially to establish a women's program in the AAF, with many accounts constructing the proposal process as a rivalry between Cochran (who directed the WFTDs and the WASPs) and Love (who directed the WAFS). There is no substantiation for this counterproductive construction. Both Cochran and Love submitted formal proposals regarding the use of women pilots by the AAF, and both had written memorandums to various military leaders in the years before U.S. involvement in the war in which they articulated the valuable contribution women pilots could make in the event of a national emergency. Neither pilot can be or should be credited with developing the idea of U.S. military use of women pilots. Indeed, these adversarial constructions only represent the negative cultural images of powerful women at that time.

The proposals submitted by Cochran and Love had distinct mission plans, which resulted in each being submitted to a different section of the AAF. Love, a renowned pilot who also was married to Colonel Robert Love of the AAF's

Ferrying Division, proposed the development of a small squad of women pilots specifically to ferry aircraft from factories to AAF bases, both in the United States and overseas. Love proposed that these pilots have a minimum of five hundred hours flying time and that they be used by the Ferrying Division exclusively.[47]

In April 1942, Love and Lieutenant Colonel Tunner, who was then commander of the AAF Ferrying Command, discussed Love's proposal.[48] In July 1942, the Ferrying Command expanded into the Air Transport Command, which included the Ferrying Division.[49] The ATC's expansion resulted from the AAF's need to transport planes to other nations as part of the Lend-Lease program, as well as to handle the transportation of planes and related supplies to military divisions.[50] Tunner approved Love's proposal and sent it to General George in June, who gave final approval to the plan.[51] In July, the proposal reached General Arnold, who replied that "prior to doing anything further along this line, it is desired that you confer with the CAA [Civil Aeronautics Administration] . . . with a view of securing every possible pilot from that source."[52]

Following General George's approval of the proposal, Love assembled twenty-eight pilots, who were required to have a minimum of five hundred hours flying time, cross-country experience, commercial licenses, high school educations, American citizenship, and be between the ages of twenty-one and thirty-five.[53] Pilots accepted into the program then received four weeks of transition training at New Castle Army Air Base near Wilmington, Delaware.[54] Transition training was not pilot training; it involved lessons specific to flying various military planes, including AAF regulations for takeoffs, landings, taxiing, and so on, and dealt extensively with the regulations involved with delivering planes, such as filling out forms and the procedures involved in maintaining the secrecy of war planes. Although their squadron was a division of the ATC, the WAFS had civilian status. The use of civilian pilots was a common arrangement with the Ferrying Division, which had also hired 3,500 male civilian pilots in the six months following Pearl Harbor.[55] For their flying services in the division, WAFS received $250 per month and a $6 per diem fee when away from their base.

Before the development of the WAFS, Jacqueline Cochran had submitted several proposals for a more expansive women's pilot program, which included the training of women pilots. She submitted her first proposal to Colonel Robert Olds of the Ferrying Command in July 1941, which called for the implementation of a squadron of civilian women pilots to handle all aircraft ferrying operations.[56] This was followed in 1942 by a more detailed proposal she submitted to General Arnold. Recognizing the limited number of women pilots with enough flight time to ferry planes with only transition training, Cochran proposed developing a division of women pilots to be trained by the AAF. She envisioned these pilots handling more than ferrying missions and proposed that eventually women pilots could handle all domestic military flights, thus releasing all male AAF pilots to fly overseas and in combat. In her 1941 proposal, Cochran had recommended that the women be civilians; after the WAFS and WFTDs were formed, however, Cochran and key military advisers realized the importance of having the pilots militarized and began to research the best possibilities for doing so.

Cochran proposed an air school for women pilots that would incorporate the same coursework received by male air cadets. Initially, pilots trained at this school would handle ferrying missions, although Cochran predicted that these women could also be used in nearly all domestic piloting applications. Cochran had first suggested that the AAF use women pilots in 1938, when she sent a memorandum to General Arnold. Arnold rejected this proposal because the need at this time was to train male pilots for combat. In anticipation of the entry of the United States into World War II, Cochran resubmitted her proposal to Arnold in the fall of 1941. Because he believed that the use of women pilots would soon be a necessity, and because he desired more information about the potential and possible limitations of women pilots, Arnold approved a request made by the British Air Commission to have Cochran recruit and direct a group of American women pilots to transport planes for the British Air Transport Auxiliary.[57] In the spring of 1942, Cochran and twenty-five women pilots went to England to join the ATA. The pilots were given eighteen-month contracts, while Cochran was issued a contract that would dissolve at the point the AAF called upon her services. She would return to the United States in less than six months.

While Cochran was in England, Love, at the request of Tunner, submitted her proposal for a small ferrying squad of previously trained women pilots. Following the establishment of the WAFS, Arnold requested that Cochran return to the United States to implement the training program she had proposed earlier. Upon Cochran's return to the United States in September 1942, Arnold appointed her director of the WFTD.[58] Within days, Cochran began interviewing candidates for acceptance into the WFTD program. The initial goal of the WFTD was to supply trained pilots exclusively for service in the WAFS. Except for the original group, all other members of the WAFS would have to be processed through the WFTD, following an order that came from AAF Headquarters in February 1943.

WASP Recruitment

Unlike the women's auxiliaries of all other military branches, the WASP program never had to establish a recruitment campaign. "The program attracted people who were willing to venture being different and to risk following the dream that they always had," said WASP Ethel Finley.[59] Relying only on personal invitations from Cochran and Love, casual conversations among female pilots, and occasional articles that appeared on the program, more than 25,000 women applied for acceptance into the WASP program, the vast majority of whom were eliminated in the first stage of processing because they did not meet the minimum flight requirements.[60] Yet, at "no time during the operation of the program was any effort necessary to secure prospective trainees, as there were always several hundred applicants on the waiting list."[61]

WASP Madge Rutherford Minton said that she and many other women pilots were motivated to join because they wanted "to see this war through and get it ended. There were thousands and thousands of women working in war plants, and every one of them was patriotic, and they were doing a job to help win the war. And the WASP also was a working woman."[62] Katherine (Kaddy) Landry Steele, another WASP, recalled, "World War II was different, it was a situation that welded us all together—men, women, and children, from all the different countries—and soon it was such a big thing, and to be a part of something that big, that important, that really set the world on the course that it later followed, is pretty important."[63]

Most trainees gave up more lucrative jobs to begin WASP training, and many sold their homes and businesses on the gamble that they would pass training and become WASPs.[64] Out of the 1,830 women accepted into the WFTD, 1,076 women graduated from WASP training.[65] Because of their civilian status, those accepted into the program had to provide their own transportation to the training bases in Texas.[66]

The backgrounds and experiences of the pilots who joined the WASP program varied substantially. As Minton noted, "The WASPs were women from all walks of life and all economic levels in the United States. We had millionaires, and we had very poor girls who worked very hard just to buy flight time. But they had one thing in common, and that was the love of flying. They were determined to fly, and they saw this opportunity to fly for our country and help win World War II."[67] Finley said, "We came from all walks of life. Many were teachers. We had everything from teachers to a Ziegfeld Follies girl, clerks, secretaries, office workers—every walk of life. But I think underneath all of it was this kind of special characteristic of the love of flying, of patriotism and also the spirit of adventure"[68]

An interest in flying and feelings of patriotic duty seem to have been the uniting principles among WASP trainees. "Flying was a very glamorous thing to do then," said WASP Clarice Bergemann. "It had a lot to do with the movies, but flying was the most exciting thing you could do."[69] "I was in college, getting a B.A. in sociology and bacteriology," said WASP Marty Wyall. "I was going to go to graduate school, but I saw that the WASPs were recruiting. I wanted to drop out, but my father wouldn't let me. So I graduated in May, soloed in August and had thirty-five hours [of flying time] by October. I loved to fly."[70] Nadine Nagle's reason for joining the WASPs was much more personal: "In the summer of 1942, my husband [a B-24 pilot] was killed on a mission in England. I read an article on the women pilots the next month. I got this patriotic feeling that I was to fly in his place." Nagle also noted that she "specifically took flying lessons because of this dramatic experience."[71]

Once they graduated from training, WASPs had civilian Civil Air Patrol (CAP) status. Their salary was $150 per month during training and $250 per month afterwards.[72] Out of this wage, WASPs had to pay for their own housing, food, clothing, transportation, and so on. They were, however, issued textbooks, flying clothes, helmets, goggles, and parachutes.[73] WASPs did not receive the same salary as male CAP pilots. WASPs earned $3,000 per year, while CAP pilots earned $3,600.[74]

To be accepted into the WASP training program, women pilots had to meet minimum requirements and pass a personal interview that was conducted by Cochran or one of her personal assistants. Because it was a civilian auxiliary group, there were no regulated requirements for the interview processes, and because of the experimental nature of the program, Cochran was very concerned about the image of the WASPs. The evaluation and interview processes were therefore very subjective and critical. The guidelines were "a matter of choosing clean-cut, stable appearing young girls,"[75] women who best fit the image of the WASPs as Cochran determined it to be. Because of the subjective nature of this process, we can infer that certain groups of women were likely excluded from the WASPs; without existing documentation, however, we do not know the extent to which an individual's class background or perceived sexual orientation determined acceptance or rejection. We do know that this subjective screening process had a detrimental impact on black women, whom Cochran removed from consideration. (Not all WASPs were white, however; two Chinese-American women were accepted into the program.)[76]

Because the application records of the WASPs have been destroyed, the number of black women who applied for WASP training is not known. We do know that several black women were rejected at the final interview stage. Cochran wrote this about the WASP policy on black pilots and the interview process:

> The so-called Negro question was laid on my doorstep in a very direct way early in the women pilots' training program. Several Negro girls applied for training but never more than one at a time out of the thousands of applicants. I interviewed these particular applicants in proper order without prejudice or preference, hardly knowing what I could do at that stage of my program if any one of them had passed the preliminaries. Fortunately for the formative stages of the work none met all the specifications. Finally one, a New Jersey school teacher who was a pilot and a fine physical specimen, made application for acceptance as a student at Sweetwater. I asked her to join me for breakfast on a Sunday morning in my New York apartment and made a special trip to New York for the purpose. I told her the manifold troubles I was having getting the program started and ended by stating that I had no prejudice whatever with respect to the color or race of my candidates but that the complication she had brought up for decision might, for one reason or another, prove the straw that would break the camel's back. This fine young Negro girl recognized the force and honesty of my arguments, stated that first of all the women pilots' program should be stabilized and strengthened, and she withdrew her application. She also saw to it, I believe, that I was left alone thereafter so far as this particular issue was concerned. I appreciate her understanding and respected her as a person.[77]

It should be noted that Cochran was not acting in a uniquely prejudiced fashion, but was following standards common in the U.S. military at this time. Unfortunately, racial discrimination extended throughout the AAF and all other branches of the American military. Despite the achievements of several black male pilots in World War I and other battlefields in the early part of the twentieth century, the AAF did not accept black pilots.[78] It was not until pressure was put on the military, organized largely by the black media, that the Air Forces began to allow black pilots, and then only in racially segregated squadrons. During World War II, the AAF assembled only two groups of black pilots: the 332nd Fighter Group, which consisted of the 99th, 100th, 301st, and 302nd fighter squadrons; and the 477th (medium) Bombardment Group, which consisted of the 616th, 617th, 618th, and 619th bomb squadrons.[79] The 99th Squadron, formed on January 16, 1941, has the distinction of being the first squadron of black pilots.[80] Members of this squadron are also known as the Tuskegee Airmen, after the Tuskegee Institute, the school at which they were first trained. Both groups suffered from documented discrimination, controversy, undue and unfair attention, and bad publicity, despite the pilots distinguishing themselves both domestically and overseas in battle with the Germans toward the end of the war.[81]

The Women's Flying Training Detachment

The Women's Flying Training Detachment received official approval on September 15, 1942,[82] and on October 7, a plan was developed proposing that the first WFTD class begin on November 15 at an air school near Houston, Texas.[83] The school was run by a civilian contractor, Aviation Enterprises. The AAF had begun using civilian contractors to train its military pilots in 1940 in order to reach its expanded goals for pilot training.[84] General Arnold developed this idea when a goal of training 100,000 pilots was established, a number that the AAF could not train internally. (In 1939, the AAF had trained only 750 pilots.) The only way to reach the new goal was to offer civilian contracts to private air schools; otherwise, the AAF would have needed to induct and train pilots to become instructors—a process that would have taken many years.[85]

Among the requirements proposed for WASP trainees were pilot's licenses and a minimum of seventy-five hours flight time,[86] which was lowered to thirty-five hours in 1943. In contrast, male pilot trainees did not need pilot's licenses or any flight experience to be accepted into flight training.

Because of the short amount of time between the proposal for the school and the date the first class began at Houston, site preparation was incomplete,[87] with necessary equipment for teaching night flying and navigation, such as Link trainers, lacking. (The Link trainer was one of the first flight simulators. It was designed to simulate blind flying, which is when the pilot relies solely on navigational instruments to pilot the plane. These skills were dangerous to learn in real flight but were necessary for night flying and for flying in bad weather.)

The problems with the site did not improve, and on January 30, 1943, a report was filed with the AAF Central Flying Training Command stating that "no dormitories or housing facilities exist for the students in the vicinity and they are being housed in tourist camp cottages at several scattered locations in the outskirts of the city and transported by bus both ways. The morale and enthusiasm of these girls under existing conditions is remarkable."[88]

On February 6, 1943, the previously established goal of graduating 396 women pilots that year doubled to a goal of 750 graduates.[89] As a result, the

AAF Central Flying Training Command began to search for other training sites. A suitable site was found at Avenger Field in Sweetwater, Texas, and a second WFTD school began. A training program for male transport pilots, run by Plosser-Prince Air Academy, already existed at this site. The first class for women pilots at Avenger Field began while male pilots were still in training, but the decision was made to phase out the male trainees and create an exclusively female flight school.[90] Aviation Enterprises opposed opening this second school, stating that the WFTD program would be "best operated and produce a more standard product" if only one contractor led training, an opinion the Central Flying Training Command believed was influenced by the director of Aviation Enterprises being "fearful of eventual loss of his own contract."[91]

The first class of women pilots entered Avenger Field on February 21, 1943, with classes being directed by Plosser-Prince Air Academy. Then, on March 10, the AAF Central Flying Training Command decided not to renew Plosser-Prince's contract because federal grand jury had indicted the company on charges of fraud in January 1943. At this point, Central Flying Training Command decided to move Aviation Enterprises and all WFTD training to Avenger Field. This move was made possible by Plosser-Prince agreeing to transfer its lease of Avenger Field and to sell all training equipment on the site to Aviation Enterprises.[92]

Curriculum and Flight Training

The program of instruction implemented by the WFTD in November 1942 put forth four general objectives:

1. Academic instruction in technical objects, proficiency which is required in ferrying training type aircraft.
2. Instruction in the fundamental principles required to pilot training type aircraft.
3. Training in accepted procedures of the Air Transport Command.
4. Physical training to maintain and improve physical and mental alertness.[93]

The first training program was twenty-two and a half weeks long and consisted of 115 hours of flight training, twenty hours of Link training, five hours of physical training each week, and 180 hours of academic instruction in five topics: navigation, weather, aircraft and engines, communications, and ATC procedures.[94] As with male pilot training, the WASPs' program of instruction underwent many changes throughout the war years. In January 1943, flight training was divided into three phases—primary, basic, and advanced; academic instruction was expanded to 230 hours, with mathematics, physics, and seven hours of military instruction added; and physical training was increased to six hours a week.[95] Physical training included calisthenics and muscle-building, with particular attention to increasing upper body strength. It should be noted that military planes in World War II did not have the technological assists of contemporary planes. Tremendous leg strength was needed to control rudders (especially in four-engine bombers), and significant arm strength was needed to control the wheel. Nagle said, "We really flew these planes—they were flown by manual movements, not technology. We manhandled those planes, if you will."[96]

Throughout 1943, the length of the training program increased. The last major change in training came in October, when training was increased to twenty-seven weeks, which was divided into three nine-week phases. Flight instruction was increased to 210 hours (from 180 hours),[97] and sixty-six hours of military training was included.[98] Academic instruction also increased substantially, to 309 hours. Instruction now comprised twelve topics: mathematics; physics; maps, charts, and aerial photography; navigation; aircraft and principles of flight; engines and propellers; weather; code practice; instruments; forms and procedures; pilots' information file; and communications.[99] The only appreciable change in the training program in 1944 was that each section of flight training increased from nine to ten weeks.[100]

Pilots entering WASP training already had pilot's licenses and experience flying civilian planes. The purpose of AAF flight training was for cadets to learn how to fly the military's single- and dual-engine planes and to learn military flying regulations and techniques. The first WFTD school near Houston lacked adequate training planes, especially cross-country and instrument training planes.[101] The move to Avenger Field not only brought better facilities, but also more and newer planes.[102] When the WFTD school in Houston opened in November 1942, there were only thirteen training planes available,[103] and when it closed in February 1943, it had 133 airplanes.[104] When the school at Avenger Field opened the same month, it had ninety-five planes, but it consistently averaged two hundred training planes in 1943 and 1944.[105] Betty Stagg Turner, graduate of the ninth WASP class of 1944, sent her parents in Columbus, Ohio, postcard pictures of her training planes. On May 15, 1944, she sent a postcard of a PT-19 (primary trainer), on which was printed an airplane insignia and the words "Lets go! U.S.A. Keep 'em flying. Uncle

Sam needs pilots."[106] On that postcard she wrote: "This is what I fly. Pretty neat huh! I really like them they're smooth. I've got about 53 hours left to fly in them, then to AT6's . . . will write to you as soon as I get a chance."[107] After she graduated to the AT-6 (advanced trainer), she sent a photo postcard of a BT-13 plane and the message: "This is the Basic Trainer I will fly after I finish my training in the AT6 the one I sent Mom. I'll take my instrument training on this ship. This is a 450 h.p., the AT6 is a 650 h.p. Will start on AT6 June 1. Will send you some picture[s] later."[108]

WFTD flight training varied only slightly from the training male AAF cadets received. The women received more navigational training but no gunnery training and less formation flight training and aerobatics—though still enough aerobatics (such as spins, loops, and stalls) to "be able to recover from any position."[109] In 1942, the flight training program began with dual flights in a basic trainer, followed by solo flights in the same trainer. Introductions to instrument training and lessons in day and night navigation were followed by day and night flights in an advanced single-engine combat trainer. The program concluded with day and night flights in a twin-engine trainer.[110]

Coursework and flight training changed throughout the WFTD's existence in response to missions being performed by the graduating WASPs. The first classes of WFTD trainees were placed in the WAFS following graduation. Beginning in September 1943, training and missions were extended to include target towing, glider towing, radar calibration flights, copiloting bombers, and flying bombardier training missions.[111]

A typical weekday for WASP trainees extended from 6:00 A.M. until 10:00 P.M., beginning with the cleaning of barracks for inspection, followed by a march to breakfast, then a day divided among calisthenics, marching and drill training, ground school classes, and flight training, with evenings reserved for study.[112] "It was very hard. I trained in Texas from May through December. It was very hot—the only relief you got was when you got in a cockpit and got off the ground. . . . You all held each other up—everyone was moral support for each other," recalled Miller.[113]

Even though they belonged to a civilian auxiliary, WASP trainees were subject to military regulations and procedures, and many trainees had joined the program in anticipation of its being militarized, like the Women's Army Corps, which had also begun as a civilian auxiliary. "We were all there for one purpose: To learn to fly the military way," Nagle said. "All of our training was geared toward the military. It was exactly the same as the men's, except they had more navigation and less aerobatics, which the men used for practicing dogfights."[114]

WASP Assignments

Following graduation from Avenger Field, WASPs were assigned to a number of AAF bases in the continental United States. Like male AAF cadets, they received additional specialized transitional training tailored to their individual assignments and the types of planes to be flown at these bases. No standard provisions were made for housing or feeding WASPs, and problems arose over these issues at some bases.[115] Few bases were large enough to provide accommodations for the WASPs. Some bases housed them with base nurses or WACs,[116] while others housed them at local hotels or civilian barracks.[117] Bases also ran into difficulties in determining where WASPs could dine. WASPs often flew missions with AAF pilots, who were officers, yet were not allowed to eat in some of the officers' messes. Bases varied in their regulations about where WASPs could take their meals. Most allowed WASPs into the officers' messes, while others restricted WASPs to WACs' or nurses' messes, or to civilian base cafeterias and local restaurants.[118]

Problems surrounding accommodations and eating were often a significant issue for WASPs on ferrying missions, particularly in the first year of their existence, when bases and airports were less familiar with them. Cross-country flights sometimes took several days to complete, and WASPs would often land at bases and airports where personnel were hostile or unsure about how to accommodate them. Many WASPs encountered problems not only with finding overnight accommodations and food, but also in obtaining permission to land and receive plane maintenance. Because the WASP program had been developed with little publicity, many base personnel did not know about it, and they refused to believe that these women were pilots. WASPs were often confused with civilian stewardesses or passengers, while some were refused service at local restaurants because they wore pants. Several even told of being arrested or detained by military base police, who believed they were impersonating soldiers or stealing planes.[119] Because of some of the problems that arose, many WASPs who ferried planes were ordered not to wear their uniforms. "When we returned to base," Madge Rutherford Minton recalled, "we couldn't wear our uniforms, but we carried a little card. And if we were going back to pick up another airplane for another delivery, this little card gave us the power to bump anybody in the nation off of a commercial airline except for members of the President's cabinet and the President himself. I only had to use it once."[120] WASPs also would find that acceptance for them varied at different bases. "The reception at no two fields is alike. Sometimes the girls are accepted without question into a fraternity that respects a good pilot regardless of sex, but often enough the atmosphere is considerably more chilly than it is upstairs."[121]

The majority of WASPs report that they received positive treatment from male AAF members. "Most C.O.'s [commanding officers] appreciated the WASPs and our abilities to perform difficult jobs well," said Wyall.[122] In final base reports, an overwhelming majority rated WASP performances as exemplary and indicated that WASPs and male AAF pilots and personnel worked together well. The final report from Blytheville AAF base noted that the "WASPS have been accepted by the military personnel in a very commendable manner as a part of the army."[123] A report commissioned by the AAF to assess the "experiment" of women as pilots was less enthusiastic, determining only that at "most of the stations no serious problems were created by the sex of the WASPs."[124] The final report from Buckingham AAF base was more enthusiastic: "Buckingham Field was sorry to lose their WASPS. The men on the line and the air crew members who helped keep the gunnery missions operating, had grown to respect the blue WASP uniform and also had grown to admire the women who wore those colors. A more enviable record could not have been left."[125]

However, some detachments were not receptive to having WASPs stationed with them, and at least one base was investigated and charged with discriminating against the WASPs stationed there.[126] Treatment ranged from commanding officers who requested that WASPs be sent elsewhere, to teasing, abusive remarks, and even sabotage. Women pilots who brought planes into airfields to which WASPs had not flown before sometimes experienced difficulties in getting permission to land. However, the most common negative treatment that WASPs described was being ignored. "Nobody spoke to us from the time we landed until the time we left. We walked into the Operations office, checked in, and still we were met only with an air of hostile resentment."[127] One AAF report noted that resentment by male pilots occurred "where the WASP's were flying 'heavier' or 'faster' ships than the ones the male pilots were flying."[128]

Captain Bob Morgan (retired) said that such resentment was limited to pilots stationed in the United States. Morgan was the pilot of the "Memphis Belle," the first American B-24 to survive its full mission tour, which was in England. (After completing their tour of duty, Morgan and his crew were brought to the United States for a motivational tour.) Morgan said that combat pilots knew firsthand that there was a shortage of combat pilots, and they appreciated the efforts of the WASPs. "The importance was that it relieved us to go off to do our combat duties and not have to ferry airplanes all over the country or test them after they were repaired—and that was very important because we were short of pilots, and we needed all the combat pilots we could possible have, and these gals could fly anything we could fly."[129]

WASP Missions

Airplane ferrying was the initial mission for which WASPs were created, and it would occupy nearly half of all active WASP graduates when the program ended in December 1944.[130] Planes produced in the United States needed to be flown from the factories to air bases at home, in Canada, and overseas. To handle this transportation demand, the ATC hired thousands of male civilian pilots to ferry planes. These male pilots were later commissioned directly into the AAF if they met the requirements and desired commissioning.[131] The WASPs were brought on as ferrying pilots, and by the time they were disbanded in December 1944, they had delivered 12,652 planes on domestic missions.[132] By that time, 141 WASPs were assigned to the ATC.[133] Although they comprised a small percentage of the total Ferrying Division pilots, WASPs had a significant impact. By 1944, WASPs were ferrying the majority of all pursuit planes and were so integrated into the Ferrying Division that their disbandment caused delays in pursuit deliveries.[134]

The days of ferrying pilots were long and unpredictable. At bases that handled a range of planes, pilots did not know from one day to the next what planes they would be flying or how long of a flight to expect. In Minton's words, "We usually reported to the flight line at seven o'clock in the morning and looked at the board to see what had been assigned us in the way of an airplane, where it went and what we would need in the way of equipment to take along, and then we would go out to find our airplane and sign it out at operations and check it over to be sure everything was okay with the airplane. And then we would take off to wherever the plane was supposed to go."[135]

Ferrying military aircraft during World War II was not an easy task. The majority of these planes were not equipped with radios, so pilots navigated by comparing air maps with physical cues (highways, mountains, rivers, etc.) or by flying the beam. (The "beam" was a radio transmission of Morse code signals. A grid of such beams was established across the United States. To follow the beam, a pilot would listen on her headphone for aural "blips" or tones to direct her. This required a great deal of concentration and was not always accurate.) Both navigational techniques were difficult, and this was compounded by the facts that many air bases and factories were camouflaged, blackouts were maintained in coastal areas, and the navigational beams were prone to breaking down. Problems sometimes arose with the planes themselves, which had been tested at the factories but never flown. Cross-continental flights often took several days, depending on the planes being flown and weather conditions.

In addition, planes equipped with top secret munitions or accessories had to be guarded while on the ground, and WASPs received orders to protect these planes at all cost. WASPs flying these planes were issued .45 caliber pistols and were trained to fire machine guns.[136]

WASPs had to be highly skilled pilots to handle ferrying missions. The planes they ferried ranged from the primary and secondary trainers they had flown at Avenger Field to fast single-engine pursuit planes (fighter planes), two-engine and four-engine bombers, and two-engine cargo planes. "I flew BT-13s and AT-6s; I flew C-47s and C-46s, and I also road the copilot's seat in the B-17s," said Minton.[137] The planes flown by the Ferrying Division were made by many different manufacturers, which meant they had different equipment and controls, speeds, maneuverability, weight, altitude ranges, take-off and landing techniques and distances, and emergency procedures.

Although the WASP program was initially formed to ferry airplanes, by 1944 less than half of all active WASPs were ferrying planes.[138] WASPs flew a wide variety of missions: they served as engineering test pilots, which included flying planes that had crashed and been repaired; they towed targets at which live ammo was fired;[139] they trained ground crews in searchlights and tracking by flying night missions; they towed gliders; they conducted flight instruction; and they performed top secret missions, including participating in the atomic bomb project, testing anti-radar devices, and flying bombers with the then-classified Norden bombsight.[140]

Cross-country navigational skills were also a necessity for WASPs who flew administrative flights, which involved transporting military and governmental personnel between bases. As their reputation grew, WASPs were in demand by AAF officers, who found them to be more reliable and consistent than the male civilian pilots.[141] Nadine Nagle piloted administrative flights and found navigation to be the most demanding yet interesting aspect of these missions. "It wasn't easy like today. You flew the beams or followed lights along the way. You don't have many landmarks in Texas to fly off of." Nagle also noted that WASPs were in demand for administrative flights: "They said it was because we didn't carry our little black books into towns, so we were on time, but I never saw male pilots missing appointments."[142] Arnold's written account of WASPs also mentions the male pilots' black books: "It was common for commanding officers to say they would rather have WASPs ferry airplanes across the United States than male pilots, because the WASP normally reached her destination a day or two ahead of the time required by a male pilot to do the same job. When pressed for reasons, the answer usually given was that the WASP didn't carry an address book with her."[143]

Although combat was the only area of military flight that WASPs were prohibited from, they did serve vital roles in training male soldiers for combat missions. For example, WASP bomber crews piloted planes pulling targets at which live anti-aircraft ammunition was fired from ground cannons. Pulling targets required precision maneuvers, because pilot error was likely to result in the plane being shot down. Even the best pilots faced the possibility of having their plane, rather than the target, shot. Kaddy Steele recalled: "You couldn't help but realize the danger, but we had a lot of confidence that the people who were doing the training were in control of what was going on, and by and large they were. But because everybody's human, and there's always human errors, there was a definite margin of error, especially in the low-altitude missions, where we were towing sleeves, because sometimes they would get overexuberant when they were firing the guns. But there were incidents where the airplanes were shot, and there were incidents where the airplanes were shot down, but not at our base."[144]

WASPs were also recruited to assist with bomber crew training, which meant piloting bombers while male combat trainees practiced as bombardiers, navigators, and gunners. They flew simulated strafing missions and dropped tear gas and other chemical agents in order to train ground troops.[145] Again, these training missions required precision and involved mock combat situations. Steele flew such missions:

> I was stationed at Biggs Field, El Paso, in an air-to-ground gunnery station, and we flew B-25s, B-26s, P-47s, AT-10s, SPDs, SP2CSs, BT-13s. We had a lot of different kinds of airplanes because we had a lot of kinds of missions.
>
> We had target-towing and radar-tracking missions. Then we had strafing missions, where we would go down and simulate strafing the troops as they would be strafed in a combat situation, and we had gassing missions, where we would gas the troops with tear gas, so they could practice using their masks—putting them on in a hurry.[146]

WASPs did not receive aerobatics training at Avenger Field because these techniques were only used by fighter pilots. However, WASPs whose missions included training pursuit plane combat pilots would later learn those techniques, so that they could practice dogfights with combat trainees. Clarice

Bergemann flew an AT-26 that pulled targets for P-46 pilots to practice dogfighting. "They used cameras, so they had on film how well they did," she said, noting that WASPs at other bases were fired on with live ammunition. "It was pretty boring: you were given the area and you flew figure-eight patterns all morning and all afternoon long. It was exact flying, not interesting flying."[147]

Base commanders sometimes used the competition that male pilots exhibited toward WASPs to the advantage of a given mission. For example, when pilots would refuse to fly a certain plane because of a known or supposed crash record, WASPs would be assigned to fly that plane at a number of bases to cajole the men into flying it as well. The four-engine B-29, which was the biggest and heaviest plane in the AAF, was one such plane. Colonel Paul Tibbets (who would later lead the B-29 formation that dropped the atomic bomb on Hiroshima) used WASPs to win over pilots who felt that the plane was too big to fly safely.[148] Tibbets subsequently used WASPs for top secret missions involved with the Manhattan project.[149]

WASPs were also used to demonstrate the safety of the B-26 Marauder, a plane that fearful pilots had taken to calling the B-26 "Murderer." The *Martin City Star* covered one such flight. In an article titled "Sugar and Spice! B-26 Gentle as Lamb in Hands of WASPS," the author pointed out that the bomber was not dangerous and difficult to fly because twelve WASPs regularly piloted it for anti-aircraft crews' gunnery practice. The piece concluded that the "announcement of young women flying the Marauder is the second piece of overwhelming evidence that proves this Martin bomber is NOT a tough plane to fly."[150]

WASP Performance

Records indicate that WASPs performed their duties slightly better than their male counterparts. Statistics from AAF Headquarters in 1944 revealed pilot error percentages at .001 for WASPs, versus .007 for male pilots.[151] The fatal accident rate for WASPs was .060 per 1,000 hours, or one fatal accident for every 16,667 hours flown, while the fatal accident rate for domestic, noncombat male pilots was .062 per 1,000 hours.[152]

Despite the low accident rates, thirty-eight of the 1,830 WASP trainees and active pilots died in service to their country.[153] Those who died received no burial expenses or even recognition. "We did, most unfortunately, lose thirty-eight of our number, some of them in ferrying planes, some of them in testing planes, a couple in towing targets, and there was one case of sabotage, where a man who didn't really feel that women had any business in a cockpit put sugar in a gas tank, and it didn't run very well, and she crashed," said Minton.[154]

Additionally, according to a report from Bryan Army Air Field, the "percentage of sick calls made by WASPs was lower in proportion to their number than the male pilots."[155] This contradicted early assumptions of medical personnel that women pilots would be grounded more frequently than male pilots because of menstruation, a factor that (after considerable study) was found to have no impact upon women pilots.[156]

Beyond these statistics are the reports and letters of commendation that arose from every base at which WASPs were stationed. Hundreds of WASPs received formal commendation from base commanders. Among the awards received by WASPs were the Air Medal awarded to WAFS founder Nancy Harkness Love and Barbara Erickson of the Air Ferrying Squadron, and the Distinguished Service Medal awarded to Jacqueline Cochran.[157] The consensus of AAF reports from all bases where WASPs served was that "women can fly as well as men."[158] These reports had tremendous impact upon the future establishment of women pilots both in and out of the military. WASPs proved, under careful study, that women could fly all military planes. Further, as General Arnold wrote, their "very successful record of accomplishment has proved that in any future total effort the nation can count on thousands of its young women to fly any of its aircraft."[159]

The official recognition of WASP accomplishments by the military meant greater recognition for women's roles in wartime efforts. Cochran noted: "The experience gained has proved that this country has an enormous reserve among our young women, available in case of need."[160] Indeed, the once top secret documents that analyzed the WASP program were written "so that when a similar program is launched in the future, as it most certainly will be if an emergency again presents itself, the new woman's program, no longer experimental, can start initially as a significant, dependable, successful, and accepted part of the Army Air Forces."[161]

Expectations for Militarization

Throughout its two-year existence, the WASP program maintained civilian status despite concerted attempts by the AAF to militarize it. The first proposals that Love and Cochran submitted to the AAF recommended that the experimental program be implemented with civilian women pilots.[162] Yet after the formation of the WAFS and WFTDs, Cochran and key military advisers realized that WASPs could serve more efficiently if they were militarized, and the AAF began to research the best possibilities for obtaining militarization.

Recruits were told that the program would be militarized,[163] and both WASP trainees and active WASPs performed and were evaluated as if they already were members of the armed forces.[164] WASPs were subject to military review, had to follow military customs and procedures, wore uniforms, and were instructed in drill and military courtesy.[165] The differences were that WASPs did not receive the money, security, and benefits of being in the military, and that WASPs could quit their positions at any time.[166] The issue of militarization constantly arose from the inception of the program in 1942 until its demise in 1944. Military protocol and drilling were part of the Avenger Field ground school, and eighty-five WASPs were sent to officer training school in Orlando, Florida, in anticipation of their becoming Army officers.[167]

Women's divisions of the Navy, Marines, and Coast Guard had been implemented as fully militarized branches, but the women's division of the Army began as an auxiliary unit (the Women's Auxiliary Army Corps) before congressional authorization changed its status to a militarized branch (the Women's Army Corps). The AAF, the War Department, and the secretary of state had all requested that the WASPs be militarized. Despite their requests, however, Congress rejected the bill for militarization, making the WASPs the only women's branch whose military status was rejected during World War II.

Gender Defines the Program's Creation

The very existence of the WASP program arose from the phenomenon in which pilots were gendered and organized according to this culturally constructed categorization. What separated the first WAFS from the male civilian ferrying pilots who were eventually directly militarized into the AAF was specifically, and singularly, their gender. Indeed, all components of the program that affected its survival, such as experimental status, media prohibitions, and incremental increases in the program following testing of pilots, resulted directly from sexist assumptions of the AAF that the program and its female pilots were likely to fail in their missions.

From its very inception, gender was the defining point of the WASP program. Women accepted into WASP training already had to be proven fliers with pilot's licenses and seventy-five hours of flight time (later reduced to thirty-five hours), while male trainees did not have to have pilot's licenses or any flight experience whatsoever to be accepted into the AAF's pilot training program.

Besides treating the male and female pilot cadets differently, the AAF handled the administration of the WASP program differently. For example, details of the WASP training program remained a closely guarded secret and the WASPs' public relations plan specifically forbade media contact. As a result, the public, the media, and Congress were not made aware of the important missions performed by the WASPs and their high level of success in completing these missions. This degree of secrecy and cautious expansion would soon cause irreconcilable problems for the Women Airforce Service Pilots program.

3

Becoming Soldiers

*Tracing WASP Expansion and Plans
for Militarization*

As the Women Airforce Service Pilots program expanded in 1943 and 1944, the Army Air Forces, realizing that the experimental use of women pilots was successful, began to examine how the newly defined program should be constituted. Several possibilities for the status of the women's pilot program existed: civil service or civilian standing, incorporation under the Women's Army (Auxiliary) Corps, or direct militarization as a division of the Army Air Forces.[1] Throughout the program's existence, concerted efforts were made to militarize it as a division of the AAF, and numerous avenues for obtaining this goal were explored. One of these, placing the WASPs under the WACs, was investigated from the beginning of the program in 1942 until its demise in 1944, but for changing reasons over the years, this option was never implemented.

Most accounts of the WASPs ascertain that the reason the program never merged with the WACs was that Jacqueline Cochran did not get along with the WAC director Oveta Culp Hobby. Records do indicate that the two women were not friends. Indeed, Cochran, in her autobiography *Stars at Noon*, described Hobby as the woman she loved to hate. However, no records indicate that the women's dislike for each other ever kept them from working together. Rather, they maintained a productive, professional relationship, regularly attending meetings together and maintaining correspondence. The Cochran/Hobby feud has the same mythic cat-fighting construction as the purported Cochran/Love feud referred to in the previous chapter. This theory also ignores numerous other documented reasons why the WASPs were never incorporated into the WACs.

The WASPs developed differently than the other women's auxiliaries of World War II, forming directly under the auspices of the AAF as a civilian group rather than by receipt of congressional approval. Other women's divisions of the military, such as the Navy's WAVES and the Women's Marines, were formed as militarized units under the authorization of Congress, and the WACs received congressional approval as an auxiliary before they were subsequently militarized by Congress. The WASPs were the only women's military branch established during World War II that did not receive congressional approval. The AAF did not submit to Congress any bills regarding the formation of the WASPs until 1944, when it submitted a bill to obtain militarization for the program. Instead, the AAF formed the WASP program under a War Department authorization that enabled it to use civilian pilots for domestic missions. The AAF frequently used male civilian pilots for ferrying missions, which meant that training and using organized groups of civilian pilots, such as the WAFS and later the WASPs, was a common procedure within the AAF. None of the AAF programs that used civilian male pilots came under public scrutiny or governmental attack. Instead, these programs were praised in newspapers and on the floors of Congress.

The first official proposal for the WASP program within the AAF called for the WASPs to be an official, militarized component.[2] This proposal, written by Cochran in July 1941, recommended that the women's pilot program be formed as an auxiliary division in the AAF and that "enabling legislation" be developed immediately.[3] This proposal was rejected by AAF Commanding General Henry H. Arnold because the United States at this point had more pilots than planes.[4]

In 1942, based on a proposal by Love, the Women's Auxiliary Ferrying Squadron formed under the auspices of the Ferrying Division's civilian pilot program. The WAFS program followed the same guidelines and principles that governed the services of male civilian pilots. On December 15, 1942, in response to AAF plans to expand the program beyond the twenty-five original WAFS, Cochran submitted a modified version of her earlier proposal, which, unlike her first proposal, reflected the AAF's opposition to militarizing women. In this version, Cochran recommended that the program not seek militarization for its pilots until at least 125 women had graduated from the program and were "working at ferrying, instructing, towing targets, and many other flying duties."[5] The major elements of this proposal were repeated in a December 19 memorandum from Brigadier General Walter F. Kraus to General Arnold, which encouraged the militarization of the program, but only after the women had proven themselves to be successful pilots.[6]

AAF officers working with the WAFS prior to Cochran's proposal had already been encouraging militarization for these women as early as November 1942, basing their recommendations on the performance of the WAFS and the needs of the military.[7] The Air Transport Command's Ferrying Division recommended that women pilots be militarized so that their standing would be consistent with that of the male civilian pilots used by the division, whom the Ferrying Division intended to militarize.[8] As more AAF leaders recognized the abilities of the women pilots and the potential for an expanded WASP program, the general staff went from cautiously releasing pilots on limited ferrying assignments to greatly increasing the variety and scope of its missions.

Based on the successes of these missions, the decreased need for combat pilots, and the Army's need for more ground forces, General Arnold announced a plan in 1944 to release all male air cadets to the Army's ground forces and expand WASP missions to include all domestic flights. At this point in the war, pilot losses in combat had been substantially less than the AAF had predicted and recruited for, and in many sectors of the globe the Allies maintained full air superiority. Therefore, the AAF no longer needed the great numbers of trainees that the Army had appropriated to it. The logical response was to transfer air cadets into the "walking army," a change that would also result in a reduced need for the AAF to employ civilian instructors.

Early Plans for WASP Militarization

When the various proposals for the development of the WASP program were written in 1941 and early 1942, there were no militarized attachments of women within the U.S. military except for the Army Nurse Corps, which was established in 1902.[9] Involvement of women in the military was initially opposed by Congress and reportedly by the American public; instead, women were encouraged to join "helping" units such as the Red Cross and women's volunteer auxiliaries.[10] Women were expected to help soldiers in the war effort but not become soldiers, which resulted in women being encouraged to participate in the war effort only within functions that did not break status quo expectations of gender roles.[11]

As WASPs successfully performed missions and were assigned to a variety of air bases, it became clear to AAF commanders that militarization was a necessary component of the program.[12] The AAF began to explore routes through which militarization could be obtained for the WASP program, such as incorporation under the WACs, direct commissioning within the Ferrying Division, and congressional dictate. In the interim, WASP training and assignments were conducted as though militarization was imminent, if not already implemented, with WASPs following military protocol and serving bases on twenty-four-hour call.[13] From the first meetings with representatives of the

WASP program, WASP trainees were told that the program was to be militarized. "We fully expected that we were going to be in the military when we joined," WASP Marty Wyall said.[14] Clarice Bergemann said: "I thought it was the military, and I was surprised when I was told that it was civil service."[15] Nadine Nagle joined the WASPs specifically to serve in the place of her deceased husband, who had been an AAF pilot: "I had expected militarization and looked forward to becoming part of the Air Corps."[16]

In anticipation of militarized status for the program, the AAF sent eighty-five selected WASPs to the Army Air Forces Tactical School in Orlando, Florida, for advance officer and tactical training in April 1944. In May, the WASP curriculum at Avenger Field in Sweetwater, Texas, was revised to include officer indoctrination training and a section on the duties and responsibilities of officers.[17] Although WASPs were behaving as soldiers, they did not receive the money, security, and benefits of being in the military. In addition, because they were not part of the military, WASPs could quit their positions at any time, which restricted the AAF's ability to discipline them.[18] Although discipline had never been a problem, the AAF believed that this complicated assignments, confused commanders as to the roles of WASPs, and increased voluntary resignations.[19]

Despite not being militarized, from its inception the WASP program had a unique relationship with the AAF. Technically civilian employees, WASPs were subject to all forms of military discipline except court-martial (but including forced dismissal), were expected to wear uniforms, lived on military bases, and worked alongside AAF personnel, following the same protocols as AAF officers.[20] But as civilians, WASPs were not entitled to the hospitalization, death, or veterans' benefits of the male pilots they served with, nor did they receive the same pay, housing, or living expenditures.[21]

The Development and Militarization of the Women's Army Corps

One means of obtaining militarization that the AAF investigated several times between 1942 and 1944 was the inclusion of the WASPs in the Women's Army (Auxiliary) Corps. Placing the WASPs as a unit of the WACs would have created for the women of both auxiliaries a structure similar to that which existed between the regular Army and the AAF.

The idea for developing the WACs arose before the United States entered World War II. On December 12, 1941, Congress introduced House Resolution 4906, the purpose of which was to establish a Women's Auxiliary Army Corps specifically for noncombat service. Those supporting the bill argued that the Army intended to use women in roles that they contended women were more skilled than men in performing. A statement issued by Chief of Staff General G. C. Marshall to Congress in support of the bill noted "innumerable duties now being performed by soldiers that actually can be done better by women."[22] The roles proposed for women within the Army auxiliary included stenographers, telephone operators, and clerks.[23] Women had performed these types of jobs during World War I in a civilian capacity, and it was because of limitations that had resulted from working with civilians that the Army wanted to militarize these positions.[24]

H.R. 4906 was replaced by H.R. 6293, which called for the development of a women's auxiliary corps that would work "with" rather than be "of" the Army.[25] This semantic distinction resulted in the greatest amount of debate concerning the bill's passage. Section 12 of the bill clearly stated the impact of the preposition: "The corps shall not be a part of the Army, but it shall be the only women's organization authorized to serve with the Army, exclusive of the Army Nurse Corp[s]."[26]

Debate on H.R. 6293 extended from January to May of 1942, and the bill went through three hearings in the House and Senate Military Affairs committees before being submitted to the General Assembly.[27] Much of this debate focused on the separate, nonmilitarized standing proposed for the WAACs. Even though some members of Congress were opposed to the involvement of women within the military, others recognized the administrative problems that would result from working with a separate auxiliary. The bill called for members of the WAAC to receive pay from the Army, be subject to some but not all military codes, and perform as voluntary employees—which meant that they could resign at any time, including when an assignment did not meet their expectations or when they wanted to escape disciplinary action.[28]

While this bill was being debated by Congress, the Army was also suggesting that an ideal situation would be to have the Women's Army Corps militarized, thus committing its members to all Army regulations. Between the authoring of the WAAC bill and its presentation to Congress, the Navy had submitted another bill, which Congress passed, that provided it with a militarized women's component, the WAVES. In 1941, when the WAAC bill was first brought to Congress, the Army had wanted a similar situation, but the climate of Congress did not favor women being militarized. In the year that had passed, that climate had changed dramatically, with Congress expressing a willingness to pass through all bills submitted by the military to keep American involvement in the war uninhibited. The Army and War Department conferred about adding an amendment to the WAAC bill that would provide for militarizing the corps, but they decided against changing the bill (which had already been held up with considerable debate at the committee level) for fear that this would further delay or even jeopardize the bill's passage.[29] Even though many members of the Senate agreed with the Army in favoring complete military standing for the corps, they voted on the bill as it stood, fearing that unnecessary delays might result if they sent it back to the House of Representatives, which had already passed the bill.[30] The Senate's decision mirrored that made by the Army, which had decided that the specific status of the women's corps mattered less than obtaining quick passage of the bill.[31] Indeed, several senators specifically referred to the Army's decision to get approval on this first bill and implement the women's auxiliary immediately and then return to Congress at a later date to improve the program's status.[32] In its presentation to the Senate, the Army indicated that it preferred militarized status for the women's auxiliary, but because it did not want any delays potentially created by including an addendum to the bill, it would leave the decision about determining WAAC status to Congress.[33]

The greatest voice of opposition to the creation of the WAAC as an auxiliary service was raised by one of the few women members of the legislature, Helen Douglas Mankin of Georgia, who had served overseas with a women's auxiliary in World War I. Mankin testified that women who served overseas during World War I had been subject to bombings, shellings, and other dangers but had not been "taken care of by the Government" because they were classified as civilian employees. Mankin stated that she was testifying because "I made up my mind at that time that, if we ever had another world war, I would do everything I could so that that would not happen again." She drew an analogy of what the Army was constructing concerning the WAAC: "making a woman's outer garments military but . . . leaving her underclothing civilian." She further asserted that because Congress was developing different legislation for women than for men, different laws would result governing the status of women, and, after the war "the women are going to be forgotten and neglected because they are going to be in the minority."[34]

Mankin's point of view was not the majority opinion within Congress. A more dominant view was the fear that if women were involved "in" the Army, there would be no barriers preventing the military from putting women into combat, which members on both sides of the debate were vehemently opposed to.[35] Some members of Congress worried that any relationship with the Army might result in women being drawn into combat and thus opposed not only militarization of the WAACs, but also women being involved in any overseas missions.[36] Army representatives at the various hearings continued to stress that the WAACs would not be soldiers but civilian employees of the Army, a relationship similar to that which the WAFS (and later, the WASPs) would have with the AAF. General Marshall was unable to testify in person because of his war duties, but he sent written statements to Congress in support of the bill. Marshall wrote, "In my opinion this proposed organization would provide a sound and practicable method for meeting military requirements with respect to the employment of women."[37] The Army also continued to support the position that the purpose of the WAACs was to focus on work that the Army felt women could do better than men.[38] At the hearing, Lieutenant Colonel Ira Swift of the General Staff Corps testified: "The Army at present time is not short of military personnel. Neither does the War Department advocate the creation of an Amazon contingent to supplement the combat forces. However, there are a great many duties in the Military Establishment which can be performed better by women than by men."[39] The duties listed were being stenographers, telephone operators,[40] stewardesses, and clerks.[41] Upon hearing this, Senator Joshua Lee (Okla.) questioned why women were not also being utilized as cooks, to which Army and War Department representative Brigadier General John Hilldring explained that cooks had to accompany their units to the field of combat.[42]

Several other points of debate arose within the congressional hearings, including the minimum age for WAAC recruits. The Army was requesting a minimum age of twenty-one, which varied from the minimum age of eighteen for male recruits.[43] The Army justified this requirement by claiming that women matured at twenty-one, making them more desirable for service at that age.[44] Several members of Congress were also concerned that the WAAC would insult "society women" who were volunteering in the war effort because the WAACs would have attractive uniforms. Stated Representative Paul Shafer (Mich.): "You are not concerned, are you, Colonel [Swift], over breaking the hearts of some of these society women who are out for a uniform?"[45] Representative Edmiston worried that the Army would become a marriage broker for single women if the WAAC program was enacted. After his questions revealed that the Army had no intention of barring these women from marrying soldiers, he asked: "You are going to start a matrimonial agency, aren't you?"[46] Colonel Swift responded by pointing out that there had never been, in World War I or thus far in World War II, problems caused by nurses marrying soldiers.[47] Throughout its congressional testimony, the Army submitted the Army Nurse Corps and Britain's use of women in its military as examples of the effectiveness and function of women within a military system.[48] Another concern expressed by members of Congress was that WAAC officers might direct orders to men in the regular Army. To prohibit this, additional wording was added to the bill, stating that "personnel appointed or enlisted under provisions of this Act will not be eligible to command outside the Women's Army Auxiliary Corps."[49]

Voices of support were raised within Congress, but they were often couched in gendered rhetoric. Representative Reynolds, chair of the Committee on Military Affairs, said: "Are we to deny the patriotic, courageous women of America the opportunity of participating in this war? It is as much their war as it is ours. It is more their war than the war of the men, because they, the future mothers of the country, will be called upon to exert their influence for right after might has been exerted in this world-wide conflict."[50] The majority of Congress kept their remarks specific to those women who would become WAACs, voicing praise for their anticipated efforts and expressing the desire to ensure them legal protection within their anticipated roles. However, some members expressed complete opposition to the WAAC. Said Representative Maloney:

> I do not want to see the bill passed at all. I think we can bring these patriotic American women into positions of importance where they may serve their country quite outside the Army. . . . It seems to me that the least that might be said of the measure is that it casts a shadow over the sanctity of the home. Women so anxious to serve, women burning with patriotism, as they are, will be afforded plenty of opportunity in the defense plants of our country and thus permit young men physically fit to go into the armed forces.[51]

Opposition to the bill was solid, but not strong enough to defeat it. H.R. 6293 was passed on May 12, 1942, and the WAAC was authorized to begin development. Although Congress placed no limitations on WAACs serving overseas, it did strictly specify that they could not perform in combat roles.

The Army began its attempts to change the status of the WAAC to a fully militarized unit as soon as H.R. 6293 passed. In January 1943, the House submitted H.R. 1188 to the Senate, a bill that would establish the WAAC as being "in" rather than "with" the Army.[52] The bill then was reintroduced as S. 495, which, in changing the women's army division to the Women's Army Corps, maintained its status as a voluntary (nondraft) organization, but one in which participants were "whole members of the Army."[53] The bill stated that all "laws and regulations now or hereafter applicable to enlisted men . . . shall in like cases and except where otherwise expressly provided, be applicable respectively to enlisted personnel and former enlisted personnel of such corps."[54] The Army pushed strongly for the bill because it had encountered a number of problems with the WAAC that specifically had to do with the unit not being militarized, such as issues of discipline and rapid turnover. However, when the Army introduced the bill to Congress, the WAAC program was being subjected to what Army reports later called a slander campaign,[55] in which rumors and then media reports alleged that WAACs stationed in Africa and the Middle East were having sexual relationships with local men both with and against their wills. Sensational media accounts alleged that there existed harems of WAACs, that women who did not want to participate in these activities were seeking shelter at various monasteries, and that the Army was shipping an excessive amount of contraceptives to the women.[56] Because of these reports, several members of Congress felt that the Army was not doing enough to protect the WAACs and were cautious about approving anything that might put additional women at risk. Fortunately, the Army had several allies in Congress who were well informed about the WAAC program and knew the fallacy of these rumors, and the Army Press Division began to confront the media allegations actively, in part by placing positive articles on the WAAC in the media. Thus, despite the slander campaign, the bill was passed by Congress, the word "Auxiliary" was dropped, and the Women's Army Corps became a fully militarized division of the Army. The program was established to last until the war's end, when it would be demobilized over a six-month period unless there was a continued need for their involvement, in which case the Army was to submit another bill to Congress.[57] Even though congressional passage was obtained, the slander campaign had a significant impact on the WACs and tarnished the reputations of all women who served in the military during World War II. The effects of the campaign were so serious that the Army believed the campaign to be the result of Nazi spies and requested an FBI investigation. The FBI traced the rumors not to enemy agents but to male U.S. Army personnel who were threatened by the incorporation of women into the armed services.[58]

Attempts to Merge the WASPs with the WACs

Because the AAF was a division of the Army, of which the WACs was an auxiliary, it seemed logical to combine the two women's programs in some fashion. From the inception of the WASPs, discussions had occurred between leaders of the two women's groups and with AAF officers to determine whether the two groups could be successfully consolidated. This option first arose when the AAF was developing proposals for a women's auxiliary of pilots. It was suggested that the WASP could be a separate but subsidiary division of the WAAC, much as the AAF operated within the Army. Before the formation of the WASPs, representatives of the AAF met with WAAC director Oveta Culp Hobby to discuss this option, and General George, Commanding General, Air Transport Command, expressed interest "that their women transport pilots be in the WAAC rather than being employed in a civil service status" because the division was attempting to eliminate all civil service employees, male and female, from its employ.[59]

Initially, these meetings seemed favorable to working out the details of such an arrangement. However, Commanding General Arnold did not approve the consolidation of the programs because he saw no benefits and several problems to placing women pilots in the WAAC.[60] A major reason for his disapproval was that the WAAC was not yet militarized, so the AAF would have no greater opportunity for enforcing orders or limiting resignations. Various AAF commanders expressed concern that this arrangement would also decrease the abilities of AAF officers to command WASPs, because the hierarchy of command would then place the WASPs under the discipline of the WAAC. Colonel Tunner, commander of the Ferrying Division, did not believe that the WAAC could meet the needs of the Ferrying Division "because of the proviso that the Women's Auxiliary Corps shall not be part of the Army but should serve *with* it. . . . The ferrying of aircraft for the Ferrying Division is not in any sense auxiliary, but is a direct function and, accordingly, the women should be directly in the Ferrying Division."[61] The requirements and missions of the two groups were so distinct that Cochran likened placing the WASP within the WAAC to putting the Air Forces under the infantry.[62] General Arnold noted that incorporating the WASP in the WAAC "would result in confusion, conflict, and inefficiency, because the women pilots would be reporting to both the Army Air Forces and the Women's Auxiliary Army Corps."[63]

Combining the WAAC and WASP programs would not eliminate the major concern the Ferrying Division had with the WASPs' civil service status, which was the need for both military and civilian commands over the women pilots. Colonel Tunner wrote:

> One of the things we hope to eliminate by militarization; namely, multiplicity of administration, would still exist were a unit to be set up under the WAAC since the Division would then have under it Army Pilots and WAAC Pilots, just

as it now has under it Army Pilots and Civilian Pilots. A more direct reason lies in the fact that if these women are to fly as a militarized duty, then they must be given a Service Pilot Rating and placed on Personnel Orders, and under AAF Regulation 507 a WAAC may not be so rated.[64]

In other words, placing the WASP under the WAAC would not eliminate any problems, and the legislation through which the WAAC had been created strictly prohibited WAACs from entering flying schools and obtaining Service Pilots Rating. The Acting Air Judge Advocate examined these regulations in 1943 and wrote that he believed that because the code AR 350-3500, which authorized aviation instruction for military personnel, had been amended to read "the Secretary of War to detail personnel of the Army of the United States as students" (thus eliminating the words "Military personnel"), there was likelihood that WAACs might not be prohibited from obtaining their pilot's rating.[65] However, this supposition was not proven, and attempts to change it would likely have also required congressional approval.

Seemingly, the AAF did not seek congressional approval for the WASPs initially because the Ferrying Division was authorized by the War Department to hire civilian pilots, regardless of their gender. The initial plans for the WASPs opposed militarizing the unit until its viability could be proven.[66] By the time reports showing the success of the program were being written, members of the AAF and the WASPs were also aware of the problems caused by the program's being comprised of volunteer civilians. The Ferrying Division, which worked with the WAFS and then the WASPs, requested that the women pilots be militarized because the difference in status between the pilots reflected a discriminatory disparity between the groups, since the women pilots "fly on military orders as do the men, and are subject to discipline and discharge as are the men."[67]

When the WAC was militarized in February 1943, the AAF again investigated the idea of placing the WASP within the WAC. However, the Air Forces discovered that there existed substantial differences between the programs that would cause problems if the two merged. For example, entry requirements for the two programs were very different. The WASP program allowed women nineteen and older to apply, while the WAC requirement, which was written into its congressional authorization, was for women trainees to be at least twenty-one.[68] In addition, the WAC did not allow women with dependent children (under the age of fourteen) to join, while 20 percent of the WASPs had such children.[69] Differences also existed between the physical and educational qualifications for applicants to the WAC and WASP programs;

however, these differences were believed to be manageable, because they were similar to the differences that existed between the male applicants of the regular Army and pilot trainees in the AAF.[70]

Another problem arose regarding how WASPs would be commissioned if they were militarized under the WAC. The bill developing the WAC specifically limited the rank and number of officers allowed. In the AAF, all pilots were officers and women pilots would have been given the same rank as male pilots if they were militarized. Therefore, the number of officers brought in by the WASP alone would exceed the total number Congress had allowed the WAC. In addition, the highest rank allowed the WAC was colonel, the position held by Hobby. Yet, Cochran had requested the rank of colonel if the WASPs were militarized because this rank was concurrent with that of male AAF officers leading similar-sized divisions. Therefore, the WASP director would have had the same rank as Hobby, who as WAC director would become her immediate supervisor.

The AAF general staff realized that there was no way to resolve these differences without having to go to Congress, so it made sense to put forth a bill to militarize the WASP as a separate program. In June 1943, following investigation into the opinions of various staffs working with the WASPs, a memorandum from General Arnold reported that

> the Commanding General, Flying Training Command, the training agency, and the Commanding General, Air Transport Command, the using agency, recommend that the women pilot group be militarized and that, for administrative and other purposes, they be incorporated into the Army Air Forces direct, rather than incorporated into the Women's Army Auxiliary Corps. The Director of the Women's Flying Training urges this procedure, which is overwhelmingly favored by the women pilots and trainees themselves.[71]

Other Plans for Incorporating Women Pilots into the Army Air Forces

The AAF investigated routes other than congressional hearings and integration into the WAC through which the WASPs could be militarized. The first avenue the AAF investigated was to award direct commissions to WASPs who served the Ferrying Division, avoiding standard channels of recruitment. The Ferrying Division was already able to avoid normal channels of receiving candidates through the Army because it could offer direct commissions to male pilots who joined the Ferrying Division as contracted civilian employees, if they met the AAF's physical, educational, and age requirements. A War Department regulation specifically authorized the Ferrying Division to induct pilots directly into its ranks, and an investigation into the legal documents behind this regulation did not find "either in the Constitution, the statutes relating to militarizing of Army personnel, or in the regulations themselves, a law or regulation to the effect that only persons of the male sex may wither be enlisted or commissioned in the Army of the United States."[72] The Ferrying Division, "in the absence of any limitations," took the position that "persons of the female sex are eligible for enlistment and commissioning in the Army of the United States."[73] Memorandums and reports indicate that the AAF gave a great deal of consideration to being able to induct the WASPs directly into the Ferrying Division in this way, but legal counsel determined that while the regulation did not specifically state that the pilots covered under this regulation were men, the understanding was that these pilots were men, and that any efforts to induct women under this regulation would not be approved.

Another avenue explored was to incorporate the WASPs into the AAF under the same legislation that allowed women physicians and surgeons to be made Army officers. Public Law 38, a one-paragraph bill, passed Congress in April 1943, thus authorizing the "commissioning of female physicians and surgeons in the Medical Corps of the Army and Navy with the same grade and length of service of men."[74] Colonel Courtney Whitney, the Acting Air Judge Advocate, reported to Brigadier General Luther Smith that this legislation had not gone through Congress smoothly and had been specifically opposed by the War Department; thus he believed that attempts to militarize women pilots in this way would also be rejected.[75]

In *Report of Investigation Regarding Proper Use of Women Pilots in the Army Air Forces*, issued August 5, 1943, Deputy Air Inspector Colonel T. C. Odum concluded: "The only way which women pilots can be brought into the Army Air Forces so as to have them comply with the requirements . . . is to have separate legislation passed providing for the establishment of a new military division of the Army Air Forces."[76] As a result, the AAF began work on a bill to establish the WASPs as a militarized component of the Air Forces. However, Colonel Whitney had predicted in 1943 that such legislation would fail: "Congress is distinctly hostile to legislation of this character. Our own experience in trying to get the Women's Army Corps incorporated into the Army has demonstrated this, and the recent experience of the Navy Department in trying to obtain certain changes in the laws pertaining to their women's reserves indicates the same attitude on the part of Congress."[77] Because the AAF had explored and rejected all other avenues for militarization, legislation was the only remaining option.

The WASP program's development was unlike that of any other women's auxiliary, but all women's detachments of the U.S. military faced opposition to their existence and continuance from the military, Congress, and the public, an opposition arose solely from the gender of those who comprised these auxiliaries. All women's auxiliaries were established as temporary contributions to a total world war, and military and congressional records indicate that there was considerable reluctance to having even the temporary participation of women in the military. The gendered rhetoric Congress used during the debate on the bills to establish the WAAC and later the WAC offers convincing testimony as to the degree to which sexist assumptions about the abilities of women determined the development of these organizations. It also provides insight into the considerable threat the involvement of women in the U.S. military posed to the continuance of normative gender constructions.

4

From Praise to Rancor

Media Opinion Changes as Men
Return from Battle

Perhaps the most important factor leading to the demise of the Women Airforce Service Pilots program was a negative media campaign precipitated in part by the return of combat pilots from overseas and the release of Army Air Forces cadets and pilot trainers into the "walking Army" for service in anticipated large-scale ground assaults against Japan's military. The male civilian pilots organized a lobbying group and discovered in the WASPs a target against whom they could articulate claims of preferential treatment, thus deflecting attention away from their real intent of refusal to serve as combat soldiers, the role in which the military had deemed that these men were needed. The male civilian pilots had avoided the draft because of their status as AAF cadets and trainers, and they had accrued enough money and resources to organize an effective lobby. A direct result of this lobby was a negative campaign in the media and to Congress against the WASPs, a campaign that was readily accepted and expanded exponentially because of cultural expectations of male superiority and privilege, much as the slander campaign against the Women's Army Corps had a year earlier. In other words, Congress and the public readily believed that the men were more worthy and talented pilots than the WASPs simply because they were men.

The War Department had established a WASP public relations plan that avoided any media publicity because it believed that the public would oppose the program, particularly if WASP deaths became known.[1] As a result of this policy, no voices were raised to counter those put forth by the male civilian pilots' lobby. Despite the need for someone from the WASP program, the AAF, or the War Department to refute untrue allegations raised against the WASP program, the public relations plan remained unchanged. The scale and tone of the media campaign was so strongly in opposition to the WASP program that in 1945 former WASP Mary B. Hillberg stated: "It is my opinion that we never had the right publicity—or *any* publicity—except bad. Like the false and misleading letters written by civilian pilots who turned down one chance to fly for the Army, but when they were faced with the possibility of being drafted into the walking Army cried for our jobs. The 'men' we were supposed to be releasing to fight a war didn't want to."[2]

The tone of media reports on the WASPs was not always negative, however. Early in the war, when American media was celebrating the efforts of all people who pulled together for the war effort, the WASPs, other women's military auxiliary organizations, and women in factories developing war materials were all portrayed as heroines dedicated to the cause of freedom. But as the war was winding down, the media began to articulate cultural anxieties about whether the country could return to its prewar standards. Women in all aspects of the war effort, once celebrated, were now attacked by the media as self-serving individuals who jeopardized the abilities of returning male soldiers to survive the postwar economy.

Life Depicts U.S. Involvement in World War II

Media support for the WASPs coincided with overall support for total American involvement in the war effort. From 1941 to 1943, the media publicly supported the war effort and the nation's military. Patriotism was a standard editorial stance, and even the most questionable battle tactics were not publicly doubted. During these first years of American involvement in World War II, the United States, which was fighting on two major fronts, was losing the war. The country had entered the war unprepared for a total world war, and efforts put forth by any citizen in support of the war were lauded.

A portal into the changing public opinion regarding women and the military is provided by *Life* magazine, which was the self-described pulse of the nation. During the war years, *Life* was published weekly and featured photographs and articles depicting the war on all fronts, including the home front. A 1942 survey revealed that 63 percent of American military men read *Life*.[3] The magazine arguably was the means by which most Americans received news about the war, and it is also an invaluable source in determining public opinion and mores because it maintained a large and popular "Letters to the Editor" section. It is of note that the depictions of those involved in the war effort were of white people. When black soldiers were represented, their race was the subject of the piece.

In December 1941, immediately following the Japanese attack on Pearl Harbor, *Life* presented some of the first War Department pictures of the attack. In the issues published in the month after the attack, articles and editorials encouraged full participation in the war effort and stressed that total commitment was needed if the United States and its allies were to be victorious. Total participation meant that the efforts of women and children were considered invaluable to the overall war effort. Stories appeared on the involvement not only of women, but also of children (usually boys), such as boys making model planes for Civil Defense identifications of Allied and enemy planes.[4]

Life first encouraged the specific participation of women in a January 1942 issue, in which a cover portrait of a nurse's aide and accompanying story encouraged women to become nurse's aides and help fight the nation's shortage of nurses.[5] Advertisements praising women war workers began to appear the same month, such as a piece for the Sanforized clothing process with the headline "Women at Work for Uncle Sam!" that features drawings of women war workers in factory coveralls.[6] An October 1942 article, "Human Resources for a Total War," directly asserted, "The ultimate solution of the manpower crisis is women," and gave war industry projections that one-third of factory work would be filled by women to meet quotas.[7] Despite its purported celebration of the potential of women to support the war effort through factory work, the article very clearly demonstrated a double standard by being highly critical of women workers who did not care about their physical appearances in the factory: "Though a man can be as sloppy as he pleases, an unsightly female, employers find, plays hell with morale."[8] The article "Girls in Uniform: In U.S. Industry They Help Make Weapons of War" suggests that industrial work was constructed as glamorous simply because the workers were women: "The woman worker in a war industry in the U.S. has acquired some of the glamor of the man in uniform. In labor's social scale, she belongs to the elite. At the very top is the girl who works in an airplane factory. She is the glamor girl of 1942."[9] Advertisements capitalized on the linkages drawn between women's war work and glamor; for example, a Munsingwear girdle ad featured a woman riveter wearing tight and fashionable coveralls and the headline "Who Says a *Smooth* Girl Can't Fight."[10]

By 1943, *Life*'s depictions of women war workers had become commonplace and included women engaged in dangerous and active roles within factories, with no mention of fashion. In "Women Now Make Tests Once Done by Soldiers," women were pictured loading and firing guns to measure shell velocity.[11] A cover photograph simply entitled "Steel Worker" featured a woman welder, wearing loose garb, whose gender is discernible only upon closer examination.[12] "Women Steel: They Are Handling Tough Jobs in

Heavy Industry" is an eight-page feature on women handling heavy steel work. The piece began: "Since the start of the war, U.S. women have quickly and ably assumed many jobs traditionally held by men."[13]

Despite this handful of portrayals of women workers that did not refer to glamor or fashion, the recurring theme in stories on women's involvement in the war effort was the impact it had on fashion. A *Modern Living* section in 1942 was titled "Short Bobs for Wartime: Women's Service Groups Require Military Style."[14] The piece discussed the uniforms not of women's auxiliaries (which had not developed yet), but of organizations like the Red Cross and American Women's Voluntary Service. Accompanying pictures showed women in these organizations' uniforms and featured detailed instructions for performing the cut. *Life* also reported on fashions that were influenced by the involvement of women in war work. The cover of the April 20, 1942, issue, entitled simply "Slacks," featured a woman wearing slacks, which had risen in popularity because, the accompanying article stated, of women's war work.[15] This cover inspired several male readers to respond to the editors. William A. Pelletier was moved to invoke a muse:

> Sirs: "Men lose their pants to slack-crazy women" (April 20) should be awarded the prize for the best title of the year. It so aptly describes the way men feel, who grudgingly suffer the passing of vests and cuffs to satisfy womanly fads which flare unabated even in wartime.
>
> As Ogden Nash said: "Sure, deck your lower limbs in pants; / Yours are the limbs, my sweeting, / You look divine as you advance— / Have you ever seen yourself retreating?"[16]

To demonstrate his aversion to women's wearing slacks, reader James Hsieh referred back to a March 9 piece, "Shape of Women," which reported: "The average U.S. female is not only short (5 ft. 3 in. tall) but chunky (133 lb.). The Department of Agriculture arrived at this deplorable conclusion in Miscellaneous Publication No. 454."[17] He wrote: "I must admit that your cover girl looked lovely in slacks, but an average woman, 5 ft. 3 in. in height and weighing 140 lb., would look like a sack of potatoes."[18]

Life was most likely to feature women who supported the war effort by maintaining stratified gender roles and encouraging their men to fight. More often than factory workers or members of the military, *Life* depicted women volunteers or women in roles as wives and mothers, symbolizing what the men overseas were fighting for. The cover "War Stamp Bride" featured a bride holding a bouquet made of war stamps.[19] The cover "USO Victory Belle" featured a portrait of a young woman who volunteered as a United Service Organizations escort to do her part for the war effort.[20] "10,000 Sub-Debs Do Hard Useful War Work As Juniors in AWVS" featured five pages of photographs depicting high school girls who volunteered for the American Women's Volunteer Services to perform traditional women's work (such as food service) in support of the war effort.[21] In the pages of *Life*, women frequently "served the war effort" by marrying soldiers and giving birth to their children. "Army Man and Wife," seven pages of women "serving" as wives to military men, began, "Plucky girls quit homes and jobs for hard camp life with husbands,"[22] and included a photograph of babies delivered in an Army hospital.

More than articles and editorials, advertisements featured women in the war effort. Camel was the first to direct its advertising toward women involved in the effort, with a series featuring spotlights on real women serving the military as, for example, a camouflage expert,[23] a Civil Aeronautics Administration (CAA) pilot,[24] and a Civil Air Patrol (CAP) pilot.[25] Not to be outdone, Chesterfield cigarettes featured a member of the WAVES smoking under the caption "More than 75,000 women in war services today. You can join now."[26] Some advertisements featured women soldiers using the sponsor's equipment, such as a Mimeograph Duplicator ad that depicted a WAAC using the machine.[27] Other ads simply placed models in uniform, maintaining the same poses and situations as before the war, such as an advertisement for Van Raalte Rayon Stockings that pictured a woman in uniform on an air base, her skirt blowing up to reveal her legs and stockings, with a smiling male officer looking at her.[28] Other advertisements featured products that could not logically be linked to women involved in the military by structuring the ads as celebrations of women in the armed services. For example, a Norge appliance ad featured a female CAP pilot flying over the ocean.[29] The piece was not about appliances, but instead offered a salute to the women in the Civil Air Patrol. Among the advertisers in *Life* magazine was the WAAC, which placed numerous recruitment ads in the publication.[30]

The first piece featuring a woman pilot working toward the war effort was a back cover advertisement for Camel cigarettes. (Throughout the war years, Camel ran a series of ads focusing on women in the war effort as pilots, civilian factory workers, and members of the armed services.) In this first ad, a bold red headline proclaimed "What! A *girl* training men to fly for Uncle Sam?" The ad featured four photographs of a woman pilot in a white jumpsuit with her plane. The copy read: "The name is Lennox—Peggy Lennox. She's blonde. She's pretty. She may not look the part of a trainer of fighting men, but—She is one of the few women pilots qualified to give instruction in the CAA flight training program. And the records at Randolph and Pensacola of the men who learned to fly from Peggy show she's doing a man-sized job of it."[31]

The first article depicting women in the military followed the development of the WAAC. The June 1942 article, "U.S. Women Troops to Enlist in Army's First All-Female Force," began: "On May 27, for the first time in history, the U.S. Army began general recruiting of women."[32] Yet, despite *Life's* assertion that the development of the WAAC was historical, the issue's cover story maintained traditional gender roles in a feature on nurses' aides that was twice as long as the WAAC piece. Another WAAC piece followed in September. "WAACS: First Women Soldiers Join Army" began: "The idea behind the Women's Army Auxiliary Corps is simply this: Women can do some of the jobs that men are doing in the Army. By taking over these jobs, they can release men for active or combat duty.[33] This article was the first in *Life* to depict black soldiers involved in the military during World War II. Within the eight-page photo spread is a photo of "Negro WAAC officer candidates," who were, according to the caption, kept segregated from white WAACs. (It is notable that the first depiction of African Americans serving with the armed forces would be of WAACs. *Life* always depicted the normalized soldier fighting for the United States as a white man.)

Life later ran features on all branches of women's auxiliaries, including women merchant marines (merchant marines were not a militarized branch of the armed forces) who had been grounded following the attack on Pearl Harbor and who were fighting to return to sea through their union (National Maritime Union): "The women members of the N.M.U. argue that since all other branches of the armed forces are open to women, the Merchant Marine should not be an exception. They underscore the fact that British, Soviet, and Norwegian women still help sail their country's ships."[34] In January 1942, a woman in uniform first appeared on the cover. While the inset reveals that the woman wearing the uniform of the British Women's Auxiliary Air Force (ground support, not pilot) was an actress in the movie *This above All,* the visual impact is that of seeing a woman soldier on the cover. This cover was followed in the February 16 "Letters to the Editors" section by a four-page feature and photograph depicting the real WAAF who inspired the posed shot.[35]

The April 27, 1942, issue featured two pieces that referenced women's involvement with the war. "Women in Uniform March for a Cause" featured a photograph of women civil defense air wardens marching in a parade, and began: "On April 11, for the first time since the last World War, 10,000 women tramped to the beat of military bands down New York's Fifth Ave."[36] In that same issue, "Civil Air Patrol: America's Private Pilots Are Mobilized for War" began: "Today, more than a third of the nation's 100,000 civilian pilots are at war on the home front. They are the Civil Air Patrol, composed of the men and women who flew for fun in days of peace."[37] Of significance is the fact that none of the article's ten photographs included a woman CAP pilot.

The women's auxiliary of the Navy, the WAVES, first appeared in the pages of *Life* in an article that focused on the designs and designers of WAVES uniforms rather than on the corps itself. "Waves Uniforms" featured three pages of photographs of the uniforms and one of their Parisian designer. The lead offered the only information specific to the corps: "On Oct. 9 about 1,600 Navy WAVES (Women Appointed for Voluntary Emergency Service) will start training. . . . They are the first of a projected corps of 10,000 enlisted women who, with 1,000 officers trained at Smith College and Mt. Holyoke, will form the first authorized women's corps in the U.S. Navy." The next paragraph established the focus of the article: "To design a functional yet feminine uniform for this newest Navy corps, the Navy turned to Mainbocher." During these same years, no articles appeared that discussed the uniforms of men in the military. Women soldiers first made the cover of *Life* in March 1943, with thirteen WAVES posed in a group shot, with an accompanying article spotlighting both the WAVES and the WAAC.[38] Photographs featured the women soldiers training, marching, and drilling, while the copy read in part: "By last week, the Waves and Waacs were no longer military experiments. They were military realities, having appeared for duty with startling effects at Army and Navy posts all over the country. Undoubtedly they were doing good work, but old-time officers and enlisted men still could not get used to them."[39]

Most of *Life*'s depictions of women in the military stressed that these soldiers were first and foremost women. Military women were frequently featured in uniform but outside of their service—for example, engaged in recreational or volunteer activities. WAVES were again featured in April 1943, this time attending a New York fashion show.[40] The next appearance of WAACs in the magazine had a similar tone: a two-page spread featured a WAAC talent show that raised money for war bonds.[41] The pattern of featuring women soldiers as society girls continued with "Sinatra Sings for WAVES: 600 Navy Girls Listen without One Hysterical Yelp," which included a photograph of uniformed WAVES gathered around the stage on which Frank Sinatra performed.[42]

In its only depiction of a woman in combat, *Life* put forth a different construction than it typically gave to male combat experience. A short piece on Lieutenant Maiya Sloboda, a Soviet combat soldier who commanded a hundred men and who had single-handedly killed twenty-eight German soldiers, provided no references to other women combat soldiers or combat pilots with whom Sloboda served, nor did it describe her acts of heroism (as was typically done with male combat stories); it simply offered a photograph of her and gave quick mention of the number she killed.[43] The article did not explain or contextualize what was a unique and newsworthy use of women in the war effort.

Just as Sloboda's accomplishments were stated with no heroic build-up, constructions of women in the U.S. military were posed very differently than those of men in the military. For example, in "*Life* Visits U.S. Army Nurses in New Caledonia, South Seas," a six-page photo spread displayed the lives of Army nurses overseas as though they were vacationing abroad. Among the photographs were shots of the women bathing outside, playing ping-pong, and relaxing. Not one photograph appeared of the nurses assisting in surgery, working in the field, or assembled under combat conditions.[44] In fact, *Life* would not print a photograph of an Army nurse actually working until April 1943, when "Flying Nurses Aid U.S. African Campaign" featured a photograph of a nurse tending to wounded soldiers on a plane.[45]

Life Depicts American Military Pilots

Just as depictions of men and women in general received differing constructions within the pages of *Life*, the magazine also depicted female pilots differently than male pilots. *Life* featured numerous stories on the growth and development of the AAF throughout the war. A February 1942 cover showed a Thunderbolt fighter, and the accompanying article began: "The air armies of America, which flew in piddling flocks two years ago, will be flying now in ever growing swarms. The gigantic specifications of President Roosevelt call for masses of airplanes which will far outmatch those of any other power."[46] Other features on the Air Forces touted the bomber task force,[47] the B-17 Flying Fortress,[48] the Chinese Airforce,[49] the "rigid training" of air cadets at Randolph Field,[50] bombardier school,[51] aerial gunnery school,[52] and aerial navigation.[53] Men were depicted in action, and no women were ever featured in these stories, even though they served as trainers and teachers and in support roles. In addition, no women pilots were featured in stories on divisions where WAFS/WASPs were assigned, such as Air Transport Command.[54]

Life first wrote about the Women's Air Ferrying Squadron in a September 1942 article focusing on women's involvement in the war effort. "Women in Action" began: "The simplest way for women—as for men—to *think war* is to get into action. Hundreds of thousands have done so. The WAACS,

WAVES, and WAFS have accepted without flinching the hard routines of military life."[55] The piece not only featured women in the armed forces, but focused on women who worked with the Aircraft Warning Service, as well as women who served as nurses, service canteen workers, and military factory workers. The same issue featured "WAFS Woman," a short piece on Nancy Harkness Love that also described the formation of the WAFS.[56] In July 1943, *Life* ran a cover story on WASP trainees, arguably the most widely read positive piece on the WASPs to appear during World War II. The cover featured a trainee in coveralls, wearing no makeup, perched on a training plane.[57] Inside, a nine-page feature entitled "Girl Pilots: Air Force Trains Them at Avenger Field, Texas" depicted the trainees on a typical day: rising at dawn, marching in formation, attending classes, bunking in barracks, walking out to the flight line, and flying training planes. The article began:

> The time-honored belief that Army flying is for men only has gone into the ash can. At Avenger Field, near Sweetwater, Texas, girls are flying military planes in a way that Army officers a year or so ago would never have thought possible. These girls, who so joyously scramble into the silver airplanes of the Women's Flying Training Detachment each day, fly with skill, precision and zest, their hearts set on piloting with an unfeminine purpose that might well be a threat to Hitler.[58]

However, not everyone read the WASP piece in a positive light. Private James D. McGilvray sent a letter to the editors stating that even bad male pilots should be flying for the military rather than women. McGilvray's letter is of particular interest because it anticipated the arguments made against the WASPs by the male civilian pilots lobby the next year:

> Sirs: Have just finished reading your article on women flying for the Army. It is very nice that our women can do such things when the need arises, but there are plenty of men that are perfectly able to do the work. Why don't they give the "washed-out" cadets a chance? There are thousands of these boys who, although they might not be good combat pilots, could perfectly well take over the job of ferrying planes.[59]

Life Champions a Return to Prewar Standards

By 1944, *Life*'s attitude toward women's involvement in the war effort had changed considerably, mirroring an overall policy change toward depictions of the war. No longer did the magazine encourage recruitment of women in the war effort—it now focused on returning soldiers. *Life* was encouraging the return to normalcy, to the mores of prewar life. Pieces on the military exuded confidence and anticipated victory. In January 1944, *Life* published "Army Air Forces Report" by General H. H. Arnold, which began: "It is now plain that, for us, the beginning has ended; for our enemies, the end has begun. The Army Air Forces are now in the process of fulfilling an historic and decisive mission."[60] The report demonstrated how the United States had risen from seventh in production of military aircraft before the war to first, and how recruitment, training and missions had been so successful that the AAF no longer needed much of its cadet personnel. Two months later, an editorial pointed out that the Army was in need of more foot soldiers and encouraged an increased draft.[61]

Advertising representations of women in the military also changed sharply in 1944. The encouragement for women to join the military was replaced by the suggestion that women return to the home and take care of their husbands. Depictions of women soldiers dropped dramatically this year, and those that appeared maintained the gender differences present before the war. For example, an ad for Barbasol shaving cream featured four attractive women in uniform saluting and the caption: "Girls in uniform salute more Barbasol Faces than any other kind for the simple reason that more men in uniform Shave with Barbasol than any other brand."[62] The women may be in uniform, but their mission no longer focused exclusively upon winning the war. Covers more often featured models instead of women actually involved in the war effort; and rather than running a cover on pants, a fashion trend that had followed an on-the-job necessity in 1942, the cover in August 1944 was on "Pedal Pushers"—shorts.[63] Women were portrayed as leisure objects rather than as skilled workers. By September 1944, *Life* was making passive objects out of women. "Which Are the Prettiest? *Life's* Camera Conducts a Test in Four U.S. Cities" featured photographs of young women from New York, Hollywood, Des Moines, and Dallas,[64] perhaps as a service to returning soldiers interested in relocating to new cities. Reader interest was high: in subsequent issues, letters to the editors (usually accompanied by photographs) continued the "experiment" in other cities.

Women soldiers were depicted less frequently, and when they were, it was with a substantially different tone than earlier in the war. An advertisement for International Sterling featured a WAC contemplating having a home with her husband following the war and suggested that her reason for having joined the organization was to have something to keep her busy while her husband was away.[65] In the same issue, an ad for the WAC followed the same theme of returning to domesticity and marriage after the war. The recruitment ad's headline reads: "I'd rather be with them—than waiting for them."[66] Women who were not soldiers were depicted similarly. A Kelvinator advertisement "Sunday. . . . Some Day," for instance, featured a male soldier and civilian woman dreamily looking toward their future fantasy kitchen.[67]

For *Life*, the critical issue in the latter half of 1944 was not winning the war but returning to prewar domesticity and productivity. "Reconversion: What Has Been Done, Who Has Been Fighting Whom and Why, and Where Do We Go from Here?" was a lengthy article discussing the reconfiguration of war factories and the expectations of a postwar economy and job market.[68] The following issue had the cover title "Special Issue: A Letter to GI's" and featured a photograph of a model wearing a bikini.[69] As the photograph demonstrated, *Life* did not mean "GI's" to include women. The issue's editorial, "Soldiers and Civilians," discussed the homecoming fears of soldiers, focusing particularly on fears that a wartime imbalance had shifted power and prestige from white men. With regards to women in the work force, it stated:

> At present women constitute a third of the U.S. labor force and many of them are keeping up their homes as well. But if any GI is concerned about a woman keeping him out of a postwar job, he can solace himself by the poll conducted by the Women's Auxiliary of the American Legion, which indicates that 54% of the women now working want to quit when peace comes.[70]

The same issue of *Life* also featured "GI's Dream Party: Beautiful Girls Made It Come True," a nine-page photomontage of a soldier surrounded by scantily clad models listening intently to his war stories and bringing him drinks.[71]

In 1945, *Life*'s only depiction of women in the military was "WACS Shiver in Paris," which featured photographs of WACs sharing a Paris apartment. None of the WACs appeared in uniform, and all the photos featured the women as domestic and romantically oriented toward men—a WAC lies in a bed loaded with covers, another irons sheets, while yet another gazes at a framed photograph because her "boyfriend's picture helps her forget the cold."[72] Throughout the remainder of the year, hundreds of pictures and dozens of articles depicted Allied victories, including the final defeats of Germany and Japan, yet women soldiers were not represented. Clearly, *Life* magazine established that in victory, American women were no longer to be soldiers or workers, but rather the wives and girlfriends who welcomed home the decidedly male victors.

Positive but Scattered Publicity Appears on the WASPs in 1942 and 1943

Early accounts in the mainstream media dealing with all aspects of the war effort, including women military pilots, were positive. In December 1941, Henry R. Luce, editor of both *Life* and *Time*, called for all Americans, regardless of gender or age, to participate in the war: "There is terrible fighting to be done. All of us will be in the fight—men, women and children, for this is indeed total war."[73] Luce did not specify exactly how women should be involved in the war, but for military strategists such as General Arnold of the AAF, a total war meant that women would have to become directly involved in the military. When Arnold announced the development of the WASPs, the first of the program's three objectives was: "To see if women could serve as military pilots, and, if so, to form the nucleus of an organization which could be rapidly expanded."[74] Military leaders of all branches of the military had similar reasons for incorporating women within their branches. As a result, the Army, Coast Guard, Marines, and Navy all formed women's auxiliaries. The media played up the formations of these auxiliaries as examples of the United States' dedication to the war effort and proof that the Allies would win the war. In the first years of World War II, articles, editorials, and even advertisements encouraged and portrayed the involvement of American women in the war effort, as members of military branches, as civilian workers in war plants, and as volunteers with service organizations like the Red Cross and the American Women's Voluntary Service. Before the formation of the WASPs, women who flew or instructed for the CAA were profiled.

In 1941, Jacqueline Cochran, who would later head the WASPs, copiloted a Lockheed Hudson bomber being delivered to the Royal Air Force.[75] The media offered glowing accounts of this feat as a demonstration of American versatility and commitment. America would win the war, the media inferred, because even its women were willing to be involved in spectacular ways in the war effort. Similar publicity followed a few months later, when Cochran assembled a group of twenty-five American women to serve with the British Air Transport Auxiliary as ferrying pilots to free British male pilots for combat duty.

When the Women's Auxiliary Ferrying Squadron was formed on September 10, 1942,[76] media attention again was positive. Accounts about individual WAFS pilots, and especially WAFS Director Nancy Harkness Love, were commonplace. Again, the stories featured the voluntary nature of women's involvement and their dedication to the war effort. Stories frequently noted that the pilots were motivated by having male relatives who were serving in combat or who had been killed at Pearl Harbor. However, accompanying the stories praising the women pilots were a significant number of articles and opinion pieces fearful of the effects of women's wartime participation. In addition, even positive accounts of women in the media contained constructions maintaining strong gender separations and naming women participants in the war efforts as temporary and exceptions to the norm.

"The Girls Deliver the Goods" was one article that appeared about the WAFS in 1942. The piece is similar to those written about the male pilots of Air Transport Command, emphasizing the skill, dedication, and discomfort involved with flying airplanes across the country on shifts that could last for days. The only source of amazement in the article was that the pilots were not just women but young women. "It was astonishing—humbling, too—to think of a girl like that flying Army planes to points all over the country, alone in the skies hour after hour, flying through rain and sleet and snow and clouds."[77] Even the photos and captions for this article avoided the glamor shots and double-entendres that would soon be the normative positioning of the WAFS. The pilots are depicted in full gear, with captions emphasizing their abilities. Appearing under a photo of seven WAFS in full flight gear walking past a trainer plane is the caption: "Aces. The squadron takes only the very best. Each girl has at least 500 flying hours."[78] Another caption, of a WAFS pilot gearing up next to a plane reads: "Solo. The WAFS fly alone for long, cold hours. Here Barbara Tame prepares for an overnight hop."[79] The tone of the piece reflects the request Love is quoted as making: "Don't present us as a glamor outfit. We're not. There's no room or time for glamor in the WAFS. We've got a serious job to do and we do it. If any girls come here with illusions of glamor, things like that mud and rain out there take it out of them quickly enough."[80]

The AAF's official press policy regarding the WAFS and the Women's Flight Training Detachment in 1942 was to downplay the programs because of their experimental nature and because both the AAF and Cochran feared public resistance toward the program, particularly if female casualties became known. In 1943, when the WAFS merged with the WFTD to form the WASPs, the first official media plan was developed. The plan was simple: Keep the WASPs out of the media.[81] Because of a record number of volunteers, the WASP program did not need media reports for recruitment purposes, as did the other women's auxiliaries. The only articles to appear about the recruiting of WASPs were short pieces appearing in 1942 announcing that WASP recruitment director Ethel Sheehy was at a specific place to accept applications. These pieces stressed that the program was looking for skilled women pilots.

For example, the piece "Seek Women Pilots to Ferry Planes" states that "licensed women pilots, with one hundred or more hours of flying time, are badly needed to ferry military aircraft in the United States."[82] Despite the clear request for only highly skilled pilots, the WASP program was inundated with applications and soon stopped all recruiting efforts. The *Washington Herald Tribune* reported: "Unlike the other women's services, the W.A.S.P. has more recruits than it can possibly use. By the end of this year there will be about 600 Wasps, with 500 more in training. Classes now are filled up until June, 1944, and no further recruitment is planned for the present. Each day, about 300 letters go out from Miss. Cochran's office, in answer to requests about the W.A.S.P."[83] Therefore, with few exceptions, articles on the WASPs were limited to graduation stories and assignment accounts in the local papers of WASP trainees, and to base newspapers and small-town newspapers where bases were located, where news of field occurrences was regularly reported.

Except at the newspaper in Sweetwater, Texas (where Avenger Field, the WASP training base, was located), WASP graduations were only news if a local woman was a graduate. Even the historical first graduation of women pilots from a military school only attracted local attention. Not surprisingly, the largest and most positive story on this historic graduation appeared in the *Houston Chronicle*, the city near the base at which the first class was trained. The full-page article begins:

> Saturday was ladies day at Ellington Field, when the first 23 women in the United States to receive their silver wings and army diplomas as full-fledged ferry pilots were graduated in an elaborate ceremony on the big ramp of the field. . . . The women have completed a seven-month rigid course training at the Houston Municipal Airport and later finished at Sweetwater, where the school was moved several weeks ago. Representatives of many states of the Union, these women have been trained to fly five different types of planes, will serve as civilian ferry pilots under army orders and will receive $250 per month base pay."[84]

One photo caption noted a physical difference experienced by some women pilots and the creative ways they found to compensate for it: "Dorothy Yang of Washington D. C., smallest of the graduates and called the 'three-cushion gal,' because she has to have that many pillows under her to see the cockpit. Since she was the first to receive her diploma and wings, she is the first woman in the United States to have that honor."[85]

The War Department's Bureau of Public Relations developed a plan for WASP public relations that encouraged media silence because it believed that the WAFS had attracted unnecessary attention, that writers wanted to do "undesirable 'glamor' and publicity-promotion types of stories," that "selection, not recruiting, is the WASP problem," and that the "program involves experimentation in training and utilization, with strong attendant possibility of mistakes and losses, with resultant public criticism."[86] The report imposed media silence on WASP activities except for stories of graduation and advancement, which were to be released to the hometown newspapers of individual pilots; WASP units' involvement in local events; and stories on WASP accidents, which were to be handled by the War Department. The public relations plan also stated that stories were to be constructed to place the role of the WASPs as supplemental to male pilots and to emphasize that the WASPs' role within the AAF was minor. Articles on the WASPs seemed to fit this construction—peripheral but laudable war efforts by those other than its principles (i.e., male soldiers). Articles described the physical attributes of WASPs, frequently dealt with their uniforms and appearances, and emphasized constantly that these pilots were, indeed, still women. As a result, the news stories that appeared during this time did little to educate the public about the range of missions WASPs performed on a daily basis or the level of skill and flying hours the pilots had before they even began training with the AAF.

One of the earliest newspaper articles to appear on the WFTD had as its theme the overwhelming interest that was expected to be shown by American women toward joining the group. The article interviewed women pilots, who gave their opinions about the newly formed women's pilot organization:

> Mae Wilson, manager and flight instructor at the Wilson airport, and nationally famous stunt flier, expressed the belief that the organization of the WAFS will meet with an excellent response among women flyers all over the country. She said: "Many of our women pilots, eager to aid in the war effort, have gone to England by Jacqueline Cochran to ferry planes for the British, but now that we have a ferrying squadron of our own, it's my guess that just about every woman flier in the country who can qualify will sign up with the WAFS."[87]

A more common type of coverage that appeared in the first months of WASP assignments to ferrying detachments were articles in small newspapers near air bases covering the arrival of women pilots. These articles almost always focused on the physical attributes of pilots and were usually accompanied by numerous pictures of the pilots, none of which ever showed them actually piloting a plane.

In a *Wichita Beacon* piece, four of the article's five paragraphs are devoted to these "attractive" women while only the final paragraph mentions the actual pilot program, as well as the related duties and expectations. The article began:

> The daily routine of delivery of military air planes to the armed forces was given the feminine touch Friday at the local Boeing plants, when a comely quartet of pilots of the Women's Auxiliary Squadron flew away four Boeing PT-17 Kaydet Primary Trainers.
>
> Friday's flight was the first time the newly-organized WAFS have operated out of Wichita. Flight line mechanics, long used to daily contact with ferry pilots, quickly broke into smiles and snapped into their duties when the able young ladies appeared. Hardened flight engineers scurried to help with luggage, and the colorful and expressive jargon of the flight hangar subsided into a good-natured bantering.[88]

"Biggs Field Male Personnel Perks Up When Expert Wasps Arrive on Scene," in the *El Paso Times*, focused on the uniqueness of having women pilots on a military base, as well as offering an accurate depiction of the WASPs' missions:

> Pilots come and go in such numbers at Biggs Field that their arrivals and departures fail to arouse much interest. But everybody looked up early this week when five new fliers check in. They were Wasps—Women's Air Force Service Pilots. . . . All of Biggs Field's Wasps, assigned to a tow-target squadron here, are experienced pilots and have been flying from two to six years. Between the five of them, they have 3500 hours in the air.
>
> . . . The general public has appeared to be a little confused about the Wasps—that they're military personnel, like WAC and Army nurses. Some persons have vague ideas that Wasps belong to the Air Transport Command or the Ferrying Command.
>
> They are civilian pilots employed by the Army Air Force. Relieving men pilots for duty in the theaters of war, Wasps are assigned to various commands of the AAF, flying tow-target planes; breaking in new engines by slow time flying; filling air courier assignments; piloting administrative personnel; ferrying ships within the Continental United States and transporting needed instruments and repairs.[89]

However, not all articles from this time focused on the novelty or physical attributes of the pilots. Some focused entirely on the pilots' skills. "Cobras have a 'Lady Pilot'" led with:

> She is the first woman ever to fly a P-39. The P-39 Cobra was in 1943 the fastest fighter plane the US Military possessed. She is a little amused at the special attention which has been given her latest assignment as a member of the Women's Auxiliary Ferry Squadron. "Men can fly the P-39 and like it," she says. "Why can't women?"[90]

The article profiled WAFS Squadron Leader Del Scharr. It is very different from other WASP articles of the time in that it discussed the gender discrimination Scharr faced previous to her assignment with the WAFS, such as her inability before the war to get a position with aviation schools despite her having earned an instructor's certificate.[91]

In "Women Train in West Texas for Army Ferry Flying," from the *Christian Science Monitor*, the WASP training program was presented as newsworthy and the pilots as groundbreakers. The article outlined in detail the duties and backgrounds of the women pilots, emphasizing the difficulty of their training and missions. It began: "Women fliers by the hundreds, sunbronzed, trim as their streamlined planes, are threading the wide blue sky of West Texas in the Army's new program to prepare them for war service."[92]

As Cochran started to pursue militarized status for the WASPs, she worked to place more stories about the program in the media. She organized a press event at Camp Davis, North Carolina, where WASPs towed targets at which live machine gun and cannon ammunition was fired. The resultant stories were the most positive and detailed articles to appear about WASP missions, and they represented the last positive series of stories on the WASPs to appear until the late 1970s.

The first story on this event, from the *Evening Star*, began with a quote from the WASP director about militarizing the program:

> Miss Jacqueline Cochran, director of women pilots for the Army Air Forces, told a group of newspaper reporters observing the Women Air Force Pilots perform their missions here at the antiaircraft training center that "if the war lasts long enough we will probably use women pilots for noncombat duties in some theaters of the war (England and Hawaii). . . . We supplement the Army Air Forces," she added, "rather than replace its personnel, for some missions for which we are capable must remain for the men as valuable experience to prepare them for combat duty."[93]

Another article began: "Women pilots, generally supposed to have been restricted to ferrying planes from factories to airfields, have, for the last three months, been performing at least six other highly specialized jobs for the Army Air Forces. . . . Eventually, it is expected, women pilots will be given a dozen different assignments with the Army."[94]

This article outlined one mission performed by WASPs with a level of detail usually reserved for the exploits of male pilots:

> As the bomber piloted by the WASPS was reported near the range, the four gun batteries trained their guns on the target—a flag of wire mesh, 35 feet by 6 feet,

about the size of the fuselage of a medium-sized plane, at the end of a 3,000 foot tow rope. Another round of gun fire, and the target snapped from its tow rope and fell into the sea. The WASP dipped her wings and turned for home.[95]

"WASPS Who Tow Air Targets May Soon Be Real U.S. Soldiers" not only reported on the missions Cochran arranged for the media to watch, but included the reason behind the media show:

> Girls will be girls and Army Air Force pilots, too. If the achievements of Jacqueline Cochran and her WASP squadron here are a sign of things to come. The WASP, Women Airforce Service Pilots, are step-children in hand-me-down clothes so far. They replace men of the First Tactical Air Force for combat by tow-target and tracking mission flying, two of the most difficult and tedious labor of flying back and forth hour after hour on a set course, making precise turns.[96]

A more common response to the media event was for reporters to enhance their news articles with references to the physical qualities of the women pilots themselves: "`We get a thrill every time we leave the ground,' says pretty Eileen Roach, Phoenix, Arizona. `The Wasps are doing a man's job, and a good one,' an attractive, blonde, brown-eyed woman in trimly tailored slack suit of blue told a visiting newspaper woman."[97] These descriptors appear despite the same WASP telling the reporter: "The Wasps are doing essential, unglamorous hard work. We are here as a small cog in an extremely important wheel of the entire Army."[98]

The *New York Daily News* handled the story by focusing on an individual pilot, Dorothea Schultz, then twenty-two: "Like all WASPS, Miss Schultz had come up the hard way, qualifying with 35 hours of previous flying time and strict physical and educational requirements. . . . `We're the luckiest girls in the world,' she commented. `Every time you take a plane up it's a thrill.'"[99]

The *Washington Daily News* offered a positive, although uniquely gendered, treatment of the media event:

> Women Air Service Pilots (WASPS) are flying target-towing and tracking missions for anti-aircraft artillerymen here. Their job has been so satisfactory that their chief, Miss Jacqueline Cochran, deemed it need no longer remain a military secret. The famous woman flier was on hand to show what her girls can do and insist it be treated "without glamor."
>
> Like WACS, WAVES, SPARS and Marines, WASPS had to win their way here. Air Corps personnel assigned to this post were quite skeptical at first. Now most of them are in the cheering section.
>
> The WASPS are from all sections, they have been drawn together by their love of flying. Under Civil Service status now, eventually they may become part

of the Air Corps. Meanwhile, they wear uniforms and take orders. They could quit—but they don't. They have made themselves at home here and new barracks are being readied for them. In the interim, they have dandied up their present quarters with chintz cot covers, curtains and other feminine touches.

Pictures line the walls—but not of pin-up men. Mostly they are pictures of various war planes.[100]

These articles, which reported an important role the WASPS had in the American war effort, represented the last time during World War II that the media portrayed the WASPs positively.

WASP Plans for Militarization Come under Attack

By 1944, media support and public opinion were turning away from all-out war efforts and were focusing instead on efforts to return the United States to an idealized prewar style of living. It was assumed that the war was won, and interest now focused on the postwar economy, particularly in jobs for returning servicemen. At war factories, women were being laid off in record numbers, and popular media, movies, and books advocated the return of women to their "rightful places" in support of men. This is the cultural context within which the issue of women piloting military planes would be debated not only in Congress, but also in the media. Congressional debate and the male civilian pilots' lobby would bring the issue of WASP militarization to public attention.

One of the major criticisms against the WASPs—that they were not needed because the ferrying of planes was being effectively handled—ironically had been contributed to by the WASPs because of their efficiency in performing their duties. By 1944, the United States and its Allies had obtained worldwide air superiority. Air battles were still being fought, but they were not of the magnitude of earlier battles, and the United States had not lost the numbers of planes and flight crews military planners had anticipated and for which they had established contingencies. As a result, greater numbers of experienced combat pilots were returning to the United States, fewer pilots and flight crews needed to be trained, and fewer planes needed to be produced. At the same time, American military planners were anticipating an intensive ground assault against Japan. The Army needed hundreds of thousands of soldiers for its ground troops. As a result of these factors, the AAF, which had conscripted men from the rosters of its parent organization, the Army, did not need significant numbers of pilot trainees and released them back to the Army for conscription into the ground forces. Schools that had been established for training pilots were closed, and the pilot trainers, who had not been drafted into the regular Army while they served as trainers, were now eligible for the draft. In addition, combat pilots who had returned to the United States were eager to perform any utility flying so that they could continue to receive flight pay. (AAF pilots received a greater monthly salary the more hours they flew. However, civilian pilots hired by the AAF, such as the WASPs, did not receive greater pay for their flight time, regardless of how many hours they flew.)

In the past, the bills to create militarized units of women's auxiliaries had met with limited opposition in the media. Editorials and articles were often incredulous of the idea of women soldiers, but tended to support the opinions and requests of the War Department. Stories covering women's auxiliaries usually appeared after the auxiliaries had been approved by Congress. However, bills authorizing all other auxiliaries were brought to Congress in 1942 and 1943, when the media generally supported increases in the military. In 1944, when the AAF brought the WASP bill before Congress, two major obstacles existed: a Congress that was concerned more with cutting military costs than with creating programs, and the thousands of men who wanted the flying positions then held by the WASPs. It would be the second obstacle that would draw public attention to the actions of Congress.

An article that appeared before the congressional debate began optimistically maintained that the men of the U.S. military supported the WASP program:

> So successful was this initial effort that the Army decided to coordinate the whole program and set it up last summer as a continuous program under Miss Cochran. So, the big-wigs are sold on the whole idea and the enlisted men have taken the girls to their hearts. A belligerent, husky sergeant who threatened to desert if a woman landed on the place now takes a personal interest and keeps on their trail.[101]

This article incorrectly predicted that male servicemen would accept the bill. While the bill for WASP militarization was still being examined at the committee level in Congress, the male civilian pilots had been laid off and were subject to draft into the walking army, and they were organizing a congressional lobby to target the WASP bill. At the same time, negative publicity toward the program was increasing in the media.

The article "Army Passes Up Jobless Pilots to Train Wasps: Prefers Women to Older, Experienced Flyers" began: "With 5,000 experienced airplane pilots looking for jobs as a result of the liquidation of the civil aeronautic commission's pilot training program, the government is training more than 1,000 young women, at an estimated cost of 6 million dollars, as ferry pilots for the army."[102] The article went on to say that "most" of the former CAA pilots felt "that the WASP training program should be stopped and experienced men pilots given the ferrying jobs."[103] The article "Men Pilots Jobless, House Unit Considers Investigating WASP" had a similar tone:

> The House Civil Services Investigating Committee, it was learned today, is considering an inquiry to determine whether the WASP (Women Air Service Pilots) program should be continued while thousands of experienced men pilots are looking for jobs. . . .
>
> Mutterings about the WASP in male flying circles increased sharply after the Army and Navy gave notice of intention to abandon the war training service program under the Civil Aeronautics Administration. This releasing approximately 900 male pilots, averaging 31 years of age and 2,200 hours in the air, and 4,167 student instructors. Many of these men will lose their deferred draft status and may be put into the "walking Army."[104]

One piece, "Lay That Airplane Down, Babe, Cry Grounded He-Man Pilots," had a more accurate focus and strongly predicted what was in store for the WASPs:

> Fiercest battle in the war between men and women, outside of James Thurber's cartoons, is being fought today in the air. Thousands of well-trained male pilots are grounded and jobless, is the masculine cry, while Jacqueline Cochran's WASPS continue ferrying planes, towing targets, tracking and doing courier work for the Army at $250 a month.
>
> The battle of the sexes has reached such proportions that mail from outraged males is piling high on congressional desks. The Ramspeck Civil Service Investigating Committee is considering an inquiry which some observers at the Capitol consider inevitable. Supporters of the ladies, seeing the handwriting on the wall, are moving heaven and earth to get thru the Costello bill that will move the winged women from Civil Service, and give them Army status and a firmer grip on their jobs. . . .
>
> Reports from around the Capitol say that some of the members are unwilling to go to bat for the ladies and support this bill while another bill before the committee to give commissions to members of the armed forces trained under the Civil Aeronautics Administration, got no action. . . . Most of the WTS instructors lack the one requirement of 200 hours in 200 h.p. planes, they say. "Most of the men wish that for the duration they could be women," wrote a group of WTS instructors to a sympathetic senator.

Some of the masculine comments aren't gallant. "Thirty-five hour wonders" is one tag they've pinned on the lady fliers.

"The taxpayers we do bleed easily," said one disgruntled male. "Costs $7000 to train every female. It's the most expensive way to ferry planes."

"If the girls were patriotic they'd resign," declared another.

"Doesn't make sense," sighed one baffled by it all. "Especially when Gen. Arnold says the Army has pilots running out of its ears."

Chances are, say Capitol observers, that the men won't go down without a fight on the floor, waged by male members who think it's time for the ladies to holler "uncle."[105]

As a result of the pressure applied by male civilian pilots, the House Civil Service Investigating Committee began an inquiry into the WASP training program. The intent of the committee, "to determine whether the Women's Airforce Service Pilots program should be continued while thousands of experienced man pilots are looking for jobs,"[106] was highly publicized in newspapers and magazines. When the committee reported that too much money was being spent on WASP training and suggested it be discontinued, the press immediately seized on and exaggerated the results. Even articles that provided positive statistics on the WASP program were distorted by irrelevant and completely gendered constructions:

Miss Cochran, who in peacetime was never too busy gathering up both men's and women's flying trophies to neglect her own femininity, is also determined that the women flying for the Air Transport Command shall not neglect their feminine allure. She has ordered them out of slacks and dungarees and into dresses at least four nights a week at the Sweetwater, Texas, Training Post. . . .

Any girl who insists on keeping on her working clothes on nights that the flag is run up for dress can't come into the mess hall unless she is on duty, nor into the recreation rooms.

Wasp uniforms for work and dress are attractive enough to make any girl want to keep them on. Santiago blue is the color for work slacks & "battle jackets" as well as the dress skirt and jacket worn with a white cotton shirt.

Women fliers have a lower accident rate than the men doing comparable work, get back from missions more swiftly and don't mind dull hops, airmen report.

Arnold wants at least another two thousand of them to replace men in permanent non combat flying jobs in this country.[107]

A *Washington Star* "Bulletin" reported that money was being spent on the WASP program while a pool of experienced male pilots existed, and that committee members were influenced in their findings by the existence of these pilots.[108] One newspaper reported that officers involved with the CAA were using public planes and funds to solicit signatures from CAA pilot instructors to present to Congress:

> Fifty Army planes carrying high-ranking officers are winging their way around the country on a whirlwind mission that may give the court to hopes of thousands of well-trained male fliers for victory in the battle of the sexes over the right to fly Army planes on non-combat duty, it was learned today.
>
> If the ladies win, it is pointed out, men fliers will have a new interpretation of "victory through air power." And in any case the Army code of "an officer and a gentleman" will have been stretched to the point of gallantry that costs the taxpayers a pretty penny.
>
> Officers of the Flying Instructor Board, appointed by the Army Air Forces Training Command, are interviewing at training centers throughout the country flying instructors of the Enlisted Reserve Corps–Civil Aeronautics Administration War Training Service to get their signatures on a document that says in effect they will be satisfied by whatever jobs they are given.[109]

At the same time, WASPs were forbidden from speaking with the media or publicly discussing the bill before Congress. "In the last twelve to fourteen months of our service in World War II, an edict came down from headquarters that there was to be no publicity and no media interviews or anything about the WASPS or by the WASPS," said WASP Madge Rutherford Minton.[110] The media silence from the WASPs during this time of crisis was itself newsworthy, and the blame for the ban was put, not on the War Department's Bureau of Public Relations, which actually developed the ban, but squarely on the shoulders of WASP director Cochran:

> Miss Jacqueline Cochran, head of the WASPs, has jealously guarded her flying women from the wrong kind of publicity.
>
> According to an air force spokesman the nationally known aviatrix feels that "glamorizing" is the worst hazard a woman flyer has to meet.
>
> Before Miss Cochran's women flying training detachment was merged into the WASPs its head had already decided that publicity for women flyers with the accent on women was "out." She had already discovered that the cameramen simply would not behave and that feature writers refused to take the proper slant on women in the air.
>
> The photographers invariably picked out the best looking girls to photograph to the discomfiture of the less photogenic of the girls with flying ambitions while the feature writers took a perverse attitude that flying was an unusual accomplishment for women and that sex should be underlined in any recital of the accomplishment of any aviatrix.

This, according to Miss Cochran's spokesman, was a false notion which must be gradually dispelled from the public mind.

Because of these strong convictions on the equality of opportunity for the sexes Miss Cochran has refused to allow her organization to be advertised as a woman's auxiliary and there has been the minimum of pictures featuring the cadets of the women air force pilots.[111]

Members of Congress likewise recognized the potential for publicity if they aligned themselves with the male civilian pilots, and they soon began to issue attacks against the WASPs. Representative Alvin O'Konski, a Wisconsin Republican, was quoted as charging that the WASP bill was "just more money for the air forces to squander," while flight instructors were "being thrown into the street."[112] In another story a Congressman explained the WASP bill with outrageous suppositions about female behavior:

And with a fine instinct for feminine psychology, Rep. May (D. Ky.), when asked why the WASPS hadn't been made part of the WACS, said, "That would be too many women in one place. The WASPS might sting the WACS." . . .

That the powder puff brigade got priority before the committee has been a matter of anguish to grounded jobless male fliers, let out when the Army discontinued the program in January, and they have been flooding congressional desks with protests.[113]

Adding fuel to the debate, the media published General Arnold's testimony before the House Military Affairs Committee, in which he said that he wanted not only for women pilots to replace men pilots, but for all women to replace all men in the United States, thus freeing the men for overseas service: "We must provide fighting men wherever we can, replacing them with women wherever we can, whether it be in factories or towing airplane targets or wherever it may be."[114]

Articles about proposed legislation to militarize the WASPs frequently focused more on the plight of male civilian pilots than they did on the WASPs. Realizing that opposition to militarizing the WASPs was largely based on concern for the male pilots, Secretary of War Henry Stimson began to address the issue. He stated that the purpose of the legislation was not to give women special privileges, nor to prevent skilled male pilots from flying, but to allow the military to take full advantage of the wartime contribution of women pilots.[115]

"Neither the existence nor the militarization of the WASP will keep out of the Army Air Forces a single instructor or partially trained civilian pilot who desires to become a service pilot or a cadet and can meet the applicable standards of the

Army Air Forces," stated Henry L. Stimson, Secretary of War, at a press conference here.

The present membership of the WASP and the women pilots in training for the Army Air Forces are employed in a civilian status by the Army Air Force, and are performing valuable services in this respect. But the rights, privileges, and benefits available to comparable military personnel are denied to them. . . . The WASP organization is small, and the women pilots are professional personnel with specialized skill, in the same sense as female doctors and female nurses. The consideration which dictates the incorporation of such professional skills directly into the Medical Corps of the Army indicates a similar disposition of women pilots.[116]

As a result of the surge in stories created on behalf of the CAA pilots, even the leader of the AAF was compelled to release a statement that modified his original intent to transfer the male civilian pilots to the Army's ground forces: "General H. H. Arnold, chief of the Army Air Forces, was reported today as willing to give male CAA instructors the same chance at Army commissions which he has strongly recommended for girl fliers in the WASPs."[117]

But these statements by Stimson and Arnold did nothing to combat the rise of negative publicity against the WASPs. The male pilots' lobby—and, subsequently, the media—had found a vulnerable target. The WASPs were accused of being excessively glamorous, and allegations arose that their uniforms were costing taxpayers more than five hundred dollars each[118] and were created by "Fifth Avenue" designers as part of the "glamorous excess of the corps."[119]

An exclusive Fifth Avenue shop is outfitting the War Department's women flyers in snappy new military uniforms at $505 per WASP, a Senate Military Affairs Subcommittee was told yesterday.

By contrast, Mr. Morrison said, male flying instructors being thrown out of jobs by cutbacks in AAF pilot training look a bit ragged in old khaki pants and "Woodtick" coats discarded by the CCC.[120]

Representative James Morrison was further quoted in another piece that focused on the WASP uniforms:

Experienced male fliers, with more than 2,000 hours in the air, may soon be cleaning windshields and servicing planes for "glamorous woman flyers who only have 35 hours of flying time," the House was told yesterday by Representative Morrison, Democrat, of Louisiana.

Declaring "this is a glamorous and unnecessary duplication," the Louisianan described the WASPS as an "elite corps," which would be made up entirely of commissioned officers if Congress approves a bill to make the group a regular part of the Air Forces.

"The WASPS are perhaps the most super-duper of all programs," he told the House. "Magazines have played them up and even the movies contributed a picture in their behalf. Their natty and stylish uniforms were tailored on Fifth Avenue in New York and cost over $500 for each WASP."[121]

Defense against the charges that the WASPs were an overly glamorized group were countered not by articles or releases from the War Department, but by Mrs. G. W. Featherhoff, a mother of a WASP who wrote a letter to the editor of the St. Louis *Globe-Democrat*:

> I have been reading with much interest the articles on the Wasps, and their so-called glamour.
> I have a daughter in the Wasps and if the life she leads comes under the head of glamour, Mr. Webster is dead wrong in his definition of the word. They fly from sun up to sun down every day, check in a hotel at night too tired even to see a movie, and even if they were inclined to do a little night life they have nothing but their flying suits to wear. Imagine spreading glamour in a bulky jacket, wrinkled slacks, helmets and maybe a decorative parachute for extra appeal. They live in barracks. Need I go into detail about this luxurious setting? . . .
> These girls were asked by their government to do this job and they are doing their very best. They are intensely interested in their work, eager to serve wherever they are needed and deeply grateful that they have been given this opportunity to fly.[122]

In addition to the attacks on the women's pilot program, WASP director Cochran also came under personalized and pointed attacks. The media displayed her as a wealthy egomaniac whose personal considerations outweighed the nation's needs. The WASPs were constructed as her pet project, supported and continued, it was alleged, because of Cochran's ability to seduce high-ranking members of the military and government. Gossip columnist Drew Pearson purported that the government was "training lady fliers, primarily at the behest of vivacious Aviatrix Jaquelin *[sic]* Cochran, wife of financial magnate, Floyd Odlum. Magnetic Miss Cochran seems to have quite a drag with the Brass Hats and has even persuaded the air forces' smiling commander to make several secret trips to Capitol Hill to lobby for her pets, the WASPS."[123] Articles further alleged that Cochran had created the WASP program not out of patriotism in support of the country's military needs, but as "a political affair."[124] Obviously, concluded these critics, this level of conspiracy could not be the act of one woman, no matter how seductive and corrupt, but must have the support of other women engaged in such devious activities. Thus, some named First Lady Eleanor Roosevelt as a "back-door" supporter of the

WASPs. One piece, "First Lady's Hand Is Seen," stated: "Suspicion points to Mrs. Roosevelt as influential in efforts to advance the WASPS, women fliers, at the expense of thousands of trained civilian pilots and instructors who possess much more experience in the air."[125] This and other pieces displayed the WASPs not as women dedicated to supporting the war effort, but as women detrimental to the war effort because they were simply the pawns of a too-powerful First Lady who wanted to unjustly further the causes of women. A sampling of headlines on the WASP bill candidly reveal the media opposition to the program and the constructions used to express this opposition: "CAA Men 'Tossed to the Wolves,' Air Staff Officer Informed,"[126] "WASP Bill Hinges on Rights for Men,"[127] "Wasps May Oust 5,000 Instructors,"[128] "Aviators Stung by WASPS: Fliers Resented Proposed Corps,"[129] and "Pilots Seek to Continue Instructing: Denied Jobs Women Pilots Now Receiving Training For."[130]

A common denominator among articles criticizing the WASP program was that the women pilots had overstepped their reason for being created and were replacing men rather than releasing them for duty. One article quoted Representative O'Konski as charging that the AAF was squandering money by training the WASPs when "5,000 trained flight instructors were being 'thrown into the street.'"[131]

Despite General Arnold's insistence that the AAF was transferring male cadets and trainers where they were needed for the war effort—which was into the ground forces—the media continued to attack the WASPs as a hindrance to the war effort. Editorials asserted that male pilots were "being converted into lackeys for the glamour gals . . . grounded to look after the glamour gals."[132] These pieces claimed or inferred that the male pilots could take up the flying jobs being performed by WASPs, never mentioning the specialized training that went into ferrying, target towing, or other missions. Some even went so far as to infer that the AAF had created artificially high standards for the male pilots specifically to prevent them from flying: "Rep. John J. Sparkman (D. Ala.) announced that he will introduce an amendment designed to stall off any move by the War Department to set the standards so high the men can't qualify."[133] Despite this assertion, the article did not point out a primary contradiction, namely, that the bill really was to provide CAA-WTS instructors and trainees with "additional training as may be necessary" to meet the minimum AAF requirements for pilots.[134]

One article even stated that WASPs were not just replacing men, but were actually preventing men from obtaining the combat training they needed: "One P-38 pilot unwilling to be named, complained that there was no room for his squadron, due in England for combat duty in nine weeks, at a southern field for much needed advanced instrument training because a WASP contingent was on hand for a six weeks' course to prepare them as instrument instructors."[135] Other articles stated just the opposite: WASPs were not flying because there were too many male pilots already flying the missions the WASPs were purportedly still being trained to cover:

WASPs themselves question their essentiality to the war effort and a sizable number may resign if Congress gives them Army status, according to Mrs. Jeanne Robertson, 26, Los Angeles, Calif., a WASP who resigned recently for "personal reasons." . . .

"All these reports of thousands of trained civilian pilots released and now grounded make them wonder how necessary they are," she said. "And there's a reluctance to fly the heavy, fast planes because they're a challenge, particularly on the part of those who have husbands and children."[136]

The same article quotes an anonymous WASP, who also purportedly resigned, as saying:

"Ever since we arrived at our ferry bases after graduation, and were promptly disillusioned as to their need of our services, the situation has been a source of discussion among the members of our class. There seemed to be no need to train women for ferry pilots as the bases were apparently overstocked with capable men who sometimes begged for a chance to fly just hours in the month to keep on flight pay."[137]

Exemplifying how strong public opinion was against the WASPs, even the release of a Hollywood film about the pilots would be turned against them. *Ladies Courageous*, a melodramatic and inaccurate portrayal of the program, unfortunately was released just as the congressional bill was receiving heated criticism. Subsequently, Washington, D.C., newspapers didn't simply review the film, they positioned it within the larger debate:

"Ladies Courageous" will arrive at Keith's tomorrow, in the midst of a Capitol Hill battle to make the WASPs a part of the Army Air Force.

Picture is a tribute to the Women Air Forces Service Pilots and has the sanction of the U.S. Army. The bill of Rep. John M. Costello of California, would swear in the WASPs as an integral unit of the Air Forces.

Lined up against the measure are the American Legion and aviation interests. The WASPs are led by the alluring Miss Jacqueline Cochran, wife of Floyd D. Odlum, multi-millionaire New York financier, possessor of many medals and honors for her feats in an airplane.

Those who have seen "Ladies Courageous" predict that the picture will do Rep. Costello's bill no particular good.

For "Ladies Courageous" careens away into telling stories about what irresponsible and emotionally unstable girls they are. Their personal problems weigh more than their careers in the air, they live in an atmosphere of petty bickering. Things get so bad that their commander resigns in shame.

Toward the end of the picture a last-minute attempt is made to hint that all these antics were just an expression of healthy, girlish spirits.

This feature arriving at the time when the debate in Congress is red-hot will be potent screen argument against Rep. Costello's bill. Personal emotions and jealousies interfere with their work, the screening at this time is a recording of the organization's growing pains. It leaves a bad impression of the women pilots.[138]

Subject and cast are far better than the film itself. Being a glorification of the WAFS—the brave, efficient femmes who ferry the planes to the fighters—it should have been a precision bomb. . . .

Tale is about the small group of women fliers who early in the war offered their services to the Government to relieve men for combat duty. Story takes you into the intimate moments of their lives in barracks, shows them on long and hazardous operational flights, dramatizes their campaign to be militarized into the Army along with the other distaff groups such as the WACS.

I think the courageous and efficient WAFS deserve a better testimonial than this.[139]

In Congress, representatives opposed to the WASP bill used the film as another example of the glamorization of WASPs, ignoring the countless movies that appeared during the war not only on male military participants, but on the WACs, WAVES, and military nurses.

The worst attacks against the WASPs came from Pearson, who, in his widely read, syndicated "The Washington Merry-Go-Round" column, aimed his vitriol not only at the WASP program, but also at the leading individuals involved in the program. Among his key contributions to the debate was alleging that Cochran, the "vivacious Aviatrix," had seduced General Arnold into using a "back-door strategy" to get the WASP program approved; that unqualified women flew in the program; that WASPs used their beauty to get by with male AAF officers; and that WASPs were inadequate pilots with an above-average fatality rate who were incapable of checking out on higher-rated pursuit planes and bombers, thus rendering them useless.[140] Among the false charges leveled against the WASPs by other journalists were that WASPs were inexperienced and bad pilots, that their fatality rates in training were excessively high, that they cost more to train than male pilots, and that they had a lower rate of passing courses and of succeeding in missions than did male pilots. One such article stated:

> Now the minimum cost of training a WASP is $20,000. Of 1313 girls who have taken such training, only 541 have graduated, 281 have flunked and the others are still trying to make the grade. It costs more to train them than to train a man for the same work and that is not the worst of it. There are thousands of men pilots with nothing much to do except to ferry the planes which Arnold wants the gals to ferry. What is behind the general's move to build the WASPs up to huge organization for which there is no earthly need?[141]

Patterns of Media Depictions of the WASPs

A careful reading of media depictions about the WASPs reveals a pattern in which the WASPs themselves were not subject to praise. Rather, during the first three years of American involvement in World War II, all efforts in support of the war, no matter how insignificant or even illogical, were praised. However, in 1944, when the war turned the Allies' way, media accounts adopted a more critical stance: battle losses were questioned; discussions arose as to the tactical values of missions; key military figures were criticized; and, in general, requests were made to return "the boys," cut losses, save money, and develop the postwar domestic economy. For the first time in World War II, the media began to criticize and carefully analyze financial expenditures on the war. In these changing media constructions toward the military, the soldier (typically defined as the man in combat or the boy overseas) was the only entity that continued to receive media support. As the year continued, the media developed as its mission the protection of these soldiers on the home front. Victory was eminent, and issues of job security and domestic appointments for returning combat veterans became primary.

The media had constructed women in the military as supplemental (following the War Department and congressional directives that defined women participants in the armed forces not as soldiers but as auxiliaries to soldiers). When full mobilization of soldiers and citizens had been called for, the media supported the involvement of these women. However, this support was guarded and constructed within gendered notions. With the war reaching its end, media opinion about women in the military shifted, and women were beginning to be constructed as unnecessary siphons of money that would be better directed in support of "real" soldiers. In 1944, the women's auxiliaries of the

Army, Navy, and Army Air Forces all came under media attack, and because women were constructed as a singular category, attacks on one branch detrimentally affected the other branches. The WAVES came under media scrutiny because the Navy planned to position them overseas. Media pieces called for the total recall of all WAVES and loudly criticized the Navy's purported attempts at putting women into combat. Following this, the WACs faced false allegations of immorality from what was later determined to have been a slander campaign developed by male Army personnel. The publication of these rumors resulted in a general call for the WACs to return to the safety of "home."

It might be argued that the WASP program suffered from bad timing. Throughout its two-year existence, there were plans to submit bills for its militarization to Congress, but the AAF did not formalize these plans and submit any bills until 1944. The introduction of the bill to militarize the WASPs came when both Congress and the media were calling for military cutbacks, and also coincided with the tremendously publicized sex scandal of the WAC. Concurrently, male civilian pilots and trainers had been laid off and faced being drafted into the "walking army," and returning combat pilots publicly complained about their need for domestic flight missions so that they could continue to receive flight pay.

All of these factors combined to initiate a dramatic media attack against the WASP program. The women pilots were depicted as a waste of taxpayers' money, as unnecessary, as lacking in skill, and as an overall detriment to the war effort. Because of a public relations policy imposed by the War Department, no media messages were issued in defense of the WASP program. Statements by members of Congress reveal that the negative publicity caused by the media campaign initiated by male civilian pilots and returning combat pilots had a profound impact on how they would vote on the bill.

5

No Allies for the WASPs

Congress Responds to Male Public Interest Groups

The powerful lobby assembled by the male civilian pilots focused its attentions on Congress as well as the media. The pilots initiated a letter-writing campaign to Congress that was backed by powerful male aviation associations and veterans groups, and they began to lobby individual members of Congress. When the group learned that House Committee on Military Affairs had recommended passage of a bill to militarize Women Airforce Service Pilots, the lobby began to attack the WASPs and pushed for the introduction of its own bill, supporting the contentions that positions be found for male pilots and that they not be relegated to the Army's ground forces.

The WASP Militarization Bills

On September 30, 1943, Representative John Costello of California introduced the WASP militarization bill, House Resolution 3358. The complete text of the bill follows, with italicization and punctuation intact:

A bill to provide for the appointment of female pilots in the Air Forces of the Army.

Be it enacted by the Senate and House of Representatives of the United States of America in Congress assembled, That hereafter during the present war and six months thereafter there shall be included in the Air Forces of the Army such licensed female pilots as the Secretary of War may consider necessary, whose qualifications, duties, and assignments shall be in accordance with regulations to be prescribed by the Secretary, and who shall be appointed and at his discretion removed by the Commanding General of the Air Forces of the Army, subject to the approval of the Secretary of War. Those appointed shall be commissioned in the Army of the United States, and shall receive the same pay and allowances and be entitled to the same rights, privileges and benefits as members of the Officers' Reserve Corps of the Army with the same grade and length of service.[1]

Following congressional protocol, the bill was referred to the Committee on Military Affairs for approval or recommendations. In an October 4 letter to WASP director Jacqueline Cochran, Costello encouraged her to ensure that the War Department would issue a favorable report to the committee, stating, "If we can get a favorable report from the War Department, I feel that I will have little difficulty in getting the Committee's approval."[2] It was six months before the Committee on Military Affairs held hearings about WASP militarization. In the meantime, Costello had submitted a longer bill, House Resolution 4219, "A bill to provide for the appointment of female pilots and aviation cadets in the Air Forces of the Army." The bill was structured similarly to the first bill, except that it provided greater detail concerning the administration of the WASP program:

> *Be it enacted by the Senate and House of Representative of the United States of America in Congress assembled,* That for the period of the present war and for six months thereafter or for such shorter period as the Congress by concurrent resolution or the President by proclamation shall prescribe, there may be included in the Air Forces of the Army such female commissioned and flight officer personnel and female aviation student personnel as the Secretary of War may consider necessary. The qualifications, duties, and assignments of such personnel shall be in accordance with regulations to be prescribed by the Secretary of War. No officer shall be appointed to a grade above that of colonel and not more than one officer to that grade, and the right of commissioned or flight officers to exercise command shall be specifically limited to personnel placed under their command.
>
> Sec. 2. The commissioned personnel selected directly from civil life, of which not less than 95 per centum shall consist of qualified pilots, shall be appointed in the Army of the United States under the provisions of the joint resolution of September 22, 1941 (55 Stat. 728), and ordered into the active service of the United States.
>
> Sec. 3. Under such regulations as the Secretary of War shall prescribe, female aviation cadets may be appointed for pilot training in the Army of the United States and, upon successful completion of the prescribed course of training, may be commissioned as second lieutenants in the Army of the United States under the provisions of the joint resolution of September 22, 1941, or appointed as flight officers of the Army of the United States under the provisions of the Act of July 8, 1942 (56 Stat. 549). Service as an aviation cadet which is terminated by discharge before completion of the prescribed course of training or before commission as a second lieutenant or appointment as a flight officer, and which is not terminated as a result of a physical disability incurred during such training shall not be regarded as service in the armed forces within the meaning of the laws granting rights, privileges, or benefits to discharged members of the armed forces.

Sec. 4. All persons commissioned or appointed under this Act shall, except as otherwise provided herein, receive the same pay and allowances as members of the Army of the United States and shall be entitled to the same rights, privileges, and benefits as are accorded the said members of the same rank, grade, and length of service.[3]

The most significant additions to this bill were the placement of a ceiling on the highest rank that could be awarded in the division (which equaled the top rank allowed in all other women's divisions within the military); a limitation that officers could command only members of their division (i.e., women could command only women); a restriction that a minimum of 95 percent of those in the WASPs would have to be qualified pilots; and allowances providing that the women would receive pay, rights, and privileges equal to those received by men of the same rank in the Army Air Forces.

The hearing by the Committee on Military Affairs lasted less than one hour, with only one witness testifying on behalf of the bill. That witness was a formidable one: AAF Commanding General Henry H. Arnold. Arnold testified that the Army was suffering from a severe personnel shortage, and that WASPs would assist American war efforts by filling all domestic flying operations roles, enabling men involved in these missions to be placed in overseas situations. He stated: "It is not beyond reason to expect that some day all of our Air Transport Command ferrying within the United States will be done by women."[4] As the *New York Herald Tribune* reported:

> The need for young infantry soldiers has become so acute that 36,000 men in the Army Air Forces pilot training pool are being returned to the Army Ground Forces; General H. H. Arnold, chief of the A.A.F., revealed today with an explanation—supplemented by General George C. Marshall, Chief of Staff— that planned requirements for air force personnel have been reduced because casualties have been fewer than expected.
>
> This disclosure of that source of combat troop supply and a statement by General Arnold that he expected women to replace virtually all male ferry pilots within the United States, serve to emphasize the seriousness of the Army's need for young foot soldiers who are now being drawn from war industry in increasing numbers.
>
> . . . The War Department explained that casualties in the air have been less than the percentages established in expectation of the character of the fighting. Also, the general shortage of trained personnel throughout the Army, due to cumulative shortages in the draft since last July, has made it necessary to utilize every available soldier to meet the current demands for pending operations.

General Arnold told the House Military Affairs Committee, however, that of the 4,687 men training to become instructors of Army pilots, 974 have qualified for aviation cadet training and 651 for glider training, 2,618 for technical training and 310 for specialist duties, and 134 were hospitalized or on furlough. Of the 615 enlisted reservists, 229 have applied for assignment to the Air Transport Command, and all will be considered for some type of work with the A.A.F. if they meet the standards.[5]

Arnold noted that the greatest shortages were with the Army's ground forces, which, he reported, was 200,000 men short of its needed personnel strength.[6] He testified that 36,000 men who had been in the Air Forces pool awaiting use as future combat flight crews had been "returned to the Ground and Service Forces," because the Army was in need of talented and educated officer material.[7] The point of Arnold's argument was that, despite what the media was reporting, WASPs would not be replacing male pilots; rather, the overall war mission called for these men to be used by the military in capacities other than as domestic pilots. Arnold proposed that all capable men be sent overseas for combat and related duties, while women handled all domestic military missions. "Arnold Visions All-Woman U.S. Air Transport," in the *Washington Evening Star*, reported the situation this way:

> Envisioning a day not far away when the airplanes will be crowded with Army planes piloted by women, Gen. H. H. Arnold, Army Air Forces commander, told the House Military Affairs Committee today he expects to have all male flyers "out of the United States and get them over fighting."
>
> "It is not beyond all reason to expect that some day all our air transport services in the United States will be done by women," Gen. Arnold said as he endorsed legislation to give Army status to the Women's Air Force Service Pilots, now composed of 534 civilian women who ferry Army planes, make weather flights and even tow targets for machine gun practice.
>
> He emphasized that "it is not proposed to send the WASPS into combat fields."[8]

Besides encouraging WASP militarization, General Arnold requested that Congress authorize an expansion of the WASP program to between 2,000 and 2,500 pilots, so that the AAF would "get enough to replace every man qualified for overseas service whose permanent duty is flying in the United States and get all of these qualified men out of the United States and get them overseas."[9] Arnold also indicated that the AAF was experimenting with WASPs as pilot trainers so that male pilot instructors could be released to "our fighting units."[10]

General Arnold countered all aspects of the arguments being put forth by male civilian pilots and instructors that the AAF did not have places for them as pilots because WASPs were filling all available flight positions. Arnold carefully traced the placement of the 13,000 male civilian pilots who had been affiliated with the Civil Aeronautics Administration and the 899 instructors from AAF-affiliated flight schools, detailing how all had been given the opportunity to join the AAF, with those who qualified being approved as pilot cadets and those who did not being transferred to flight crew or ground crew positions or receiving medical discharges.[11]

Arnold stressed that the male pilots were not being replaced by WASPs, but that most of these men did not meet the pilot requirements established by the AAF. (Their previous positions had been with the CAA, which had lower requirements than the AAF.) "If they cannot qualify according to our standards in one of these capacities [as pilots, copilots, bombardiers, gunners, or navigators] then we offer them other training in the Army Air Forces. We cannot lower our standards because a man has had a few hours in the air. They must meet our standards," Arnold testified.[12] Thus, in order for the AAF to accept the pilots who were publicly demanding to be given places, it would have to lower the standards established for pilots—standards met by the WASPs.[13]

One committee representative told General Arnold about an instructor with 1,900 air hours who was turned down by the Air Forces because he was not in the Reserves, and asked the general what he could do to help that individual. General Arnold responded: "We don't consider we owe them anything because they were offered a chance to join the Reserve and did not take advantage of it. And now when they see they are likely to be drafted they want to come in and it is too late."[14] General Arnold was testifying about a side of the issue that the media was not reporting. The Army had plans to use the male civilian pilots in overseas roles, probably in combat positions for which they were both qualified and needed, and these men were resisting this necessary transition. The stance of patriotism put forth by the male civilian pilots and their lobbyists in the media was a false one. The purpose of the civilian pilots campaign against the WASPs was not to support the war effort, but to avoid the draft and combat service. Their positions as instructors and CAA pilots had protected them from being drafted; when the AAF removed their draft-exempt status, they were faced with the possibility of serving in combat. In addition, the Air Forces had given them the opportunity to serve in active duty as pilots, but the majority of the pilots now publicly vying for the jobs held by WASPs did not meet the qualifications necessary to place them in those roles.

General Arnold also testified about the reasons why the Air Forces had chosen to develop the WASPs as a separate division from the Women's Army Corps. "For a while we thought we might be able to put the women pilots in the WAC's, but we have an entirely different type of personnel. The women pilots are professional, with specialized skill, in the same sense that nurses are," Arnold testified. (The Army Nurses Corps was also an autonomous military division, which was entirely separate from the WAC.) "And there are also certain basic provisions in the WAC legislation that prevents them taking over the WASPS we now have."[15] The differences Arnold listed were minimum and maximum age requirements and the WAC ban on women who had children under the age of fourteen. Other differences between the two organizations had to do with minimum education requirements, WASP training requirements, and a rider in the WAC bill that specifically prohibited WACs from being pilots. In concluding his testimony, General Arnold encouraged passage of the bill not only so that the AAF could expand the WASP program and eventually replace all male pilots flying domestically, but also to enable the AAF to better utilize WASPs who were already active:

> In connection with the WASP bill we are waiting now, holding over certain of our decisions pending the passage or nonpassage of this bill. From our point of view with the present terrific manpower shortage we should use every means we can to put women in where they can replace men. This bill will help not only to do that but will also make far more effective the employment of the present WASPS that we have in our service. . . . It is an emergency proposition so far as I am concerned.[16]

This echoes the sentiment expressed by Secretary of War Henry Stimson, who submitted a letter in support of enabling WASP legislation dated February 16, 1944, when H.R. 3358 was still under consideration. Like Arnold, Stimson expressed the need for the WASPs, outlined the benefits that militarization offered the AAF, and provided reasons why incorporation into the WAC would not work. Stimson also pressed for a quick resolution to the bill:

> The War Department believes that presently qualified female pilots and such necessary female administrative personnel should be commissioned in the Army of the United States without delay, and that provisions be made for additional appointments as the need arises. . . . The organization is small and is composed of women who are offering a special skill in connection with the prosecution of this war.[17]

On March 22, 1944, the same day General Arnold testified to the Committee on Military Affairs, the committee issued a report recommending the passage of H.R. 4219. The committee cited two arguments in support of the bill: that recognized personnel shortages in the war effort warranted the existence and expansion of a program of women pilots; and that because of the necessary services being performed by these women, they deserved the medical and other military benefits provided to members of the armed services. The report stated:

> There is no controversy over the fact that there exists in this country an acute shortage of manpower necessary for the armed forces and essential industry. . . . In recognition of these principles, the Army Air Forces now employ as Federal civil-service employees over 500 women pilots. . . . The present organization and procedure is not well adapted to the peculiar and special nature of the duties performed and most efficient personnel administration.[18]

The report noted that the WASPs were not receiving needed benefits "merely because of the lack of enabling legislation"[19] and suggested that the militarization of the WASPs would benefit the war effort by streamlining the administration of the program:

> It should be pointed out, however, that passage of the proposed legislation would not result in the creation of another separate women's corps. To the contrary, it eliminates an otherwise necessary separate civilian organization now attached to the Army and provides for the incorporation of this personnel in the Air Forces in a manner similar to that whereby professional female personnel with specialized skills are assimilated by the Medical Department of the Army.[20]

In other words, the WASP would not perform like the WACs—as a segregated unit—but would instead be integrated with male pilots, as they were already operating. The committee submitted its report along with H.R. 4219 for consideration by a House vote.

On March 24, 1944, Senators Joseph Hill (Ala.) and Harold Burton (Ohio) submitted Senate Resolution 1810, "A bill to provide for the appointment of female pilots and aviation cadets in the Air Forces of the Army." S.R. 1810 was the Senate version of H.R. 4219 and contained the same elements as the House bill.

Male Pilots' Lobby Presses House Civil Service Committee into an Investigation

Expectations for passage of a bill to militarize the WASPs were high. Congress had never rejected a bill supported by the War Department or commanding generals during the war,[21] and the bill had been endorsed by the Committee on Military Affairs. Within the AAF, plans were being made to accept the WASPs as Army officers, including the enrollment of twenty-seven women into officers' training school in Orlando, Florida. The only voices of opposition raised against the WASPs were those of the unemployed male civilian pilots, but it was expected that their voices would soon quiet as the public came to the realization that they were only attempting to avoid the draft and receive flight pay. But between March and June of 1944, the male civilian pilots began to get substantial and sympathetic media coverage. They were joined in their attack against the WASPs by military pilots who were returning from the various war theaters, who wanted to guarantee that they kept their flight pay. "The men pilots were coming back from the various theaters of war and they found that we were flying the hottest and the heaviest and the fastest airplanes, which they thought were their private property, and they wanted their flight pay. And flight pay for flying those kind of airplanes was a choice morsel. So they just lobbied against us," said WASP Madge Rutherford Minton.[22]

They formed a powerful lobby, supported by several civilian aviation organizations and veterans' associations. The lobby found an ally in the media, which was advocating an end to the war, a return to prewar standards, the reduction of military expenditures, a return of soldiers from overseas, and, significantly, a return of women from factories and the military to their homes.

The male civilian pilots' lobby approached Representative Robert Ramspeck, who chaired the Committee on the Civil Service, formed for the purpose of streamlining and accounting for civil service components of the war effort.[23] Directly because of requests from the group of male pilots whose specific intent was to eliminate the WASPs, Ramspeck's committee began an investigation of the WASP program.[24] The report issued by the committee, commonly referred to as the Ramspeck Report, was created without any members of the investigating committee visiting the WASPs' training school at Avenger Field or any bases to which WASPs were assigned to active duty.[25]

Two investigators for the Committee on the Civil Service did meet with WAFS director Nancy Harkness Love on April 16, 1944. In a résumé of the conversation written by Love the following day, she noted that the majority of the questions were about alleged incompetency of WASPs, purported failures with WASP training, and assumed resentments from male pilots toward the WASPs as well as between Love and Cochran, all of which Love denied.[26] A substantial portion of the "facts" gathered by the committee were submitted by the male civilian pilots' lobby.[27] Indeed, the structure of claims raised against the WASP program was directly attributed to the pilots' group within the committee's own report:

> Essentially, the mass of this correspondence addressed to the Congress protested that—
>
> 1. Army Air Forces had embarked upon a costly and unnecessary program of recruiting inexperienced young women for training as noncombat service pilots.
> 2. Simultaneously, Army Air Forces was dismissing, or failing to properly utilize, large numbers of male civilian pilot-instructors, who had been trained at a cost of millions of dollars.
> 3. While insisting upon high qualifications as prerequisite to the retention of these male civilian pilot-instructors, Army Air Forces was lowering the standards for female civilian recruits to an almost irreducible minimum.
> 4. The program was highly experimental.
> 5. The alleged manpower shortage given as a reason for the recruiting and training of inexperienced personnel was not, as claimed, being alleviated, but instead was being further confused and aggravated.[28]

The thirteen-page Ramspeck Report addressed each of these claims and found, with little reference to AAF documents, that the claims of the male civilian pilots were upheld. Indeed, the report was as much about the male civilian pilots and their supposed plight as it was about the WASPs. Although it contained several statements claiming that it was not about women as pilots, the report focused on gender issues. It stated: "This is not a question of the utilization of male or female personnel, but is a question of the utilization of experience and capabilities before resorting to the use of inexperience and costly training."[29] Despite the claim that the report was to investigate disparities between pilots' programs, no reference was made to the male pilots of Air Transport Command who had been recruited and inducted just as the WASPs had, but who were later provided commissions in the AAF. (At the time these male pilots were commissioned, the AAF had wanted to extend commissions to the women pilots as well but was prevented from doing so only because the pilots were female.) Indeed, the report opened by alleging that the women did not possess the skills to be AAF pilots because they had previously been employed in work attributed to women.

> The implication contained in the proposal, that it is now either necessary or desirable to recruit stenographers, clerks, school teachers, housewives, factory workers, and other inexperienced personnel for training at great outlay of public funds as pilots for the military planes of the Government, particularly when there already exists a surplus of personnel to perform these identical duties, is as startling as it is invalid.[30]

The committee did not find it at all as startling or invalid to recruit "inexperienced personnel" who were men and who had come to the Air Forces from traditionally male jobs just as removed from piloting as the career fields listed above. Several pages of the report dealt exclusively with issues surrounding male civilian pilots rather than the WASPs, and alleged that these male pilots had the same skills as WASP graduates. The report contended that women pilots were being given preferential treatment:

> It is not understood why the qualification for both men and women should not be identical, and why the proven experience of this available male personnel is not being utilized. It is impossible to escape the conclusion that this discrimination attempts to demonstrate that the millions of dollars of public funds, spent with the approval and at the insistence of the War Department, to train these civilian instructors has been unwise and unavailing.[31]

The report published statistics provided by the male civilian pilots to demonstrate that thousands of male pilots were out of work. Nowhere in the report did the latest figures provided by General Arnold about the true hiring patterns and skill levels of these pilots appear, nor did the expressed request of the War Department for these men to serve in the Army ground forces.

Allegations of the Ramspeck Report

The Ramspeck Report published many purported findings about the WASP program, which had considerable influence not only over how Congress voted on the WASP bill, but also on the anti-WASP media campaign. The Ramspeck Report gave journalists more material for stories, and following the release of the report, the media campaign against the WASPs escalated dramatically. The report made numerous allegations about the incompetence of the WASPs and the unnecessary role they performed. It presented facts about the program in a distorted and negative manner, with misleading and negative headings. To begin with, it alleged that women recruited into the WASPs lacked aviation experience.[32] Although the WASP program had lowered its requirements for acceptance into the training school from seventy-five to thirty-five flight hours, male pilot recruits were not required to have any previous flight time or even to have pilots' licenses. The report also alleged that the Women's Flying Training Detachment was formed specifically so that unqualified women could fly planes for the military, when in fact the program

All photographs and identifications are from the WASP Photo Collection, Women Airforce Service Pilots. Air Force Museum Archives. Wright Patterson Air Force Base, Ohio.

1. The first WASP classes, known as the "Guinea Pigs," were trained at the Houston Municipal Airport. Here, acting commanding officer Captain Henry Gibbons greets Ann Johnson, Jane Straughan, and Mary Lou Colbert Neale, members of the first WASP graduating class.

2. The main gate to the WASP training center, Avenger Field at Sweetwater, Texas. Note the depiction of the WASP mascot, Fifinella, a Disney design, that tops the sign. Aviation Enterprises, Ltd., the civilian contractor responsible for training the WASPs during most of their existence, also trained male Army Air Force pilots.

3. Graduation day for WASP trainees at Avenger Field, May 1943.

4. Nadine Nagle appears in an Avenger Field barracks doorway wearing her flight gear, including the leg-strap map pad used for navigating.

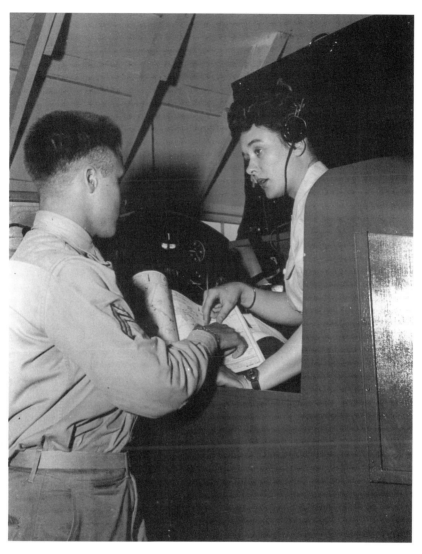

5. Joanne Trebtoske appears in a Link Trainer with an Army Air Forces instructor at Romulus Army Air Field.

6. Velma Morrison Saunder qualified in the P-39 at Harlington Army Air Field.

7. Three WASPs in cold weather flight gear pass a BT-*13*, also known as the "Vultee Vibrator."

8. WASPs of Buckingham Army Air Field converge around B-17s to discuss the day's mission: Dawn Rochns Balden, Blanche Osborn, Julie Ledbetter, Virginia Acher, and Charlotte Mitchell.

9. Elizabeth Gardner walks across the wing of an AT-23, which is a stripped-down B-26.

10. Shirley Slade (*Life's* WASP cover girl) sits awaiting departure of her B-24 at Harlington Army Air Field before flying a gunnery training mission.

11. An A-24, commonly called the "Dauntless," flown by Elsie Dyer returns from a tow target mission pulling a target sleeve, used for training anti-aircraft troops.

12. Dora Dougherty Strother, Joyce Sherwood Succhini (seated), and Florence Knight with a line-up of A-25As prior to a tow-target mission at Davis Army Air

13. Mary A. Nelson awaits take-off in an A-25 "Helldiver," March Army Air Field.

14. Three unidentified WASPs check a map on the wing of an A-25 "Helldiver," March Army Air Field.

15. WASP Director Jacqueline Cochran with Commanding General Henry H. Arnold at Avenger Field on December 6, 1944, for the final WASP graduation. Note Arnold's modified B-25 in the background.

16. Commanding General Arnold awards wings to the final WASP graduates at
Avenger Field, December 7, 1944. WASP Director Cochran appears to the immediate left of the WASP who is receiving her wings.

began to expand the pool of available domestic pilots and to fit more closely the training demands and expectations of the AAF. The report stated: "In September 1942 the organization known as the Women's Flying Training Detachment (WFTD) was established for the purpose of training young women who could not meet the qualifications for duty in the Women's Auxiliary Ferrying Squadron (WAFS)."[33] This overlooked the fact that the programs were organized separately, for two distinct purposes, and with different organizational futures planned. The WAFS were designed as a small and elite group of women pilots who were to remain as civilian contractors to the AAF, while the WFTD was formed to develop a larger core group of women pilots to handle most or all domestic flights.

The report also questioned the legality of the organization of the WASPs by arguing that the program was unnecessary. The report acknowledged that the secretary of war had the authority to "appoint trained civilian personnel to such duties in the War Department as he sees fit," but claimed that because the "necessity for this training program has not been demonstrated," the War Department was not specifically authorized to create the program, because the law under which authority was given stated "salaries and wages of civilian employees as may be necessary."[34] Therefore, by drawing conclusions about the necessity of the WASPs (conclusions opposite to those reached by General Arnold, the AAF, and the War Department), the committee claimed that the War Department was in violation of standards for developing a civilian program.[35] Under the heading "Standards Lowered," the report listed that the program had lowered its age limit from twenty-one years to eighteen-and-a-half years, without mentioning that this was done to bring the WASP program requirements in line with those of male pilots' training requirements. It also listed that required hours had been reduced, without giving the reasons for the reduction or mentioning that male pilot trainees were entering AAF schools with no pilots' licenses and zero hours of flight time.

The Ramspeck Report took figures about WASP pilot training out of context, without comparing them to figures for male trainees, and then developed negative conclusions about the statistics. For example, the report stated that only 80 percent of trainees completed the training program at a total cost per graduate of $12,150.70.[36] The report declined to provide comparative statistics for male graduates, which would have revealed that WASP candidates had a higher graduation rate than male pilots and were trained at approximately the same cost. The report also provided WASP casualty figures without comparing them to male casualty figures, claiming that such a comparison was not equitable because the training of the two was not identical. The report then went on to make a supposition about the casualty rate: "It is authoritatively stated, and there is every reason to believe, that the induction of additional unskilled personnel into this program will accelerate the accident and fatality rate."[37] However, this contradicted AAF reports, which concluded that the WASPs had lower accident and fatality rates in training and on operational missions than did male pilots.

In a further allegation of the WASP program's failure to train its pilots effectively, the Ramspeck Report included a chart and descriptive copy that purported to show that WASPs could not successfully progress to higher pilot rating. The chart showed that as of March 1944, only three out of 532 WASPs qualified on four-engine bombers, and only eleven qualified on twin-engine pursuit planes and bombers.[38] Again, while these figures are accurate, they leave out a great deal of information, such as the fact that the AAF had placed restrictions prohibiting WASPs from getting rated on four-engine bombers, and that the program for WASPs to transport pursuit planes had only started immediately before the statistics were gathered. So, while the numbers were correct, the assumption about why the numbers were at those levels was incorrect, yet was printed as being factual. To back claims that a lack of transitional rating was the result of WASP inability, the report published hearsay: "A substantial number of candidates for the higher rating experience difficulties in making the transition, and officers in charge of WASP operations state that there is a lack of sufficient experience upon which to base an estimate of probable results."[39] The report furthered the supposition and hearsay in the section "Eliminees Total Losses," which began: "Authoritative sources are definite in their opinion that a large percentage of WASPS will never qualify to pilot the faster or heavier" planes.[40] As a result of this, great numbers of WASP training eliminees were assumed, for whom the report calculated a projected loss of $3,558,600 if the WASP program was expanded to 2,500 pilots. Again, the report presented this conjecture as fact.

The Ramspeck Report concluded by alleging that because women were getting preferential treatment, trained men were left with no jobs, and the WASPs were wasting millions of dollars raised from "the war stamps of school children, the taxes of the farmer, the savings of the wage earner, deductions from the pay envelope of the laborer, and the earnings of the industry."[41] The report alleged that the WASPs were destructive forces in the war effort. It also reflected public fears of a postwar United States suffering from economic problems escalated by women in the workplace when it stated: "At the end of this war there will be tremendous surpluses of trained and experienced pilots throughout the world. Utilization of these surpluses will constitute an acute post-war problem. To now seek out and train, at Government expenses, additional inexperienced personnel would add another surplus to this recognized post-war surplus."[42] The report ended with three conclusions:

1. The proposal to expand the WASP has not been justified. Therefore, it is recommended that the recruiting of inexperienced personnel and their training for the WASPS be immediately terminated.
2. That the use of the WASPS already trained and in training be continued and provision be made for hospitalization and insurance.
3. There exist several surpluses of experienced pilot personnel available for utilization as service pilots.

    Therefore it is recommended that the service of these several groups of experienced air personnel be immediately utilized.[43]

It is notable that of the three recommendations, only the first was dealt with extensively. The report did not mention why the WASPs needed provisions for insurance and hospitalization, nor did it address the costs of doing so. Although the report focused nearly half its space on the purported plight of male civilian pilots, it recommended that the AAF use these pilots without examining the training necessary to bring them up to a functional level, the costs involved in executing such training, the means by which these individuals should be used, and the provisions needed for implementation. Indeed, the conclusions of the report continued to reflect the biases of the committee and the lack of documented evidence and investigation in support of its claims. It is very telling that five representatives—one-third of the committee—issued a minority report that clearly stated their disagreement with the Ramspeck Report and indicated that "the termination, the continuation or the further development of a woman's flying program is a matter for the Army Air Forces to determine."[44]

The House Committee on Appropriations Addresses the CAA and WASP Programs

At the same time the Ramspeck committee was publishing its findings, the House Committee on Appropriations addressed the WASP program but arrived at substantially different findings. In "Military Establishment Appropriation Bill, 1945," a report issued in June 1944, the committee found that there were valid reasons for the termination of the CAA and AAF schools, which resulted in the redirection of thousands of instructors and cadet trainees into the

Army's ground forces. Indeed, the committee found that the "considerable criticism" that arose publicly was unwarranted, and that "the matter has been handled with reasonable dispatch and as fairly and equitably as consistency with appropriate military considerations would permit."[45] In its analysis of the WASP program, the committee found that despite the allegations, no WASP "has displaced or will displace a male pilot meeting the single standard maintained for both sexes."[46] This committee, unlike the Ramspeck committee, reached 100 percent agreement about the WASPs. Its conclusion about the value of the WASP program was completely opposite to that reached by the Ramspeck committee. The Committee on Appropriations reported:

> The members of the subcommittee having jurisdiction of the accompanying measure are a unit as to the genuine value of these women fliers to the war effort and agree with General Arnold that they should be given a military status and have the same responsibility as male pilots flying military airplanes, and, along with it, the same rights, privileges, and benefits to which such male pilots are entitled.[47]

The committee approved the requested amount of $6.4 million to fund the WASP program in 1945.[48] This compared with an allotted amount of $12.6 billion approved for the AAF and a total military appropriation of $49.1 billion for 1945.[49]

Congress Introduces the Ramspeck Report and Media Accounts into the House Debate

The findings of the Committee on Appropriations would not receive media coverage nor was the full report introduced at the hearings on the bill to militarize the WASPs. Yet the conclusions and figures from the Ramspeck Report were quoted in great detail by the media and also made their way into other governmental reports and congressional testimony, to the detriment of the WASP program. On June 16, 1944, one week before the WASP bill was to be voted on in Congress, Representative James Morrison of Louisiana voiced his opposition to the militarization of the WASPs and entered the entire Ramspeck Report into the public record, urging all members of Congress to read it, claiming it was "concise, exact and to the point."[50] The extensions of Morrison's remarks were listed under the heading "Ramspeck Committee Urges Army Air Forces to Utilize 10,000 Instructors and Trainees of WTS Program and Curtail Further Expansion of WASP Program."[51] On June 10, Representative Costello, author of the WASP bill, mentioned the errors and discrepancies in the Ramspeck Report. His "Extension of Remarks" was listed under a more simple heading: "The WASP Bill."[52] In his remarks, Costello focused on the report's claim of a pilot surplus: "the most astounding part of this report is the assumption that there does exist a vast pool of well-trained pilots ready to serve the Army Air Forces at a moment's notice. This is an error that I would like to correct now."[53] Costello provided documentation of the true status and availability of male civilian pilots, and urged congressional support for the bill:

> We have placed General Arnold, with perfect confidence, at the head of the 16 air forces now functioning throughout the world. The records of these forces speak for themselves. General Arnold himself has requested the passage of the WASP bill in order that the civilian women pilots now serving with our air forces and those hereafter to be trained might be removed from their civilian status and placed in a full military status. The desirability of this change cannot be questioned by anyone. Even the report of the Civil Service Committee urges in their second recommendation that "provision be made for hospitalization and insurance." The effective utilization of these women pilots can only be accomplished if they are made a part of the military organization. Having seen the development of the WAC's, WAVES, SPARS, and MARINES, I know no reason why this group of women pilots alone of the various military-service organizations should not be given the same status as had been accorded those other groups.
>
> In conclusion, let me explain that the sole effect of the WASP bill is to bring these civilian women completely under military jurisdiction as they should be. Likewise, let me point out that the Army Air Forces have been more than pleased with the splendid success of the WASP program and its accomplishment, and this program shall be continued whether it remains in a civilian status or becomes a military organization. It will be continued because the Army leaders are satisfied as to the necessity for the organization and because it will aid materially in benefiting our aviation activities in this country and likewise relieving many pilots qualified for combat activities and enabling them to hasten our day of victory in this war.[54]

However, Costello's facts were no match for the cultural fears being raised in the media and among members of Congress. Morrison used newspaper opinion pieces and editorials to bolster opposition to the WASP bill. In all, he cited three op-ed pieces, one personal statement, and one letter in the weeks prior to the House's vote on H.R. 4219. Under the heading "Bradley Taylor Explains in Detail the Whole WASP Situation—Says W.T.S. Men Got Raw

Deal," Morrison gave expert standing to a member of a special interest group, entering into the record a letter written to him by Bradley Taylor, who represented a group advocating for the male civilian pilots. The letter filled two pages of the *Congressional Record* with hearsay and innuendo.[55] In a statement labeled "Why Waste $273,355,225 of Our Taxpayers' Money and Spend Another $100,000,000 To Train Personnel for the Same Jobs?—Something That the WASPS Can't Answer," Morrison not only failed to mention where he acquired these dollar figures or what exactly they referenced, but also failed to mention the WASPs.[56] He instead focused on the "plight" of the civilian pilots and concluded: "Not only in fairness and justice but from the standpoint of good old-fashioned horse sense, I say that the men we have already trained should be commissioned and given the jobs for which they were trained."[57]

On June 8, two weeks before H.R. 4219 was slated for a House vote, Morrison condemned the bill widely under the heading "Dimples and Glamour Evidently Have Devastating Effect Even on General of A.A.F."[58] The sole evidence that Morrison presented in defense of his condemnation of the bill was newspaper opinion. Morrison read from op-ed pieces, so that they would be included as "Extension of Remarks" in the *Congressional Record*. Among the headings given to Morrison's remarks were: "The Evening Star, One of the Leading Washington Papers, Says WASP Program Is Wasted Money and Wasted Energy"[59] and "Why Spend $100,000 on the WASP Program?—Read What Miss Cassinni Says."[60] The latter piece alleged that the AAF was backing the WASP program because Cochran had seduced General Arnold:

> In the last week the shapely pilot has seen her coveted commission coming closer and closer. * * * One of the highest placed generals, it seems gazed into her eyes, and since then has taken her cause celebre very much "to heart" * * * She's such an attractive composition of wind-blown bob, smiling eyes and outdoor skin nobody blames him.
>
> It's whispered he's battling like a knight of olde, or olde knight, for "the faire Cochran." So the announcement can be expected any day that Jackie's commission has been approved, if the captivated general is victorious in his tournaments.[61]

Morrison was not the only representative to quote opinion pieces instead of facts. After the initial vote on the WASP bill, Representative Edward V. Izac of California included a piece by gossip columnist Drew Pearson, who had issued a series of attacks against Cochran and the WASP program. The heading for Izac's remarks was taken directly from Pearson: "Arnold Faces Congressional Uproar Over His Continued Use of the WASPS—Miss Cochran's Lady

Fliers Now Replace Instead of Release Men."[62] Morrison was, however, the most prolific in submitting materials against the WASPs. Among these was an editorial piece published in the *Idaho Statesmen* on May 12, 1944. The editorial not only made unfounded allegations about the WASP program and misquoted AAF statistics and requirements, but it offered a distinctly sexist shaping of all women. Because the allegations and tone of the article were echoed by members of Congress in the debate over the WASP resolution, the entirety of Morrison's quotation follows:

> *Priority on Women*
>
> Several times we have heard servicemen, usually back on furlough, complain about women in the service. Sometimes we felt that they were merely prejudiced, but sometimes it seemed to us that they had a valid gripe. A recent happening supports the latter position.
>
> Some weeks ago thousands of experienced male pilots were grounded, presumably because we had trained more pilots than we shall need. Nevertheless, Jacqueline Cochran's WASPS are getting a priority of a very special kind. There is a bill before Congress to commission women pilots, and some have already completed their first weeks of schooling. General Arnold told Congressmen the women pilots will be needed for combat. That's a strange statement to make when thousands of men pilots are now out of jobs, or soon will be.
>
> The men are angry about it, and they seem to have additional reasons. For instance, WASPS qualify for transport training after 35 hours of flying time, whereas men must have 1,000, including 200 in heavy craft. We don't know what the explanation is. Probably it is the sentimental softness of American men in regard to their women. In colleges the smooth, good-looking gals can get A's without a lick of work; and in the armed services it may be that dimples have a devastating effect even on generals.[63]

The rhetoric of this piece strongly implied that the WASPs had somehow, through sexual seduction, received undeserved privileges. In addition, by comparing these highly skilled pilots of military planes with college girls, the author even refused to characterize the WASPs as adults. "Priority on Women" also included inaccurate data about the requirements of the WASPs, comparing the hours of flight time needed simply to join the WASP training program with the total transitional hours needed by any pilot to ferry military aircraft. Men who entered the AAF cadet training program did not need pilots' licenses, let alone any hours of flight time, while WASP trainees had to have licenses and a minimum of thirty-five hours of flight time. By comparing statistics from two different stages of pilot training, the author constructed something that looked like the prejudicial treatment contended in the editorial. Many other media pieces would make similar comparisons, which members of Congress would later quote as fact in their arguments against proposed legislation for WASP militarization.

The House Considers the WASP Bill

Neither Costello nor any other supporters of H.R. 4219 introduced any media opinion pieces, letters, or testimony in defense of the WASPs. The bill was introduced for consideration by Representative Roger Slaughter of Missouri on June 20, 1944, who simply defined the parameters of the bill and explained, at the request of other members of Congress, the impact it would have on civilian male pilots. After hearing arguments raised by Slaughter about the bill's importance, the House agreed to consider the bill the following day.[64] Highlights of Slaughter's arguments follow:

> There is no question but that there is a shortage of pilots, although there may be some difference of opinion as to the proper method in which this shortage should be met; nevertheless the Army, and when I say the Army, I mean General Arnold, General Giles, and the Secretary, Mr. Stimson, are strongly in favor of this bill and have recommended and asked for its passage. . . .
>
> While they [the 500 WASPs in active service] have done a splendid work, according to the Army and according to those individuals who are informed, there are very definite drawbacks to the present arrangement, not only from the standpoint of the Army, but of the women themselves. For instance, these female pilots come into various Army posts and after they ground their ships there are no facilities for taking care of them. They are not permitted to go into the officers' clubs; they are not permitted to buy from the post exchange; they are not permitted to go into certain portions of the Army reservation; and, although they are doing work identical with that of certain portions of the Army fliers, they are not eligible for certain benefits, including insurance. The Army, on the other hand, complains that while these women who enjoy a civil-service status are doing this highly important work, the Army does not have the necessary and essential control over them which it should. In other words, while they are closely connected with the Army, in truth and in fact they are completely outside so far as authority is concerned, and for that reason the Army through General Arnold is urging the passage of this bill. . . .
>
> One argument which has been raised against this bill is totally erroneous, and that is, if this bill is passed, it would create what would be in effect another branch of the Women's Army Corps. The very contrary is the case, because as matters now stand these women of civil-service status are set off in a sort of

group by themselves. This bill, if it passes, will absorb this group and amalgamate them and bring them into the Regular Army Air Corps.[65]

On June 21, the House went forward with its consideration of H.R. 4219, "To Provide Appointment of Female Pilots and Aviation Cadets in the Army Air Forces." The debate did not focus on the WASPs, however, but instead became a forum for Congress to placate the demands of the male civilian pilots' lobby, in which issues affecting not the WASPS but the male pilots were raised and debated. Throughout the debate, it became clear that many members voting on the bill did not even understand that it was specifically about WASP militarization.[66] Indeed, it seemed that for many, their sole exposure to information about the WASP program was through the strongly biased and inaccurate report written by the Ramspeck committee, or through opinion pieces and editorials published in newspapers or submitted to the *Congressional Record.*

In a turn that virtually guaranteed that the measure would not pass, the debate over the WASP bill was chaired by Representative Ramspeck.[67] On top of that, the debate was attended by members of the male civilian pilots' lobby, who filled the gallery of the House and vocally expressed their opposition to the bill.[68] "They didn't know what they were talking about with regards to our work," Nadine Nagle said. "Our work was different than theirs."[69]

Representative Robert Sikes of Florida opened the session by criticizing the report issued by the Committee on Military Affairs that recommended passage of the bill because the hearings "comprise a little more than 9 pages" and did not provide enough justification for the measure.[70] Sikes went on to praise the Ramspeck Report, which at "13 pages in length . . . is very complete in its study of the WASPS."[71] Sikes added:

> I do not believe we are ready to say to the Congress that we know the WASPS as a military organization are needed now and that we can justify the expenditure of $50,000,000 for training of limited-service personnel. I do not use that term in a derogatory sense, because this is a fine group of ladies. They have done a splendid job. I commend them for their service to the war effort. But nevertheless, their service is going to be limited. They cannot be used in combat theaters.[72]

Sikes then encouraged the passage of a bill relating to "the utilization of the C.A.A. and W.T.S. trainees and instructors,"[73] who, based on no reports issued by congressional committees, Sikes determined were deserving of military commissions. Following the introduction of the topic of male civilian pilots by Sikes, Congress began a lengthy discussion that would extend through seven pages in the *Congressional Record.* Of the fifty-five columns reporting the House debate on the WASP bill, twenty-six mostly or entirely involve discussion about the WASPs and/or the proposed bill, while twenty-nine columns mostly or entirely involve debate about the situation of male civilian pilots. Although members of Congress needed to understand the status of these male pilots (since it was being alleged that WASPs were taking their rightful places in the cockpit), to devote more than half of the debate on the WASP bill to the issues of male civilian pilots, without requiring that detailed reports and data be submitted, was a grievous error. Indeed, because the decision of whether to pass the WASP bill was motivated by issues surrounding the male civilian pilots, it was unjust to reach such a decision based upon figures and notions supported by special interest groups and a biased media presentation. Despite his stated opposition to the WASP bill, Representative Sikes argued specifically for this level of fairness in the debate:

> The C.A.A.-W.T.S. groups should have their day in court on the merits of their case, and not as we propose to bring them in today, as an appendage to the WASP bill. The entire bill should be recommitted to the Committee on Military Affairs for further study, and during the period of that study the War Department will have a full opportunity to utilize the C.A.A.-W.T.S. trainees to the greatest possible extent. Then we can consider the WASP bill on the basis of the actual need for that group alone.[74]

Despite Sikes's request, the debate continued to focus on the male civilian pilots and the legitimacy of their claims. Even Costello, the bill's sponsor, entered into the discussion of the male civilian pilots, stating that another bill (which had been proposed but had not yet been debated) would give those male civilian pilots who were physically qualified AAF commissions, but that it was unreasonable to ask the AAF to lower their standards to those of CAA instructors.[75] "There are any number of diseases and disabilities that these men suffered with and now have, and whom he would bring into the service,"[76] Costello argued, noted that these pilots, like the WASPs, were not eligible for combat service. Costello also pointed out that the current policy of the military was to place qualified male civilian pilots into the AAF as pilots: "If the men are qualified to fly planes, we want to put them in the Army flying planes. If they cannot qualify to fly planes, we want to put them in as Army navigators and bombardiers. We want to use every man that is qualified."[77] In the ten minutes allotted to him, Costello at least managed to bring the discussion back to the WASP program:

> Let me call your attention to this one fact. The sole purpose of this bill is simply this, to take these women who are now with the Army Air Forces in a civilian capacity and convert them into a military capacity. That is the sole purpose

of the WASP bill and nothing else. This should be done, because these women at present are denied hospitalization; they are denied insurance benefits, and things of that kind to which, as military personnel, they should be entitled, and because of the work they are doing, they should be receiving at this time. Likewise, these women then would be subject to military discipline.

May I point out that right now the Government can go out and spend $12,000 for training one of these women and, if you do not pass this bill, she can quit after she receives that training. You have spent $12,000, and you do not have anything to show for it. If we make them part of the military, we will retain them as part of the military, and they will be subject to military discipline. That is very necessary. Might I emphasize that the cost of training one of these women is no different from the cost of training a man. It is approximately $12,000 for each, whether they go through Randolph Field or whether they happen to go through the women's pilot training program. The cost is approximately the same. The cost for the uniforms is the same. There is actually no difference. The casualty rate is approximately the same. There has been no difference whatsoever between the men and the women.[78]

Despite Costello's attempts at defining the bill and directing House debate to its particulars, members of Congress returned to the emotional topic of women taking over the roles of men. Explaining his position in support of the male civilian pilots, avid editorial reader Representative Morrison of Louisiana claimed that the men had been unfairly asked: "Would you qualify for combat duty?" He explained that either way a pilot answered the question would get him thrown out of the Air Forces, which Morrison compared to asking a man: "When did you stop whipping your wife?"[79]

Costello failed to evoke feelings against the male civilian pilots regarding their lack of devotion toward the war effort because he simply gave the facts, rather than powerfully challenging the men in a condemning oration. Unlike his opposition, Costello did not make sweeping statements, link the plights of WASPs with young women throughout the United States, or confront the cowardice of the pilots by reading an account of a brave young man who did not flee his duty. Costello's presentation lacked the emotional appeal necessary to combat the allegations against the women pilots, who were supposedly unnaturally claiming that which was not theirs. His only plea to enforce patriotism was brief and lost among questioning about the particular status the pilots might hope to achieve in the ground forces. Costello stated:

We are in war. You very often have to change the rules of the game in the middle of a war in order to win. What are we in the war for, anyway?

I have not had much complaint from the fathers of these young men when I explain the situation. These men were transferred to the ground forces because they were needed there.[80]

Morrison, on the other hand, was zealous in his use of sweeping generalizations and personalized accounts. He introduced an amendment to the bill that would limit the total number of WASPs to 1,500, so that the male civilian pilots could have the opportunity to fly missions as well. He claimed that the men had "gotten a raw deal and this WASP program makes it worse," because they had been promised entry into the Army with commissions and were only given entry into the Army.[81] In other words, the "raw deal" Morrison was submitting was that these men were not making enough money during a time of war. To bolster sympathy, he told how trainees received only $50 a month plus room and board while they were training. (WASP trainees received $150 a month, but had to pay for room, board, travel, and clothing.) As a result, Morrison claimed, "Many lost their homes and lost their automobiles and almost lost their wives, because when the money situation became so acute they had to go and live with their own families."[82] Members of Congress gravitated toward Morrison's stories, never asking for references or statistics, and never reasoning that the women of the WASP program would have had the same hardships, for they obviously did not expect women to own homes or automobiles.

Representative John Vorys of Ohio rose in opposition to Morrison's amendment, arguing that it "is an attempt to write physical standards into this bill by saying that the physical characteristics of women are such that we need only 1,500 of them."[83] Vorys, who was an active CAP pilot, stated that Congress did not understand the physical qualifications needed for flying and was attempting to apply "outmoded" standards onto the situation at hand. He went on to say:

> Women can qualify for flying and they cannot qualify for ground fighting. . . . I have found out, on a number of airfields in the past few months, that the flying people grudgingly admit that these girls can fly and do the kind of flying that they are assigned to do, and therefore in some way release a man, to do what? Release a man someplace along the line to fight in the air or on the ground.[84]

Representative Compton White from Idaho addressed Vorys's remarks by citing the Ramspeck committee's allegations of waste and incompetence within the WASP program. Representative Karl Stefan of Nebraska offered statements of support for both groups, but he also wanted the House members to use correct figures concerning the male civilian pilots rather that the outrageously overblown numbers that Morrison and others were claiming.[85] In support of the WASPs, Stefan gave a speech, recorded under the heading "Work of American Women," that celebrated not only the specific work of the WASPS, but the wartime contributions of all American women. It began:

> I feel that the women pilots who are now doing such valuable work for our Army Air Corps should be commended. I hope that nothing be done here to eliminate them and that those women who are now flying transports will not only be retained but be given the rewards to which they are entitled. I have first-hand information as to their great ability, and I resent insinuations that these or other women have not rendered tremendous service to our Nation. . . . That women are rendering outstanding service should not be denied, but it should be acknowledged again at this time when we are dealing with legislation affecting their future. This does not detract from the grand service which has been rendered by the instructors referred to in this debate.[86]

Stefan went on to discuss the many other invaluable contributions made by American women toward the war effort. He concluded:

> In the homes of America, Mr. Chairman, the fires of hope are burning because the American women are making that hope live. In these few minutes allotted to me I wanted to add my word of homage to American womanhood and give thanks to the Almighty that American men honor and respect our women. For their great service I voice my appreciation and thanks.[87]

Representative William Miller of Connecticut also voiced his support of the WASPs, and stated Morrison's opposition to the proposed amendment, which would limit the WASP program to 1,500 pilots and trainees. He also inferred that other members of Congress had not gotten the facts on the WASPs and in his statement summed up what was truly at issue in this debate—the use of the WASPs as bargaining chips to guarantee the commissions of the male civilian pilots.

> I have taken the trouble to talk with men in the War Department who have assured me, and proven to me, that they have a real need for these WASPS. They are doing a good job; they have demonstrated that they can do a good job. . . .
>
> It seems to me that the House is in a bargaining mood today. We are saying to the Chief of the Air Corps: "If you want 5,000 WASPS, we will let you have them, but if you get them you have to take this other group of students and instructors that you say you do not want at this time."
>
> I agree with those who say that a promise should be kept, but above all, a promise that may be made to any particular group about what commission they

would get when they completed a certain course of training is subordinate to our over-all promise of 100 percent support of the war effort. . . . So the War Department had to say to these men in the schools and colleges: "We are sorry, but our job is to win the war and the greatest contribution you can make toward winning the war is to now go into the Infantry." Most of them went willingly.[88]

When the House finally got around to discussing the components of the bill, it became obvious how much their ideas about the program and the bill had been influenced by newspaper opinion pieces. For example, Representative John Hinshaw of California objected to the section of the bill that provided for commission of a colonel, which was "reserved and intended for Miss Jacquelyn Cochran, a famous woman flier."[89] This was the allegation made in several opinion pieces, including "Why Spend $100,000 on the WASP Program?—Read What Miss Cassinni Says," which Morrison had submitted into the *Congressional Record*.[90] However, the bill clearly stated that colonel was not a required rank, but would be the maximum rank possible in the organization, and had Hinshaw read any documents pertaining to the WASPs, he would have recognized that Cochran was not just a famous woman flier but the current director of the WASP program.

Debate then focused on several aspects of the WASP program, all of which had been raised by the media and the Ramspeck Report: that the WASPs should be placed under the WACs, that unethical if not illegal developments had occurred because Congress should have previously voted on the development of the WASP program, and that the program was unnecessary. Concern over the question of rank was so great that Representative Samuel Hobbs (Ala.) introduced a bill to limit the highest rank possible within the WASPs to captain.[91] Hobbs suggested that this would be more fair, since the WAC colonel commanded 75,000, while the WASP director would only be in command of 2,500. He also suggested that having "a sprinkling of captains along with the rank and file of lieutenants" would settle the whole issue of rank.[92] Representative Costello then stated that it was necessary to have a single officer in command, and that the "rank of colonel in the case of the WAC's, the WAVES, the SPARS, and the MARINES"[93] was consistent to facilitate functioning among those divisions, and therefore it was important to do the same with the WASPs. Representative Edward Rees of Kansas raised the specter of the program having been wrongly created without the vote of Congress, to which Representative James Wadsworth of New York answered: "The use of women for ferrying piloting was an experiment, therefore authority was not asked for in the statute. It has now proven to be a success, and they want the authority to put them in the Army."[94] To this, Rees replied that the experiment had been "carried" too far.[95] Representative Joseph O'Hara of Minnesota interrupted the debates and issued a strong condemnation of the entire bill, which he described as being "a piece of social legislation."[96]

> As far as I am concerned the bill is about as unpalatable as it can be, no matter how much it is amended, because I think you are overlooking some very, very serious things. . . . This bill is apparently for the purpose, not of creating a WASP organization—that has already been created—but to commission these very charming young ladies. . . . I am wondering what we are going to say to these boys who have been combat pilots and have been wounded, and come back, and want to keep on flying? They cannot go into combat flying because of their injuries, and perhaps because of the nervous strain they have undergone. But they can do the very things that these girls are doing. No: they cannot do that because they say, "We have to have somebody in there who is a very attractive lady pilot."[97]

By constructing the WASP militarization bill as "social legislation," O'Hara shifted the focus of the bill from legislation that was developed to further the American war efforts to legislation that was shaped as governmental sponsorship of leisurely activities for a privileged group. The assumptions of members of Congress about the intentions and abilities of women pilots specifically and women generally clouded their abilities to recognize the resolution as it was submitted—as enabling legislation sponsored by the AAF and the War Department.

O'Hara's statements were followed by support for his position from Representative Walter Brehm of Ohio: "I agree with the gentleman that this legislation is very unpalatable. I think it is time to forget the glamor in this war and think more of the gore of war."[98] Costello followed with a rebuttal of these statements, arguing that Congress needed to rely on the military experts who were requesting the bill, because it was they who understood the demands and needs of the war effort:

> I, for one, would not want to try to tell the Army Air Forces when they say they want 2,500 of these WASPS, that they will have to get along with less. I am not going to tell General Eisenhower, when he says he needs 5,000 tanks to carry on a battle, that he can get along with 500 tanks and like it. I am perfectly willing to rely upon the judgment of the men who are engineering this war. I am not going to set myself up here and state that because you give a uniform to these women pilots, just as you have given a uniform to the women nurses or to any one of all the other women's organizations, you are creating some glamorous organization or some social organization. If you like to be covered with grease, if

you like to sweat out piloting an airplane through stormy weather from one coast to another, and call that a social activity, very well then, vote against this bill. Then that is a "social activity." But if you want to try to help to carry on the war effort, if you want to release a few more men to do some of the ferrying in combat zones, to engage the enemy themselves, then pass this bill and release another 2,500 pilots who otherwise will have to stay in this country.[99]

Representative Forest Harness of Indiana followed Costello by stating that if there was such a need to release pilots for overseas duty, the instructors could be utilized, and "they may not need all the WASPS they intend to bring in."[100] Representative Ed Izac of California offered a motion to strike out the enacting clause of the bill. "My object here is to kill this bill because we do not need such a bill. It is the most unjustified piece of legislation that could be brought before the House at this late date. I know that any woman would like to have 2,500 girls under her and be a colonel."[101] He concluded by stating:

> You are not going to make it any different for these women because 500 of them are already serving under civil service doing this identical, utility work. No change, except the change that comes by putting on a manikin's uniform. It is not going to help the course of the war one bit, and I am sorry to see Hap Arnold lose his balance over this proposition.[102]

The atmosphere of the congressional hearing was rather circus-like, with members of the male civilian pilots' lobby cheering, booing, and making other outbursts. When Izac, in offering a motion to kill the measure, said, "This is the most unjustified piece of legislation that could possibly be brought before the House at this late date. It is an unconscionable bill," many House members applauded his remarks, and male civilian pilots cheered.[103] WASP Madge Rutherford Minton said: "When the bill came up in the House of Representatives, the galleries were full of pilots returned from war theaters. And they vocally shouted and expressed themselves and lobbied against the bill."[104] The disturbance created by the pilots was so great that "about 20 soldiers were asked to leave the gallery when they continued to applaud anti-WASP remarks from the floor."[105]

Testimony over the bill concluded with Representative Robert Thomason of Texas asking for the other representatives to return to the bill at hand and consider it intelligently:

> Mr. Chairman, I think I sense the temper of this Committee and I am taking these 5 minutes to beg and plead for clear straight thinking without any bias and without any prejudice. . . .

While I am not in sympathy with everything that is in the bill, yet I am not willing to go on record as saying that the head of the greatest air power in the world should have his official request turned down. We are not military experts. Our military leaders are now on the way to a glorious victory. Our brave boys are fighting and winning on every front. The least we can do is to back them up. . . . He [General Arnold] can be depended upon to treat them all fairly, and we will be hastening the day of victory.[106]

Following Thomason's statements, Ramspeck called for votes on Izac's motion that the enacting clause of the WASP bill be stricken out. The first vote was divided. Representative Andrew May of Kentucky called for tellers, and another vote was taken, which this time showed that the motion was agreed to by "119 ayes and 102 noes."[107] The House then voted on the recommendation that the enacting clause be stricken out. The roll showed that there were 188 yeas and 169 nays, with 73 representatives not voting.[108] The House had effectively killed H.R. 4219, "A bill to provide for the appointment of female pilots and aviation cadets in the Air Forces of the Army," by a margin of nineteen votes. Not since the beginning of the war in 1941 had any legislation supported by the Army Air Forces been turned down.[109]

6

They'll Be Home for Christmas
The WASP Program Disbands

Following the defeat of the House Resolution 4219 on June 22, 1944, the Army Air Forces was faced three choices regarding future actions for obtaining WASP militarization. First, it could push for passage of Senate Bill 1810, a WASP militarization bill that had been submitted to the Senate Military Affairs Committee and was awaiting debate. If the War Department encouraged its submission, and if it passed the Senate, then the issue could be resubmitted before the House, because the House had technically not voted against the bill but had, in a legislative maneuver, simply removed its enactment clause. Second, the AAF could stop WASP training, in accordance with the recommendations of the Ramspeck committee, maintain the WASPs on active duty, and seek medical and insurance benefits for them. The third choice was to disband the entire program.

While the WASP bill was being debated before the House, Commanding General Henry H. Arnold was in Europe directing the air operations for the D-Day attack, still recovering from a heart attack he had suffered immediately before the European mission. The D-Day operations had been very successful. Allied troops had landed in Normandy with fewer losses to the Air Forces than had been anticipated. The Allies were now moving toward Germany, and the American media was predicting a quick end to the war.

Upon his return to Washington, D.C., General Arnold ordered on June 26 that, in compliance with the recommendations of the Ramspeck committee report, the training program of the WASPs be discontinued as soon as those currently in classes finished.[1] Because of the time involved in training, this meant that the training of women pilots by the AAF would end in December 1944.[2]

In July, R. Earl McKaughan, president of Aviation Enterprises, the civilian firm responsible for training the WASPs, and his attorney, Ed Ponder, began an inquiry into the facts surrounding the order to end training, with the hopes of getting Congress to reconsider the WASP bill so that the firm's pilot training school at Avenger Field could remain open.[3] In the meantime, McKaughan had solicited Avenger Field to the AAF Training Command as a training facility for male pilots and WASPs engaged in transitional training.[4] After the AAF Central Training Detachment indicated an interest in using Avenger Field for the training of male pursuit pilots, McKaughan no longer made any attempts to address Congress about the WASPs.

The "Lost" Class of WASPs

The next class of WASPs (which would have been the first class to graduate in 1945) was scheduled to begin training at Avenger Field on June 30, just four days after General Arnold issued the order to conclude training.[5] On June 26, Telegrams were sent under General Arnold's name to the women who were to be part of this class, telling them that the training program had been canceled. The telegram read:

> Due to the recommendations of House Civil Service Committee and unfavorable action of House of Representatives on WASP bill your orders to report for WASP training thirty June nineteen forty four are cancelled.[6]

Because of the uncertainties of travel schedules during the war, most women who were in this class had already left their homes for the WASP training field in Texas. The telegram reached Eleanor Watterud at the Bluebonnet Hotel in Sweetwater, Texas. Many of the women who had been scheduled to begin the next class had, like Watterud, already arrived in the town nearest the training field or were well on their way to Texas when the announcements were sent out. All of these women were traveling at their own expense. Even many of those more fortunate candidates who had not already left for the training field had quit their jobs, sold their homes, and purchased the clothing and supplies they needed for WASP training.[7] "When the girls that would have been in 45-1 came in, and were told, it was terrible. Some of them had sold their homes, because they were going into the service; some of them had made arrangements for their children; and there were so many things that just broke their hearts. It was so sad for us," said WASP Betty Stagg Turner.[8]

For the next several days, the office of WASP director Jacqueline Cochran was inundated with calls from these women and their families. Some families, like that of Elizabeth Wadlow of Pleasant Ridge, Michigan, came from seeing their daughter off at the train station, only to return home to a telegram announcing the cancellation of the program.[9] Some women found out about the cancellation of the program en route, such as Elaine Scull, whose father sent a telegram to her at a train station on the way to Sweetwater.[10] Scull called Cochran to find out what to do about transportation, because she had already traveled from Atlantic City to St. Louis, where she had received the telegram. She was calling not only for herself but for four others scheduled for the June 30 class who were at the station with her.

Cochran told Scull that if she continued on to Sweetwater, transportation would be provided to her, not to her hometown, but to the base nearest to her home. To receive this transportation, Scull and her companions would have to travel to Sweetwater, because transportation was only authorized from there. Cochran added: "You won't get any money refunded if you go back from Sweetwater, but we are going to give the girls transportation from Sweetwater to the nearest point to their home. For instance, you're in Atlantic City; you'd probably be dropped off at the nearest point the airplane passes over— probably New York."[11] A woman traveling with Scull, Joan Bogart, called back to the WASP offices to see if travel expenses to Sweetwater would be reimbursed. She asked: "Well, if we went down there we'd go on our own money, wouldn't we—from St. Louis?" To which she was told, "Oh yes, you'd have to go on your own money and of course if you came back from St. Louis you'd have to come back on your own money."[12]

Cochran also informed Scull that she and the other scheduled trainees would not have any of their travel expenses refunded. When directly asked about a refund, Cochran stated, "No. There just isn't anything they could do; they've been told to stop training, and they stopped training in accordance with their instructions from Congress."[13] The women were given a choice of bad options. Either they would pay for a return trip home, or they would pay for the remainder of the trip to Sweetwater, fly to an airfield near their homes, and pay for transportation from there to their homes. Cochran also received telephone calls from women who were scheduled to be in later classes and who had already taken their physicals at Army bases or who were scheduled to do so. Cochran told them not to take their physicals, that all future classes were canceled—a fact that she said would not change unless Congress changed its decision.[14]

The plight of the women of the WASP class slated to begin June 30, 1944, who were stranded without transportation on their way from the training field, did not escape mention in the press. One of these pieces, "Congressmen Clip Wings of 9 Wasps: Detroit Girl Fliers Downed in Texas," appeared several days before the class was to have started, and before the WASP trainees had made any decisions about what they would do. The piece began:

Word received by parents of the Detroit girls indicates that most of them have refused the Army's offer to fly them home because they are just too embarrassed to come home. Some of the girls gave up jobs, others disposed of their civilian clothes, and all of them were given farewell parties by their friends and gifts by their relatives.

The plight of the girls was described by Mrs. Mary Wadlow, 24 Kensington Avenue, Pleasant Ridge, whose 18-year old daughter, Elizabeth, is at Sweetwater.

"Elizabeth's preparations for joining the Wasps," Mrs. Wadlow said, "cost us almost $1,000. I think that figure must be about average for the group. It includes 35 hours of flight training which the Army required before it would undertake its own training of the girls. . . . They had to pay their own railroad fare to Avenger Field."[15]

This same group of WASPs would soon become the only organized opposition to the disbandment from within WASP ranks, as those women already in training or having active mission status were strictly prohibited from speaking to the media. The women first organized a protest, as reported in the *Detroit Free Press*:

The WASPS, seven from Detroit (by latest count) staged a sit down at Avenger Field, Sweetwater, Texas, over the weekend while friends and congressmen flooded Washington with telegraphic, oral and written protests.

Meanwhile, Mrs. Mary Wadlow, 24 Kensington, Royal Oak, Mother of Inductee Elizabeth Wadlow, said that the girls, who represent almost every state, are planning a special lobbying committee to march on Congress in September.[16]

Marty Wyall, WASP and official historian for the program, said of the many WASP trainees who did not receive notice of disbandment and showed up at Avenger Field: "They were mad, and refused to leave. The only way to get them out of there was to get a DC-10 and fly them to California at the Air Forces' expense."[17] A dozen WASPs demanded flight to Hollywood, and then began a media crusade from there. The lead for one article about them was: "Jobless, deserted by their 'rich uncle' and a long way from home—that's the plight of a dozen attractive girls at the women's division of the Hollywood Guild Canteen."[18]

Another article revealed that the Hollywood protest had its pleasurable side, and that the women pilots were being approached by recruiters from other women's military auxiliaries:

Hollywood is proving to be the ideal place for 114 would-be girl pilots to forget their troubles. The girls were stranded in Texas a week ago by Army orders halting their inductions into the Wasps. They are now in Hollywood being treated like celebrities according to Dorothy Moon of 15458 Nowda.

"We are having a gay time," Dorothy wrote her mother, Mrs. Morton Moon. "At the Hollywood Canteen one night, Joan Crawford and Alan Ladd came over to see us and Peggy Ryan invited us to lunch at her studio."

"This morning I expected to sleep, but three newspapermen and photographers came to see us, and later officers of the Army and Navy came over to try to enlist us in the Air WAVES and Air WACS," she said.[19]

Despite the Hollywood fun, the losses to the women trainees were not to be taken lightly. One woman told reporters about how she had gotten a release from her war job to join the WASPs, while another said that she had spent five hundred dollars of her own money to get the flying hours needed to qualify for WASP training.[20] Another article asserted that more than fifty separate bills before Congress were expected to be filed by the women who had traveled to Sweetwater, so that they could recoup their travel money. The article began:

> Congress, which washed up the Wasp training program just before recess, will find quite an aftermath waiting on its return.
>
> Fifty-odd private bills for reimbursement of travel expenses of that half of the new Wasp class which did not get their telegrams saying it was off, and so arranged for training at Avenger Field, Sweetwater, Tex., are almost certain to be introduced at the earliest possible moment.
>
> The War Department has already been besieged for a return of the money. Its answer, of course, was that the only way such reimbursement would be possible would be through the introduction of a private bill in Congress. Each of the fifty-two disappointed Wasps would thus have to get her own member of Congress to put in a bill for her.[21]

The women of what would later become known among former WASPs as the "lost" class of WASPs continued to address the curtailment of their training in the media and toward Congress.

The Media Continues to Attack the WASP Program

Despite this slight peppering of articles, what happened to the training program and to these women did not arouse the same outrage from the media or the public as had the plight of civilian male pilots. The only media that consistently argued on behalf of the WASPs were aviation journals and magazines. For example, *National Aeronautics* magazine correctly stated the impetus behind the WASP bill and offered a balanced opinion: "As far as the conflicting claims of the WASP and the CAA-WTS men are concerned there is justice on both sides. Patently, justice must be done for both groups. The women now flying for the WASP or in training deserve military status. Those CAA-WTS men who are qualified for flight duty deserve flying jobs in the armed services."[22]

Another publication, *The Service Woman*, offered articles fully in support of the WASPs:

> If there is anything to that old superstition there must be a number of legislators in Washington with burning ears. To put it mildly, WASPS—Women Air Force Service Pilots—in training here are darn good and sore. In fact they're hopping mad. . . .
>
> The feelings of the girls at Avenger Field might be summed up in the words of one petite WASP.
>
> "What the heck," she said, "why do CAA pilots have to be afraid of us? If they're better pilots than we are let them prove it. And if they're better then it's a cinch that the Army would take them instead of us."
>
> The girl, who asked that her name be withheld, referred to the argument presented to Congress that CAA pilots have to have 1,000 hours flying time as against 35 hours required of a girl before WASP training. She mentioned one friend of hers, Marcella Fried, now stationed at the U.S. Army Air Field, Greenville, Miss., who has logged almost 2,000 flying hours.
>
> "Marcella's a test pilot," the petite WASP said, "and I'll stack her up against any man flyer alive. And he can choose his own plane and distance."[23]

But these treatments were the exception, and because they appeared mainly in trade journals, they did not affect public or congressional opinion. The mass media did not complain that patriotic individuals had been let down by their country or that governmental money was being wasted in a time of national crisis, as had been stated in support of the male pilots. In addition, editorials did not lament the losses of jobs, money, and homes by these women who had sacrificed a great deal to join the war effort. Despite the facts that were publicized about the WASP program, and despite public support for programs designed to put a quick end to the war, the media still did not acknowledge that these women were soldiers with important missions and valuable skills who were being let down by their government and thus were not contributing to the U.S. war effort. Instead, the media continued their negative publicity against what remained of the WASP program. Opponents would not be satisfied until the entire WASP program—both training and active assignments—was ended.

As the media announced the rulings of the congressional committees and the full votes of congressional members, the tone continued to be poised against the WASPs:

> The Civil Service Investigating Committee this afternoon recommended to the House that recruiting of inexperienced personnel for training with the WASPS be terminated and that the service of experienced air personnel now available be utilized immediately in the jobs for which women pilots are being prepared.[24]

Newspaper articles continued to perpetuate rumors and spread incorrect information about the WASP program. One such article began: "Reliable information from Washington indicates the WASPS (Women Air Service Pilots) are in a nose dive from which they will not recover."[25] With headings such as "Not Created by Congress" and "Scores Are Killed," the article maintained that the WASP program had been created illegally and that the women pilots were so unskilled that they were dying in record numbers.[26] It also alleged that the women pilots cost more to train than men and stated that most WASPs were still in training because they weren't competent enough to graduate. It also quoted unnamed sources, giving them the status of experts: "They are on their way out and, to quote one who knows, 'we'll wake up one of these mornings and discover there are no more WASPS to sting the taxpayers and keep thoroughly experienced men out of flying jobs'."[27]

As early as July 1944, rumors were being printed in the media that the entire WASP program was going to be disbanded, rather than just the training program. *Aviation News Magazine* reported in its "Washington Observer" column that "it is only a matter of months until the whole program will be washed out."[28] The article went on to state that while Cochran was making "a flying 'stumping' tour to various states, in order to drum up congressional support for her organization," the American Legion and other veterans' groups were supporting a House bill introduced by Representative Harness to immediately abolish the WASPs.[29]

Gossip columnist Drew Pearson returned to his attack on the WASP program in August, claiming that the Ramspeck committee report originally had stated, "We urge that the Wasps be wiped out completely," but that General Arnold had made a trip to Capitol Hill and prevented that sentence from appearing.[30] Pearson alleged that WASPs were still in training and still flying missions while "more than 5,000 trained men pilots, each with an average of 1250 flying hours remain idle," and that General Arnold was going against the congressional ruling and was attempting to have the WASPs incorporated under the WACs.[31] Pearson's column was flagrantly incorrect and deliberately omitted that the AAF had concluded new training and recruiting. However, response to the rumor issued by Pearson and other reporters was so strong that the War Department issued a press release denying that incorporation of the WASP into the WAC was under consideration.[32] Another rumor that arose during this time was that the call for WASP militarization was not based on need or prior plans, but on the AAF's desire to have its own women's auxiliary, like the rest of the military divisions. One article blamed the controversy on "an over-zealous, 'Party line' kind of mentality on the part of some of Arnold's subordinates. They reasoned that if the Army and Navy have their auxiliaries, therefore the air force should have its separate auxiliary."[33]

Yet another line of negative reasoning was that the AAF and General Arnold knew that the WASP program was not viable or reasonable, but that AAF leaders had pressured for military recognition of the pilots in order to overcompensate for their mistake:

> But at this stage of the war, the renewed effort to commission members of the WASPS is more indicative of a desire to vindicate the wisdom of an experiment of doubtful value than to meet any valid need. On a "long-term" basis, it is said, full effectiveness of the WASPS requires militarization of the organization. The question is whether long-term use of woman pilots in the Army is really under serious consideration by anybody.[34]

Another situation that damaged the program's reputation was that the media continually compared the WASPs, who performed relatively risky missions, with other women's auxiliaries whose missions were not at all similar, simply because all maintained the same gender. For example, the *Washington Daily News* noted that the "25th WASP girl-pilot death has just been reported" and added, "Some critics of the WASP program have compared these 25 deaths among the less than a thousand WASPS in service with 40 deaths in the entire personnel of the WACS, WAVES, SPARS and Army nurses combined."[35]

The result of this inequitable comparison of fatality figures among the women's auxiliaries was to shape the WASPs as being incompetent. It also reflected a cultural construction in which men and women were perceived as being such separate categories that it was deemed more logical to compare the WASPs with women who served as clerks, nurses and secretaries, rather than with male pilots stationed at the same bases as the WASPs. Had the WASPs been compared with these male pilots, instead of being constructed as incompetent, it would have been revealed that the rate of accidents and deaths was lower for WASPs than for male pilots in training and performing similar missions.

Cochran Releases Report on WASP Program

On August 1, 1944, Cochran issued an eleven-page, two-year status report on the WASPs to General Arnold, which was written, in part, "to determine their future in light of today's known factors."[36] The report provided a thorough history of the program, an administrative background on the organization, and costs of training and program maintenance, and it listed the objectives and missions of the WASPs. Cochran concluded that the program was successful in meeting its stated objectives[37] and described the range of missions being performed by WASPs, which included ferrying, instructing, engineering flying, target towing, testing flight clothing and equipment, and liaison flying.[38] She noted: "The usefulness of WASPs cannot be measured by the importance of the types of planes they fly, for their job is to do the routine, the dish-washing flying jobs of the AAF, that will release men for higher grades of duty."[39] In discussing WASP missions, the report noted that many WASPs had received commendations, and that the accident and fatality rates were lower for WASPs than for male pilots of the Continental Army Air Forces who were performing similar missions.[40]

Either to counter the negative publicity surrounding the WASPs and the bill for militarization or in a calculated attempt to bring about the conclusion of the program, the Press Branch of the War Department released the two-year status report in its entirety and attached to it a two-page news release that highlighted, not only in its text but in its headline, a single suggestion made in the report by Cochran, which was that "serious consideration should be given to inactivation of the WASP program if militarization is not soon authorized."[41] This suggestion was seized upon by the media as an ultimatum issued by Cochran to force the AAF into giving her and "her girls" officer commissions, and would lead to the final demise of the WASP. A substantial portion of the report dealt with the issue of militarization—whether the pilots should be militarized, if the WAC was an acceptable option for obtaining militarization, and if the program should continue. Cochran came to several conclusions, which were that the program should be militarized, but not as part of the WAC, and that despite the success and value of the program, without militarization it should not continue once an evaluation had shown that the WASPs were no longer needed. She noted in a section about militarization that:

1. The loss of funds expended in training civilian WASPs and the unreliability of flying personnel in a civilian status, as indicated by the high resignation rate, are factors to be considered in using civilian WASPs in any AAF activity. . . .

2. The difficulties of providing proper administration of a civilian organization established to perform a military mission have proven to be almost insurmountable. WASPs are assigned to military units, perform the same jobs as commissioned pilots, and are associated wholly with military personnel. However, as civilians they are subject to an entirely different set of laws, rules, and regulations. . . .

3. Difficulties encountered in utilizing the WASP civilian personnel as outlined above and mentioned throughout this report indicate that the only effective means by which the AAF can obtain efficient and economical use of women pilots is through a militarized program which makes the WASP a part of the AAF. Simple justice for the WASPs themselves also dictates such a step. They are doing the work of an officer freed to serve elsewhere. They get none of the benefits of military status, not even the right to a military funeral. As a WASP's pay is less than the income of a second lieutenant on flying duty, it follows that the AAF is getting results at less cost. This would presumably continue if WASPs were militarized, as it is believed that most WASP commissions would be in the lowest grade. They are entitled to equal pay and equal recognition for equal work.[42]

With regard to when and how the WASP program should be concluded, Cochran wrote:

The WASP should, of course, be demobilized quickly when no longer needed. To say that they should be the first pilots to be demobilized does not necessarily follow. At present each WASP saves one less-qualified man from being withdrawn from private life or releases one already-trained pilot for other duties. The question needs to be raised and settled whether WASPs should be retained temporarily during early stages of demobilization so that male pilots who wish to return to their normal civilian occupations can do so that much earlier. Certain it is that the WASPs will have no useful place with the AAF when the male pilots who wish to remain in service are sufficient in number to perform all the duties.[43]

Cochran concluded the report with four recommendations: that the WASPs be militarized and commissioned at the lowest grade possible; that no decisions be made about program expansion until projections were established about future need for pilots; that the civilian WASP program be continued until a final decision was made about militarization; and finally:

Under a civilian status, so many elements of the experimental project are lost or weakened, and there is such lack of control over permanency of work by individual WASPS after they are trained, that serious consideration should be given to inactivation of the WASP program if militarization is not soon authorized. If such action should be taken, and effort should be made to obtain military status, if only for one day, and resulting veterans recognition for all who have served commendably.[44]

The media leapt on this recommendation solely. With headlines like "WASP Director Demands Army Status for Group,"[45] "WASPS Ask General Arnold for Bars or Discharge,"[46] and "Miss Cochran Would Commission Wasps or Junk Organization,"[47] the media asserted that Cochran was issuing an ultimatum to secure commissions and that the WASPs were not professional or devoted to the cause of winning the war, because they were already resigning and were willing to stop flying if they did not receive commissions. One such piece, "The WASP Row," claimed that General Arnold was hardly aware of the WASPs, had been drawn unfortunately into the dispute, and along with male pilots, would gladly use the threat to disband the WASPs. The piece began:

> It is unfortunate that Gen. Arnold, chief of the United States army air forces, should have gotten himself involved in a dispute over the military status of the WASPS. The best available information from Washington on the row kicked up by Jacquelyn [sic] Cochran, director of the women's air force service pilots, is that it is a petticoat fuss from which Arnold would gladly withdraw.[48]

Occasional pieces that supported the WASPs did appear, but never with anywhere near the sensational headlines, size, frequency, or placement of the opposing pieces. "A Fair Proposal" ran only four paragraphs and stated that Cochran's report "reviewed the two-year history of the Wasps and the splendid record they have made ferrying all types of aircraft from factories to stations throughout the country and towing targets at aerial gunnery schools."[49] The piece concluded by noting that Cochran's "recommendation" that the WASPs receive military status for at least one day, in order to receive veteran's recognition or end their service, was "a fair proposal and one on which Congress should act promptly. These young women either have proved their worth or they have not. If they have, they are entitled to the same consideration which already has been given women volunteers."[50] Another editorial that supported the WASPs, "WASPs Deserve Army Status," ended:

> The women fliers should be recognized. They do a task equally as important as the WACs, WAVEs or SPARs. They are entrusted with exceptionally valuable fighting aircraft. They must be efficient. Their record is superb.
> The members now are deprived of military benefits since their status is that

of civilians. They cannot be used to fullest worth in the air forces because they are not under military discipline. The House was wrong in June. It's time to give these young women their due recognition.[51]

AAF Sets the Stage for Disbandment

An August 24, 1944, memorandum from the office of the assistant to director for the Army Air Forces on outlined plans for disbanding the WASP program and suggested that the conclusion of Cochran's report, which requested militarization or cancellation, arose from a source other than Cochran's own hand. The report began by focusing on media activity surrounding the issue of WASP militarization. In referencing what he called the "WASP Project," Major Richard Elliott, special assistant to the director for Army Air Forces, stated that various phases of the "project" were completed. Those phases included: "issuance of articles on CAA-WTS Trainees, on Civilian Instructors, on WASP training in Orlando, and of Miss Cochran's report to the Commanding General. . . . Facts of the WASP situation have been clarified, success of the experiment partially told, and the issue outlined as one of militarization or of cancellation."[52] Cochran's purported ultimatum seemingly was not even her own, but part of a plan devised by the AAF.

Major Elliott's memorandum went on to explore continued lobbying for legislation benefiting the WASPs and considerations about the continuation of the program. It stated that there was considerable opposition to the WASP program on Capitol Hill, and that only sustained public relations and legislative campaigns combined with provable needs for pilots might result in militarization of the program. The risk was that "any campaign to obtain militarization could result harmfully for AAF public and legislative relations."[53] The AAF was gearing up for a larger legislative campaign to obtain separate standing from the Army following the war, so it did not want to make enemies in Washington. The report suggested that WASPs could be used for a short time as civilians if "no action is taken to project them before the public's eyes,"[54] but that the deactivation process should be started. The report concluded with two recommendations:

a. Announcement be made that all basic flight training of WASPS at Avenger Field will be concluded as of 6 September 1944, with the class graduating that date to be utilized, with all other students in training to be dismissed. Announcement will be tied to "changing pilot situation in anticipation of fall of Germany," and "undesirability of continuing to expend funds for training."

    b. Announcement be made that immediately—or following fall of Germany—the WASP program will be cancelled.[55]

In an attempt to direct some of the public attention away from the WASPs, Elliott suggested "that any action in regard to cutting back or cancelling the WASP program be tied in with similar action in regard to other women in AAF service, to civilian male pilots, to civilian specialists."[56] The plan for ending the WASPs was written. If the program received little media attention, then it would be continued temporarily as a civilian program.

However, the editorials and articles opposing WASP militarization continued in greater numbers than those in support of the program. Washington newspapers frequently ran articles against the WASPs, which alleged, like Pearson's piece, that the WASP program and the AAF were engaged in illegal activities by attempting to go against a congressional order. The *Washington Daily News* ran a piece that began: "Undaunted by Congress' emphatic no vote in June, advocates of giving Army status to the WASPs, Air Force civilian fliers, have begun a pressure campaign to get Congress to reverse itself."[57] "Inside Washington," a syndicated piece that ran throughout the country, succinctly put forth all the opposing arguments against and incorrect assumptions about the WASP program:

> Despite a Congressional ban on WASPS in the U.S. Army, there is a move under way to incorporate the women pilots in Uncle Sam's fighting force anyway.
>
> Ever since being given the cold-shoulder by Congress early this summer, the WASPS have been buzzing angrily, recently issuing an ultimatum of their own.
>
> In an 11-page report, Jacqueline Cochran, WASP director, demanded the "Girls" be made part of the Army or given their discharge. The top air chief, Gen. H. H. Arnold, always was friendly toward the idea of women pilots to fill out the need for "manpower" in his flying forces.
>
> And if the women pilots are disbanded, Jacqueline adds, they should be given military status if only for a day so those who have served can be recognized as "veterans" of World War II.[58]

Media pressure was relentless, and on September 12, Major General M. A. Craig, assistant chief of Air Staff, issued a memorandum to the office of General Arnold that recommended that "the WASP Program be discontinued on or immediately after the day Germany is defeated," because of continued opposition against the program from the media and members of Congress.[59]

Arnold Disbands the WASPs

On October 1, 1944, General Arnold issued a memorandum to WASP director Cochran stating that the WASPs had successfully completed their mission
and, because of the "changing war situation," would "soon become pilot material in excess of needs."[60] He wrote:

> I have therefore directed that WASP be deactivated as soon as consistent with
> giving adequate notice to the WASPs and to the Commanding Officers of the
> bases where they are employed, and that you submit promptly to me your plan
> for such deactivation to take place not later than 20 December 1944.[61]

Cochran responded that same day, offering five recommendations: that the
program end on December 20 to give base commanding officers adequate
time to arrange replacements and return the WASPs home by Christmas; that
any WASP resigning after November 20 not have her performance status affected by her resignation; that all phases of the WASP program be continued
until that date; that each WASP in service until her release be issued a certificate similar to an honorable discharge; and that all WASPs be given a card
confirming their pilot ratings, to assist them in obtaining commercial pilots'
licenses.[62]

The same day, General Arnold authored a letter to be sent to all WASPs,
which announced the inactivation of the program on December 20. He
stated:

> The WASP became part of the Air Forces because we had to explore the nation's
> total manpower resources and in order to release male pilots for other duties.
> Their very successful record of accomplishment has proved that in any future
> total effort the nation can count on thousands of its young women to fly any of
> its aircraft. You have freed male pilots for other work, but now the war situa-
> tion has changed and the time has come when your volunteered services are no
> longer needed. The situation is that if you continue in service; you will be re-
> placing instead of releasing our young men. I know that the WASP wouldn't
> want that.[63]

Cochran included Arnold's letter along with a letter she sent out to the
WASPs on October 2. Her letter outlined the conditions of disbandment she
had submitted in the October 1 letter to Arnold and directed the WASPs to
update their logbooks to help the AAF issue a horsepower-rating card to
them.[64] The following day, Cochran wrote a letter to the WASPs training at
Avenger Field, notifying them of the upcoming disbandment and assuring
them that they would be allowed to finish their training.[65] Cochran also vis-

ited the WASP trainees at Avenger: "Jackie Cochran came to the field, and she announced to us that we would no longer be flying after December, that Congress had decided that they no longer needed us that the war was winding down. There was a lot of crying," said Betty Stagg Turner.[66]

On October 4, the Press Branch of the War Department issued a media release announcing that the entire WASP program would be concluded on December 20. It began:

> Unless there are unexpected and much higher combat losses in the air war over Germany, the Army Air Forces will inactivate the Women Airforce Service Pilots (WASP) on December 20, 1944, General H. H. Arnold, Commanding General, announced today.
>
> The decision to release volunteer women pilots from further service with the AAF was based on present indications that by mid-December there will be sufficient male pilots available to fill all flying assignments in the United States and overseas.
>
> General Arnold said:
>
> "I am proud of the WASPs and their record of skill, versatility and loyalty. They have done outstanding work for the AAF, even exceeding our expectations when the program was begun in 1942.
>
> "The WASPs were accepted as volunteers at a time when the nation faced total mobilization and when a pilot shortage would have imperiled this mission of the AAF. They have been as much an integral part of the AAF as their civil service status would permit and have not only performed highly essential service but also have established previously-unknown facts concerning the capabilities of women in highly specialized military flying jobs. Their knowledge will be of inestimable value should another national emergency arise. Together with the women fliers of our Allies, the WASP have proved that women have the ability and the capacity to perform the most difficult jobs in flying."[67]

The press release did nothing to counter the arguments that had been raised against the WASPs. Indeed, it furthered the argument that the WASPs were not needed by incorrectly stating that there existed enough pilots to fly all domestic missions. The release also contained minor errors, including an incorrect figure for WASP deaths.[68] The public announcement of the disbandment of the WASPs did not achieve its intent; media attacks against the program continued. In an article on Arnold's announcement that the WASP program would soon be disbanded, the *Washington Daily News* wrote: "The decision came after several months' controversy about further expensive training of women pilots at a time when several thousand male civilian fliers were available as the result of discontinuance of the civil pilot training program."[69] An editorial in the *Washing-*

ton Post furthered the allegations, claiming that the "Wasps' controversial career" ended directly because of Cochran's ultimatum. The piece was titled "Men Take Over: Army to Drop Women Fliers Next Dec. 20."[70]

Even with the program slated to end, and with it the threat posed by the WASPs, some positive articles began to trickle into the media as well. "'Let Us Fly,' Plea of WASPS: Grounding of 1,000 Girls Brings Many Heartaches" quoted two WASPs as saying that the training of WASPs was wasted, and that the WASPs had no hopes of finding commercial flying jobs following disbandment. WASP Nancy Hanks was quoted as saying: "the airlines don't want us. One of the girls was told when she inquired about a job, 'The only place we want women is scrubbing out the planes, or maybe an office if you can type!'"[71]

Cochran had been quoted the previous spring as saying that the WASPs would have no future in flying:

> Jacqueline Cochrane *[sic]*, director of the Wasps, declared yesterday she can see no future for women in commercial aviation after the war. . . .
>
> "I don't believe many women will be used actively in aviation after the war because there will be too many pilots available to the aviation companies who will need jobs.
>
> "Airlines, too, will consider the hazards of hiring women who may marry and have to take time out to have children. Flying is nothing you can put on the shelf for six or eight months and then take up again."[72]

As the date for disbandment neared, the percentages of positive media pieces about the WASP program increased, because the male civilian pilot's lobby, which had achieved its goal of ending the WASP program, pulled back its media campaign. For the first time since the debate over the program began, the WASPs themselves were interviewed and the media reported on the nature of their missions. Among those who wrote in praise of the WASP was popular USO and Hollywood entertainer Bob Hope:

> We were flying in the lead ship in a formation of B-17's the other day on our way to the Army air base in Clovis, N. M., and after we had been in the air about an hour I went up to the cockpit to talk to the pilot and discovered a girl flying the plane. Imagine my amazement! I should have know it was a woman pilot because another B-17 was flying along side trying to rub noses. This girl, Mary A. Gresham of Plainfield, N. J. is a Wasp, one of those girls who have been flying planes for our Government these past few years and have been making a great contribution to the war effort.
>
> I found out from one of the crew why they call them "Wasps"—If you get too close they sting. I understand the Air Force is going to drop all the civilian

girl pilots this year and before it's too late I think we all should make them take a bow because any time a girl can pilot a lead ship of a formation of Flying Fortresses it certainly makes a sucker out of the phrase "weaker sex."[73]

Stories commonly focused on what the WASPs would do after the program disbanded. One story reviewed the findings of a War Department survey of WASPs, which revealed, not surprisingly, that the majority wanted to continue flying after disbandment.[74] The story noted, however, that it was unlikely that any WASPs would find such employment, and that those WASPs who had been trying to find civilian flying jobs were already giving up. The story also noted that Cochran had written to the embassies of Allied nations to see if they would hire the WASPs, in much the same manner as England had hired American women to transport planes before the formation of the WASP program, and that other WASPs were looking toward South America as a possible place to fly commercial transport planes.[75] Other pieces also speculated on what the future would hold for the disbanded WASPS:

> The wonderful Wasps (they fly B-29's, pursuits and other heavy planes) will try to connect with the Red Cross, driving ambulances. They are all miserable because the Government is inactivating them on December 20. None can get a job at any plane plant, either. Fine way to reward these girls who risked their lives for all of us. Here's a salute to the 600 of them.[76]

> Now there is no place for these 1,000 girls, the greater majority of whom want to keep on flying. Many seeking jobs as commercial pilots have been turned down because there are so many male pilots. It seems unfortunate that this situation exists. These girls gave up good jobs, in many instances, and they have done valuable work. They deserve better treatment.[77]

WASP Disbandment Costs the Army Air Forces Time and Money

One of the most positive pieces on the WASPs was a syndicated column by Gill Robb Wilson. The piece not only pointed out the successes of the WASP program, but stated that the disbandment of the WASPs would prove costly to taxpayers because the male pilots taking over their positions ferrying airplanes would need training, which would cost time and money. Wilson acknowledged that expected wartime pilot casualties were not as high as had been anticipated and planned for, but he was not convinced that the WASPs were not needed, particularly since they were "ferrying more than 80 per cent of all ships produced."[78] Among his arguments for continuing the WASPs was the range of planes they were capable of flying:

> I take up no cudgels for women pilots because they are women nor for men because they are men, but only to get on with the winning of a war, the toughness of which is not yet generally comprehended. Approximately two hundred of the nine hundred Wasps can fly expertly any plane that is used in battle today, including jet-propelled aircraft. Training of men to take their places will require a million dollars, from four to six months' time, and even then will not replace the broad experience which the women have built up on pursuit aircraft. I just do not think the United States is rich enough to throw away two hundred expert pilots, regardless of who they are. . . .
>
> In their two years' existence the Wasp organization as a whole has logged better than half a million air hours on almost every type of mission except combat. In ferrying they have flown all the aircraft from the biggest bomber to the hottest pursuit, and their low accident record is a joy to behold. But, as previously indicated, the question is not of demobilizing the Wasps, but of firing the experts among them who can not be replaced in full and whose partial replacement will be expensive and slow.[79]

Appearing in the same issue of the *New York Herald Tribune* was an editorial in support of Wilson's piece:

> The necessary waste in prosecuting a war is appalling. Appalling too, is its corollary—callousness toward unnecessary, entirely avoidable waste. Captain Gill Robb Wilson points out elsewhere on this page that the demobilization of the Women's Airforce pilots scheduled for December 20 will, unless prompt measures are taken to avoid it, deprive the Air Transport Command of 200 expert ferrying pilots; cost a million dollars to train men to do their jobs; hamper the delivery of planes during the four to six months required to train replacements; and prevent the men who are transferred to ferry duty from completing training for specialized combat tasks.
>
> The decision to discontinue training women pilots and to disband the Wasps was no doubt based on the fact that Airforce casualties were not so great as estimates and the resultant prospect that there would be plenty of available men pilots. As Mr. Wilson makes clear, however, there are not men already trained to do the specialized flying which the two hundred women have been doing for eighteen months. They have flown almost every type of war plane and they have done half of all the ferrying of pursuit planes. Moreover, their enviable safety record is one which it will be next to impossible for flyers who have not had their accumulated experience to match.
>
> What is needed is (1) authorization for the Air Transport Command to hire pilots in a civilian capacity and (2) the money with which to pay them. There

are unused funds appropriated for the Wasps training program which might be allocated for at least partial payment. Neither requirement should present insuperable difficulty. What is unthinkable is that the Transport Command be forced now to dispense with the services of 200 expert pilots who can be replaced only at a very high cost in time, money and personnel. This surely is waste that can and should be avoided.[80]

It is probable that someone from the Ferrying Squadron or the Air Transport Command leaked certain information to Wilson, because the figures used, as well as the angle of the story, replicated a memorandum that had been sent by Ferrying Squadron Brigadier General Bob Nowland to the Commanding General of the Air Transport Command. The Ferrying Squadron had proposed to General Arnold that certain experienced WASPs be allowed to continue their services past the disbandment of the WASP program. In addition, several WASPs made an offer (which they publicized) to the AAF to continue their flying services throughout the war years for payment of one dollar per year.[81] One article focused not on the patriotism of these particular women, but on an inferred lack of support in the war effort from other women:

> The offer of some 20 Women Air Service Pilots—who have been known as Wasps—to serve for $1 a year if they can continue their work of ferrying planes from points of manufacture to points where they are needed, and its rejection by Gen. H. H. Arnold on the ground that there are now plenty of male pilots is in contrast with the situation that exists in other branches of war work.
>
> The Army Nurse Corps, the Wacs, the Waves and the Spars all need recruits and women workers are needed in many war industries but sufficient volunteers are not forthcoming. The shortage in the Nurse Corps has been so acute that talk of drafting nurses has been heard and extension of the draft to women to fill up the other branches has been discussed.[82]

Other articles, however, focused on the misused patriotism of the WASPs:

> To be qualified and anxious to do an important war time job but being barred from it's the plight of about 1,000 patriotic American young women.
>
> Members of at least two of the deactivated squadrons have requested that they be allowed to continue the work, at $1 a year pay. . . .
>
> Most of the ex-WASPS expect to enter commercial aviation. Whatever their choice, they again will select something of direct benefit to the war effort.[83]

One article noted that offers had been received from WASPs at three different ferrying bases, and that the "Air Forces said the offer was appreciated but that enough men pilots were available to carry on the ferrying operations which the women civilian pilots had been performing."[84] However, this publicized statement was very different from the reality, which was that trained male pilots were not available to take over the positions of the WASPs, and that serious backlogs would result because male pilots needed additional training to replace the more than 800 WASPs who were engaged in active service. Of particular concern to the Ferrying Squadron was the loss of skilled WASPs to deliver pursuit planes, because at the time of their disbandment, WASPs were ferrying all P-47 Thunderbolts and nearly all of the other fighters.[85]

On November 1, 1944, Brigadier General Nowland, commander of the ATC Ferrying Division, wrote a memorandum detailing the hardship that the loss of the WASPs would cause to the division and to the male pilots who would have to take their places. The most significant points raised in the memorandum follow:

> The announced inactivation of the WASP on 20 December 1944 will have a pronounced effect on the ability of the Ferrying Division to meet its commitments and to deliver pursuit type aircraft. Since June 1943 women pilots have been delivering fighters in increasing numbers, and at this date 117 WASPs, or 82 per cent of the total number assigned this Division, are "frozen" on pursuit planes. They represent 49 per cent of our total "frozen" pursuit pilots in the five Groups to which WASPs are assigned. It was planned to keep this group of civilian pilots on pursuit deliveries permanently, thus releasing men for progressive upgrading in order to meet our quotas. . . .
>
> Replacement of these experienced pilots with an equal number of male pilots will entail a month's training at Brownsville for each male pilot. These replacements must be chosen from the ranks of our more experienced personnel, since it has been demonstrated that a minimum of 400 hours and an instrument card are necessary prerequisites for pursuit training and subsequent safe delivery of fighters. The 117 WASPs we have been using on pursuit deliveries are already experienced in this specialized type of flying and have established a remarkably low accident record. . . .
>
> The cost of training a fighter pilot at the 4th OTU is approximately $9,336.00, or $1,085,312 for the 117 replacements required upon the discharge of the WASPs. . . .
>
> The loss of the women pilots in the Ferrying Division will effect a definite hardship upon the operations of the Groups. The discharge of the WASPs in December will necessitate the immediate freezing on pursuits of 117 male pilots to replace them. These officers will consequently be ineligible for upgrading and foreign quotas for a minimum period of five months, since pursuit training consumes one month, and a period of four months of pursuit flying has been demonstrated to be the minimum period to insure effective utilization.

These pilots, even after training, will not be as efficient, due to lack of experience, as are the WASPs who have been specializing in this type of flying over a period of eighteen months. It is obvious that the elimination of this group of pilots will not only seriously hamper the Ferrying Division in performing its ferrying mission, but will result in needless expenditure of a considerable amount of money in training and replacements.[86]

The memorandum reached the attention of General Arnold, and under his command, a terse reply was issued to the ATC stating that hiring WASPs after the disbandment date would not be approved and strictly prohibiting any discussion about the costs or delays that the WASP disbandment would cause: "Evaluation of this program in terms of dollars and cents is not the immediate issue at stake and personnel under your control should scrupulously avoid any discussion along this line."[87]

Had similar assessments of the costs and delays of WASP disbandment not been forbidden, the high cost of disbanding the WASPs would have become a matter of record, revealing that disbandment had not saved taxpayers any money, but most likely had cost millions. By using the dollar figure provided by the Ferrying Squadron, a rough figure of the costs of replacing the WASPs can be assessed. The true cost is likely to be even higher, because male pilots would also have received a higher monthly wage than WASPs, as well as flight pay and the costs of benefits. The training costs of all WASP replacements would also vary slightly from the Ferrying Division figure, because WASPs in different divisions flew different planes and missions, which required the introduction of other types of transitional training. However, while not all WASPs were engaged in ferrying pursuit planes, WASPs did have specialized training in bombers, experimental planes (including jets), and as trainers serving as tow target pilots, instructors, test pilots, engineering pilots, and so on. Using Nowland's assessment of $9,336 to train a pilot to ferry pursuits, a rough calculation reveals that the estimated cost simply to train male pilots to replace the 850 WASPs active at the time of disbandment was $7,935,600. (This figure does not include increased monthly wages, flight pay, health insurance, life insurance, and other benefits accorded to military pilots.) The amount requested by the AAF and approved by the Congressional Appropriation Committee to run the entire WASP program throughout 1945 was only $6,391,250.[88]

The memorandum issued by General Arnold's office ordering silence about the costs of training male pilots to replace WASPs is official acknowledgment from the AAF that the WASP program was necessary, that its disbandment would cause delays of military planes in reaching their destination and cost the country millions of dollars, and that male pilots were not actually trained to do the jobs of the WASPs. However, a position of enforced silence from AAF Command Headquarters would ensure that problems caused at various domestic bases by the recall of WASPs would not be documented.

In the meantime, Cochran was trying to locate other flying positions for the WASPs, but without success. She gathered a list of WASPs willing to fly planes for Allied nations, then approached the embassies of these nations, but none followed through on the offer.[89] Rumors of potential flying jobs circulated frequently among the WASPs, as well as rumors that the program was going to be continued or resurrected. One such rumor circulating after disbandment claimed the WASPs could be incorporated in the WAC as rated flying officers.[90] This rumor was so strong and continued for so long that Cochran sent a letter to all former WASPs in February 1945 explaining that it had no factual basis, and that the WASP program was not going to be continued.[91]

Even as the WASP program ended, there was no official acknowledgment of the value of the program in the public sphere, and the media continued to issue negative and exaggerated pieces attacking the WASPs. One such piece was "Passing of WASP Mourned by Ardent Few Who Created This Un-Needed Service." It began:

> With the advent of Dec. 1, the futility of the WASP will disappear into the void of Washington records, mourned only by its creators and remembered wistfully by few.
>
> No dimming of the glory and courage exhibited by those keen-eyed girls who entered the WASP, who flew for it, studied and died for it. They only read the posters, then crawled into dungarees and training planes to fill a need that never existed.
>
> The Women's Airforce Service Pilots, brainchild of American aviatrix Jacqueline Cochrane [sic], blundered through a series of official okehs, was patterned after the highly useful and efficient British Women's Ferrying corps. Outwardly a vitally needed home front organ, the unit actually added turmoil to the overfed pilot training program, embittered experienced pilots who were thrown out of jobs because of its existence, and worst of all, disillusioned a lot of stout-hearted U.S. maidens who were in there pitching for a No. 1 cause. . . .
>
> In spite of unenviable training records, the WASP turned out girl pilots. These superficially trained fledglings, although earnest in their desire to help, were in the majority not qualified to fill ferry and instructor jobs assigned them. Those who did make the grade forced veteran instructors out of long held positions and generally created pandemonium in the ranks of home front aviation. Worst of all, 24 girl pilots were killed by Jun. 21, 1944.
>
> Fortunately, all efforts to incorporate the WASP as an intrinsic part of the

army, failed months ago. Termination of army contracts and War Training ser-vice training schools for military pilots further lessened the need for more air manpower. With more than 6,000 capable male instructors facing induction as buck privates in non-flying GI capacities, the WASP withered and died. As of Dec. 1, 1944, the organization will disappear.[92]

The Final WASP Graduation

On December 7, 1944, the final class of WASP trainees graduated. Their grad-uation date had been advanced to coincide with the third anniversary of the attack on Pearl Harbor and to allow these final graduates to be deemed active WASPs before disbandment. Seventy-one women graduated in this class—seventy-one pilots who would not return the twelve thousand dollars in train-ing costs invested in each of them.[93]

Perhaps in an attempt to demonstrate publicly that the WASP program had indeed been disbanded to placate critics of the program, the WASP graduation was designed to be a publicity event for the AAF. Lieutenant Colonel Manning D. Sell, Public Relations Officer, Flying Training Command, was in charge of the ceremonies.[94] A number of AAF generals and commanding officers were in attendance, and General Arnold, Lieutenant General Barton Yount (Com-manding General of AAF Training Command), and Brigadier General Walter Kraus (Commanding General of Central Flying Training Command) spoke to the graduates, along with Director Cochran.[95] In attendance were Army film-makers and military and civilian reporters. Lieutenant Colonel Roy Ward, Commanding Officer of Avenger Field, introduced the graduation ceremonies of the nineteenth and final graduating class, noting that the ceremony was also a final tribute to the WASP program.[96] He commented that

> the war situation has changed since the WASPs volunteered their services. Combat losses have been unexpectedly low. The vast AAF Training program, has been amazingly successful; so that now we find ourselves in the happy po-sition of having enough trained pilots on hand to meet all needs here and over-seas. The WASPs themselves have contributed no small part to the present fa-vorable picture and though it means that their own beloved program is no longer needed, they share the nation's thankfulness that we are moving toward victory ahead of schedule.
>
> I know I speak for everyone at Avenger Field and our many friends in the City of Sweetwater when I say that we sincerely regret termination of the WASP program here.[97]

General Kraus followed Colonel Ward by presenting a review of the training program. Noting that 1,076 WASPs graduated in the two years of the program, he added: "In relation to the overall AAF Training effort, this WASP program has been conservatively small. However, from the standpoint of those directly responsible for the conduct of the school, the operation was a sizable one. The graduation rate of 1,000 in two years equals the entire Air Corps pilot training production rate of the peaceful years prior to 1939."[98] General Yount provided a summary of the missions of active WASPs and asked for remembrance of those women pilots who gave their lives in service to their country:

> Let us acknowledge the measure of their sacrifice by honoring them as brave women, and by honoring them as women who served without thought of the glory which we accord to heroes of battle. The service pilot faces the risk of death without the emotional inspiration of combat. Men who battle in the sky have the grim, triumphant knowledge that their bombs and bullets are destroying the enemy, and their courage is sustained by the emotions of conflict. These women have given their lives in the performance of arduous and exacting duties without being able to see and feel the final results of their work under the quickening influence of aerial action. They have demonstrated a courage which is sustained not by the fevers of combat, but by the steady heartbeat of faith—a faith in the rightness of our cause, and a faith in the importance of their work to the men who do go into combat.
>
> Let us pay tribute to these women by honoring their memory. . . . Let us treasure their memory as women whose sacrifice has brought honor not only to their country, but also to their organization. . . .
>
> We shall not forget the accomplishments of our women fliers and their contributions to the fulfillment of our mission. And we shall always keep and remember the brave heritage of the women who gave their lives. It is the heritage of faith in victory and faith in the ultimate freedom of humanity.[99]

General Arnold spoke next, outlining the history and accomplishments of the program, as well as his own initial doubts that "a slip of a young girl could fight the controls of a B-17 in the heavy weather they would naturally encounter in operational flying."[100] He countered those doubts: "You and nine hundred of your sisters have shown that you can fly wingtip to wingtip with your brothers. If there ever was a doubt in anyone's mind that women can become skillful pilots, the WASP have dispelled that doubt."[101] Director Cochran concluded the remarks, and she and General Arnold handed out diplomas and WASP wings to the seventy-one WASPs who would never serve their country. An AAF directive sent graduates of the last WASP class to the stations nearest to their homes or the areas to which they intended on moving after disbandment.[102] For the next two weeks, WASPs at various duty stations tried to get in as much flying as they could, but their abilities to do so depended on the graciousness of their commanding officers.[103]

The official "AAF Policy Governing Separation of the WASP" dictated that "WASP in good standing be given the opportunity to ride in military aircraft to their homes or to the vicinity of their homes, provided space is available and no additional expense to the Government is incurred."[104] Because of this caveat, the policy was open to interpretation by base commanders. Most WASPs were fortunate to serve on bases where commanders and base pilots empathized with their situation, so they did get flights home, with some even piloting or copiloting the planes. Marty Wyall (who only had eleven days from graduation to disbandment) not only received a flight to a base near her home, but she also got to copilot the plane. She noted that male pilots from her base sympathized with graduates who didn't get to serve as WASPs, so they let them fly as many missions as possible in that short time, including on the flight home. "There were six of us WASPs on the plane to New York," she said. "Each got to copilot."[105]

Unfortunately, this was not the situation for all WASPs. Some were returned home by other means of transportation, often at their own expense, because their bases didn't have outgoing flights to their home areas. "I went home on a train, because there weren't any planes going near my home," said Betty Stagg Turner.[106] Even worse, in a situation reminiscent of the plights of those women scheduled to be in the June 1944 training class, many WASPs were stranded after disbandment at bases far from their homes. "We were dropped—out of the blue—with no benefits," said Clarice Bergemann. "We were just told to leave—there was no 'we'll take you home' or anything. We had to get home as you could."[107] Wyall, WASP and program historian, added that while she was flown home, "A lot of gals did have problems getting home. Some were stuck or stranded in places."[108]

However, at least one base at which WASPs were stationed ignored the edict against incorporating WASPs into the base staff as civil service employees. Ethel Findley, a Link instructor at Shaw Field, South Carolina, said: "The war was still going on, and it was still a basic school, and I was classified as civil service. They needed [Link] instructors, so we stayed down there."[109]

After Disbandment, the Media Lessen Their Attacks

Only after disbandment did the media begin to offer realistic and factual depictions of the WASP program. Most of these pieces conveniently forgot the barbed attacks those same newspapers had led against the pilots just several months earlier. Stories about the final WASP graduation included more positive data about WASP duties and missions than had been previously revealed:

> The Chief of the Army Air Forces said the record of the Wasps is "valuable information for the archives as we enter the air age."
>
> He added that "we haven't been able to build an airplane you can't fly" revealing that women have flown the big B-29's and the new jet propulsion planes. . . .
>
> Miss Cochran said the women's flying program will go down in history and "will mean more to aviation than anyone realizes."[110]

The most laudatory media pieces about the WASPs appeared on or after the day they disbanded—when there was no threat of women "taking over" men's flying jobs. These stories quoted from the graduation speeches and emphasized the roles the women pilots played in the domestic war effort, their range of skills, and their patriotism. Most articles emphasized the point encouraged by both Cochran and Arnold, which was that the WASPs would be home in time for Christmas, a symbolically important goal for most servicepeople, one so important as to be immortalized in song.

"Although they never actually got into combat but did valiant duty in important war training missions and other war service, the Wasps will be home for Christmas," began the article "Wasps Go into Retirement after Valiant War Service."[111] Added another: "Disconsolate Wasps who have lost their Army flying jobs with the recent disbandment of their service are coming home in time for Christmas, soothed only by that fact. The only other thing that could please them at this point is to find a new assignment that will keep them busy flying planes."[112] Notably absent from this final batch of stories was any mention of the organized opposition to the program from male civilian pilots, returning combat pilots, and Congress; allegations of ineptitude and wrongdoing; and insinuations that the women pilots were detracting from the war effort.

Indeed, an effort seemed to have been made to celebrate the WASPs with convenient forgetfulness:

> On Wednesday 1,000 pilots of the Women Air Force Service—the WASP—will leave their ships for good. The service is disbanded because there are enough men pilots available now to do the job. Meanwhile, let's look at the record.
>
> The girls made good. Flying in fair weather and foul, they delivered fighters and big transports far and wide; they served in the ferrying command, they did a hundred odd jobs of the air that had to be done in the press of organizing the

Army's striking power of the skies. Thirty were killed in the line of duty. And all the while they were civil service pilots. The pity is that they were not given equal status with the WACS while they did their bit for Uncle Sam. But the rumpus over their position is all in the past. The record remains—a golden chapter of America's marshaling air fleet. A grateful nation says: "Thanks, girls."[113]

Another article, "Women Pilots out of Work as Wasp Quits," began:

The Wasps—more than 1,000 of them—succumbed yesterday to the cold of a congressional edict. Women's Army Service Pilots, who for 18 months have served in domestic ferrying, target towing, as instrument flying instructors and couriers for the Army Air Forces, have taken up their last plane as members of an organization which never attained Army status.[114]

An editorial piece, titled "The Gentler Sex: Women Unafraid," approached the WASPs from an angle of what they symbolized to current and future generations of women:

The Wasps are not needed, says the Army, because there is a surplus of veteran men pilots to do their work—to ferry planes on non-combat assignment. So the 1,000 or more young women who participated in one of the most venturesome jobs of the war will receive certificates of service and return to move traditional and possibly "lady like" pursuits. . . .

However, the Wasps will not be forgotten. They will live as a symbol of woman's military trail-blazing into the air and particularly of women's conquest of physical fear. . . .

Should this peace be only another armistice, swarms of Wasps will fly again—and probably not only in non-combat areas. A peaceful world, young women will find in commercial aviation a new outlet—even though they may have to fight at first to break down barriers.

In feminine tradition the Wasps symbolize the beginning of a new era—that of the woman who scorns to use fear as an adjunct of personal charm.

The Wasps have made such fears seem silly. The increasing number of young, attractive, even fragile young women who rally forth into the air is making feminine physical fear seem antiquated. Last bulwark of the women who clung to the precarious economic security of helplessness, such fear has become nothing more than a maginot line to the dauntless feminine generation that this war has sent into the air at home and into the combat areas abroad.[115]

But it was not until 1945 that newspapers would report that WASPs had not received commercial airline jobs and were upset about their status:

After flying the Army Air Forces' biggest bombers and piloting jet propulsion planes, the disbanded Wasps are plainly discontented on the ground. . . .

Typical of the group is Miss D'Ambly, who remarked: "The men pilots said that 1000 Wasps were keeping 5000 of them from jobs. Maybe we're even better than we thought."

One of the most annoying Congressional Statements to the girl fliers was a remark that "This is just social legislation to glamorize the war."

The Wasps maintain there was little glamor attached to their jobs. No uniforms were issued to them until the last few months of their careers, they point out, and most of their time was spent in coveralls, "either flying or waiting to fly."

They had not military status, and their pay as pilots was less than a second lieutenant's.

"We were taken as a matter of course on the airfields," said Miss D'Ambly, "as soon as the pilots recognized that we were capable of doing a good job. We lived in barracks on the field, but we never rated a salute." . . .

Two hundred of the women have been rated as top pilots of fighter planes, as part of the $21,000,000 spent on their training in the corps.[116]

Despite General Arnold's support for the WASP program, public opposition had been too strong and had arisen from too many sectors for him to be able to combat it. In addition, in an Air Forces of 190,000 male pilots,[117] the program of 1,074 WASPs was relatively minor, and because of the public attack the program was receiving, it began to demand more assistance than it provided. Timing was also bad for General Arnold to offer dedicated support, because the congressional bill was defeated immediately following D-Day, for which Arnold led the Air Forces' participation. Because the WASPs never attained Army status, they were destined to fade from public attention despite the assertion by General Yount that the country "shall not forget the accomplishments of our women fliers and their contributions to the fulfillment of our mission."[118]

When Germany surrendered in May 1945, no one remembered the WASPs. When Japan surrendered in September, thus ending the war, the AAF did not mention that WASPs had been part of the top secret planning missions of the crews who had dropped the atomic bombs. In the hundreds of pages of stories in magazines and newspapers across the country that celebrated the soldiers of the U.S. armed services, none remembered the WASPs. In cities and towns across the United States, more than a thousand former WASPs were trying to begin their lives again in a nation that now wanted women out of the military and out of the workplace. They were unable to put their tremendous skills to use, and because they were not veterans, they could not use the GI Bill to obtain new skills and educations. Faced with a country that had never celebrated their contributions and wanted to forget their existence, most WASPs packed up their wings, their uniforms, scrapbooks, and pictures, and tried to fit into postwar American society. As Katherine Landry Steele said, "The WASP program was over; we got on with our lives, and nobody knew who we were and nobody cared, so I didn't care either."[119]

7

On a Different Battlefield
The WASP Fight for Militarization after the War

The disbandment of the Women Airforce Service Pilots and the Allied victory in World War II did not end WASPs' attempts to receive veterans' status or other recognition for their wartime service. In 1945, former WASPs placed their hopes on the Senate WASP bill that had been introduced at the same time as the defeated House bill, but because of the great media opposition to the program, no senator would sponsor the bill. WASPs attempted to obtain sympathetic publicity about their plight, but theirs was not the story the media wanted to tell. As World War II ended, the focus of the media and Congress was on victory, returning servicemen, and the postwar economy. There was no room for accounts of women pilots, particularly when they were claiming that their government had let them down. The media spotlighted the return of women from war roles back to the household. Individual members of the WASPs pressed their congressional representatives for a bill in support of the WASPs, but no one would introduce such a bill.

The WASPs pursued lobbying campaigns pressing for veterans' status. Many WASPs remained organized after their disbandment through the Order of Fifinella, a WASP service organization, which had been formed in October 1944 following the announcement that the program was to be disbanded. "In the first years after the war, everybody had gone their own ways, but a few people kept holding small core groups together and organized what was called the Order of Fifinella," said WASP Ethel Finley.[1]

Named the Order of Fifinella after the WASP insignia character, the organization was formed with the purpose of informing WASPs about employment possibilities and the continued fight to get reinstated in the Army Air Forces.[2] In 1947, the Order of Fifinella approached its members to support a resolution it submitted to Edith Nourse Rogers, chair of the Veterans Affairs Committee of the House.[3] The resolution was for WASPs who had completed the program in good standing to receive full veterans' rights and for the next of kin of WASPs who had died "in the line of duty" to receive compensation.[4]

Despite the involvement of the Order of Fifinella and backing the by numerous former WASPs, the resolution did not receive enough overall support in Congress to be introduced.

The Women's Armed Services Reserve Bill

In 1948, Senate Bill 1641 was introduced in Congress "to establish the Women's Army Corps into the Regular Army, to authorize the enlistment and appointment of women in the Regular Navy and Marine Corps and the Naval and Marine Corps Reserve."[5] The bill came at a time when the contingent arrangements provided by World War II were ending. All military branches had been satisfied with the performance of women soldiers and wanted to maintain a regular component of women soldiers in the peacetime military. If approved, this would be the first time the U.S. military would have positions for women in the regular peacetime military branches.[6] Representative Charles Brooks (Ill.) stated: "Mr. Chairman, this bill marks an epic in the development of our armed forces. For the first time during the period of peace we are authorizing organizations of women in our armed forces."[7] The Senate passed the bill to allow the women into the "Regular Army," but the House held up the measure, introducing a compromise bill aimed at keeping the women in the Reserves.[8] Some members of the House clearly believed that there existed tremendous differences between men and women, and expressed reservations over the "many considerations involved in the problem of placing women in a permanent status in the service."[9] Just as the congressional debate during World War II over the development of women's auxiliaries centered on fears that women would be negatively affected by their wartime involvement, the 1948 House debate focused on the propriety of women serving in the Regular Army. Unlike their wartime predecessors, however, the members of Congress who opposed the measure could not argue that women were incapable of military service, for the World War II records of women soldiers in all branches had been impeccable. Said Representative William Miller (Conn.):

> Certainly they have demonstrated during the war period and in the months and years since the shooting war ended that there is a place for them in the armed forces, that they can do a job fully as well as any male soldier can do it, and in certain positions and categories, particularly in hospitals, they can do their job better than any man can do it for them.[10]

Indeed, it seemed that all of Congress solidly approved of the involvement of women in the military throughout the duration of the World War II, when all of America was mobilized, but with a postwar return to normalcy, however, many felt that women should no longer be part of the armed services. For these members, the permanency of women in the military offered by this bill was perhaps its most frightening aspect. Representative Paul Shafer of Michigan was also worried that permanent women's divisions would keep men who desired commissions out of the military,[11] a position very similar to the one that turned Congress against the WASPs. This time, however, there was no vocal and organized opposition to women serving in the military; instead, a number of civilian organizations endorsed the bill.[12] Indeed, other members of Congress offered an opposite argument, on the basis of other bills up for consideration that involved a civilian draft. Asked Representative Lyndon Johnson of Texas: "How can the gentleman vote for a draft of 19-year-old boys to fill places that we refuse to let women voluntarily fill."[13]

Because of the distinguished service performed by women in World War II, members of Congress who were opposed to women serving in the military couched their opposition in laudatory praise. Said Representative Adolph Sabath of Illinois:

> Personally, I am satisfied that the women have served the country well, but that was during the war. I feel now that the war is over—and I hope there is no danger of another war—that it will not be necessary to expand the women's branches of the armed services.[14]

One member of Congress spoke against the bill because he believed it would result in women being drafted into the military. Representative Noah Mason (Ill.) concluded: "I certainly would not want my daughter to be drafted into the Army against her will, and I certainly would not vote to make it possible to draft another person's daughter into the Army against her will."[15] However, most members of Congress expressed support for the bill and were upset that the measure presented before the House was designed to keep women only in the Reserves. Representative Margaret Chase Smith of Maine, one of the few female members of Congress, proposed an amendment for the House to adopt the bill that was before the Senate, which maintained the existence of women's branches in the regular armed forces.[16] In support of this amendment, Representative William Miller of Connecticut followed with a celebratory speech:

> I can see no justifiable reason for discriminating between men and women in their privileges, opportunities, and duties to preserve and protect our country. . . .

There are many women who are ambitious to make military life their permanent careers. Unless the Smith amendment is adopted, and in the event the House bill becomes a law as written, women will not have the same opportunities as are accorded men. . . .

American women are not bystanders of war. They play a vital role in virtually every phase of its prosecution.

War has a curious way of speeding up all historical processes and pushing people and their societies much more rapidly into the future than they would ever move under normal peacetime processes.

For instance, it speeded up, even more rapidly in the last war, the revolution in the life of women. We forget that it is not only about 100 years since women were first admitted to any universities in America; that they obtained the franchise only after World War I; and that only during the Second World War were all restrictions on their possible activities lifted, with their admission into the last hitherto exclusively male occupation: the armed forces.

War is inevitably a revolutionary force in the life of women. There are those indeed who, like Max Lerner, go as far as to say that "when the classic work on the history of women comes to be written the biggest force of change in their lives will turn out to have been war."[17]

The records of women during the war and in the three years since, which many members of Congress cited as their reason for supporting the Smith amendment, provided solid statistics and reasoning that the opposition could not rally against. When Representative Dewey Short of Missouri (a member of the committee that rewrote the bill to limit women to the reserves) tried to bring up allegations of immorality concerning WACs, Representative Miller stated: "the behavior record of the women on the basis of the records of the War Department is better than the record made for behavior by the males."[18] A congressional slander campaign against women in the military was not to occur in 1948, because at this point a solid record of participation by thousands of women belied such erroneous assumptions. In fact, the debate on the Women's Armed Services Reserve Bill began with condemnation of the way that Congress had dealt with women in the military during the war years. Said Representative Wadsworth:

> Just a word about the measure itself and perhaps its origin. I am sure a great many of you will remember the discussions which took place back in 1942 and 1943, while we were at war, with respect to the admission of women to the military services of the United States. I can remember very well at that time there were a good many cynical remarks made, some were very unkind remarks, with respect to the ability of women to serve faithfully and efficiently in the armed forces.[19]

The bill received substantial and vocal support during the House debate, and it passed on April 21, 1948, thus allowing women entrance into the regular military branches in a permanent capacity. The measure did, however, place a 2 percent cap on the number of women allowed to participate in the military.[20] Within the House measure, the possibility of reintegrating the WASPs into the Air Force (which had become a separate military branch in 1947) was discussed. Representative Charles Fletcher (Ga.) named WASPs "the unsung heroines of the last war"[21] and detailed the events in Congress that led to their demise. Following this, Fletcher requested clarification that the provisions of the Women's Armed Services Reserve bill would allow former WASPs into the Air Force Reserves. He provided statistics about the costs of training the WASPs and noted that if they were allowed to participate as pilots in the Air Force Reserves, their training costs would be put to good use.[22] After receiving confirmation that the bill had no sections that would exclude WASPs, Fletcher read a subsection of the bill that he purported would allow the WASPs to return to military flying:

> May I call the attention of the Members that the bill further provides in subsection (f) of section 301 that—
> "The Secretary of the Air Force shall prescribe the military authority which any female person of the Air Force Reserve may exercise, and the kind of military duty to which such female persons may be assigned: *Provided*, That female persons of the Air Force shall not be assigned to aircraft while such aircraft are engaged in combat missions."
> I think that clearly shows that it was the intention of the committee to include WASPS in the Air Force Reserves.[23]

Despite Fletcher's assumption, it was not the intention of the Air Force to utilize WASPs or any other women as pilots. The Air Force was, however, interested in integrating former WASPs into the Women's Air Force (WAF) as nonflying officers, and Air Force officers had been meeting with ex-WASP director Jacqueline Cochran to establish provisions for doing so. Although former WASPs were invited to join the WAF program, they suffered yet another indignity because appointment of officers in the WAF was limited to women who had military service in World War II.[24] Because the WASPs had never been militarized, they could not be commissioned as officers, "except as newly appointed second lieutenants in competition with other women having no military service."[25] Even in the Air Force, the WASPs had no recognized status, and no women, including former WASPs, were to be appointed as pilots.[26] Despite this, about three hundred former WASPs joined the Women's

Air Force Reserves, including Cochran and WAFS leader Nancy Harkness Love.[27]

Air Force Deputy Chief of Staff Lieutenant General I. H. Edwards encouraged the Secretary of the Air Force to give preference toward the former WASPs:

> The WASPs did a good job during the war. As a body, they were high type women, and we would be well advised to offer them an opportunity for commissions in the reserve. I feel they should be given constructive military credit for their service during the war. Many of them have skills and techniques, other than flying proficiency, that are very usable. However, our position should be definite that they are not eligible for a pilot status.[28]

Four years after their disbandment, the WASPs were given an opportunity to be involved in the Air Force, but only in the reserves, without earned commissions, and not as pilots. For most former WASPs still fighting to receive militarization, when the integration of women into the armed services in 1948 again excluded the women pilots and officially denied the wartime service of the WASPs, it meant the end of any expectations of ever obtaining militarization. Clearly their battle was over. The experiment they had participated in had irrevocably concluded, and the women who had once flown military planes were now, without a doubt, expected to return to their civilian lives.

Nearly thirty years would pass before the former WASPs would again come together and fight for the militarization that had been promised but denied them. In these thirty years, some stayed in the military, and some continued to fly; however, most of the women married, had children, and did not talk much of their contribution in World War II. Most unfortunately, the WASPs lost track of each other. Because they were not veterans, no system was in place to maintain their records, and because most who married changed their names, keeping track of each other was nearly impossible.

The WASPs Reunite

In the 1960s, one former WASP, Marty Wyall, a member of the final graduating class of December 7, 1944, began to assemble the addresses of former WASPs. In 1964, twenty years after the program disbanded, Wyall organized the first reunion of the WASPs.[29] She planned another reunion in 1969, which was better attended than the first because many women she could not locate had heard about the first reunion and contacted her. This was the first time many former WASPs had discussed the disbandment of the program. Most had been unaware of the situations surrounding their demise, and those who were had been forbidden by the AAF to discuss what they knew. Despite the passage of time, their anger was still acute. Obtaining militarization became a central issue at reunions, and many women began to work individually, approaching politicians, the media, and veterans' organizations in an attempt to obtain their standing as veterans.[30]

In 1972, the WASPs held their largest reunion thus far. Marking the thirtieth anniversary of the program's beginning, the reunion was held in Sweetwater, Texas, where most of the WASPs had trained.[31] Again, conversations of the former WASPs turned toward militarization. Several WASPs had been lobbying for a militarization bill, and one bill, House Resolution 15035, had been introduced by Representative Patsy Mink of Hawaii. However, like the first Senate bill in 1944, this bill never reached the floor of the House for debate, but was instead refused consideration by the House Veterans' Affairs Committee.[32] As a result of these discussions, the first national organization was formed to obtain militarization, the WASP Military Committee.[33] Nancy Crew, then president of the Order of Fifinella, organized the committee in February 1973 and named as its chair retired Air Force Colonel Bruce Arnold, the son of deceased Army Air Forces Commanding General Henry H. Arnold.[34] "Senator Barry Goldwater and Colonel Bruce Arnold, the son of Hap Arnold, helped investigate our getting veterans status, and this is when the WASPS again became more active and started have biannual meetings," said WASP Ethel Finley.[35]

The committee began its work by organizing former WASPs, assembling documents about the WASP program, publicizing accounts of the program in the media, and lobbying the Pentagon and Capitol Hill. Members of the WASP Military Committee pored over earlier congressional documents and media accounts to determine the sources of opposition and mistakes that had previously been made. The failure of the 1972 bill to even reach the House floor provided the committee with an indication of the opposition they could anticipate receiving in Congress.[36] In 1975, the efforts of the WASP Military Committee resulted in the introduction of WASP militarization bills in both the Senate and the House. Representative Mink again sponsored the bill, House Resolution 6595, while Senator Goldwater (who had served as a Ferrying Squadron pilot in World War II) sponsored Senate Bill 1345. However, neither bill made it past their respective veterans' affairs committees because of opposition to the bills in both military affairs committees.[37]

The "First" Women Military Pilots

In 1976, the Air Force announced a major policy change—women would be allowed to serve as pilots. That summer, ten women officers entered flight screening at Lackland Air Base.[38] In September 1977, the women pilots graduated from the Air Force Pilot School.[39] These announcements generated a great deal of media attention—because, it was claimed, women were going to pilot U.S. military planes for the first time.

The climate for women had changed tremendously in the thirty-two years since they had last flown military planes. In 1944, the media pressed for women to return to their homes and maintain peacetime gender roles. Stories about the WASPs in 1944 had headlines like "Glamorous Fliers"[40] and drew upon opinion rather than documentation in condemning the women pilots. Because of wartime restrictions on the WASP program, the story of their missions had never been told during the war; after the war, there was no interest in telling their stories.

In the 1970s, there was significant media interest in stories about the accomplishments of women, particularly in fields previously or commonly believed to be nontraditional for women. The women entering the Air Force Academy as pilots received a substantial amount of publicity because their achievement was believed to be a first. Many WASPs who read or saw stories on the Air Force's latest women pilots were upset and angered by the positive attention these women pilots now received, but they and the WASP Military Committee recognized that the opening of Air Force pilot positions to women in the 1970s was an opportunity not only for those women, but also for the WASPs. Katherine (Kaddy) Landry Steele said:

> When the Air Force Academy decided they were going to take women, and they made the announcement that for the first time in history women were going to fly military aircraft, it really set a bomb under all of us. I thought: Come on, after all we put into that program, and all of the—I won't say sacrifices, because it wasn't really much of a sacrifice, but it certainly was a big effort, and we did a very, very good job. So I then decided that we all had to get behind our militarization.[41]

The WASPs now had an angle with which to approach the media. Soon, stories began appearing in newspapers and magazines and on television about the women who truly were the first to pilot military planes. Connections were made between the achievements of the WASPs and the achievements of the newest incarnation of American women military pilots. "If we had been called in and asked to do the missions we had done, and we made a bloody mess of it, then this would have been delayed another fifty years. But because it was successful—is the important issue—they had no problems," said Steele.[42]

It was a first for the WASPs as well. For the first time, they were able to tell the complete story of their service, their achievements, and how they had been let down by the government in 1944. They were able to explain in personal and tangible terms what the loss of military benefits meant for many of them. And, for the first time, America listened.

The headlines of WASP stories in 1976 and 1977 were dramatically different from those that appeared during and immediately after World War II. "The WASPs: Maybe They'll Get More, But All They Want Is Recognition"[43] and "World War II's Women Pilots Feel Forgotten, Their Benefits Ignored"[44] are typical of the headlines written during this period. Stories published in the 1970s followed similar structures: the history of the WASP program was given, emphasizing that these were the first American women to pilot military planes; stories of individual WASPs were told; and the pieces concluded with a discussion about the lack of militarization, its effects, and efforts being made to remedy the situation. These stories were very different from previous coverage, both because the complete history of WASP achievements was being told (as records and reports became declassified) and because there was a distinctly sympathetic and supportive tone to the pieces.

In the 1940s, the media was incredulous that the WASPs would demand or expect veterans' benefits; by 1977, the media was incredulous that they had not received these benefits. In 1944, editorial writers offered WASP deaths as proof of incompetence and used them to dissuade the public of the value of the program. In stories from the 1970s, the deaths of WASPs were offered as proof of their claims and as the strongest validation that these women were indeed veterans, who had offered the greatest sacrifice to their country. One piece began: "Thirty-two years after they flew for their country and sometimes died in flaming crashes, more than 950 former wartime fliers who had been attached to the United States Air Force feel they are not gone but that they are forgotten."[45] Another piece detailed the tragic effects the lack of benefits had when a WASP was killed in the line of duty:

> Because the WASPs were officially still civilians, there were no benefits. In fact, as Pat [Pateman] and Ellen [Evans] told, the WASPs would sometimes have to pass the hat for enough money to send the body home.
>
> "Everywhere I went, people were killed," Pat said. "And every time it seemed an injustice because we had no benefits. . . .
>
> "There was no insurance or anything to cover the death of a woman pilots. We collected money among ourselves and at the officer's club. One of the offi-

cers took leave to take her [a WASP test pilot who had died in a plane crash] body home. Most of the men were surprised that we had nothing.

"We served our country, and when one of us died the parents were met with a pine box saying, 'Thanks a lot, here's your daughter'. It was pretty earth-shattering."[46]

In the years immediately following Vietnam, many Americans were demanding that the military be held accountable for the deaths of soldiers and citizens alike. In the WASPs, the public recognized a group who had received no compensation for its wartime effort more than thirty years earlier. The WASP Military Committee welcomed the change in media temperament but did not rest its case on that alone. It continued to encourage former WASPs to get their stories told in the media, and it worked with the media to counter any opposition that arose.[47] In 1972 and 1975, three WASP bills had failed to reach the floor of Congress due to a lack of public pressure. The WASP Military Committee did not want this to happen again.

While the cause of the WASPs had public support, it also had official opposition. The Veterans Administration, American Legion, Veterans of Foreign Wars (VFW), and President Jimmy Carter were opposed to the measure, and, as another WASP bill was proposed, they began to publicize their opposition. One opposing piece, very interestingly entitled "Woman Opposes WASP Push for Vet Benefits," focused on the Veterans Administration opposition— as voiced by Dorothy Starbuck, the "first woman to head the benefits division of the Veterans Administration."[48] Citing Starbuck's testimony before the Senate Veterans' Affairs Committee, the piece noted that the Veterans Administration's opposition rested with the civilian status of the WASPs. The Veterans Administration's position was that the WASPs did not differ from other civilian groups who had supported the U.S. war effort and that if the WASPs received veterans' benefits, those benefits would then likely have to be accorded to all other civilians who belonged to support organizations.[49] Despite its slanted headline, this story did provide the WASP position regarding militarization, which was that the WASPs had performed as though they were militarized.

Part of the WASP media strategy was to keep public the legislative maneuvering that accompanied the bill for WASP militarization. Working out of the Washington, D.C., offices of the Army-Navy Club, the WASP Public Affairs Office provided continual media updates regarding the progress of the bill, arranged for interviews with individual WASPs, and provided photographs and fact sheets to members of the media. In 1944, the WASPs had lost their bid for militarization because the public was both misinformed and uninformed about the missions performed by the WASPs and the impact caused by a lack of militarization. In 1977, the WASPs, no longer under AAF orders to maintain their silence, were going to ensure that they were not overlooked this time around. An intensive media campaign placed stories about individual WASPs in Sunday papers across the country, in regular news features in print and on radio and television, and even on the national television entertainment series *Real People.*

While the WASPs were well represented in the mass media, opposition to WASP militarization was arising not from the average American voter and television viewer, but rather from the veterans' organizations. In 1975, both the House and the Senate had shut down the WASP bill in their respective veteran's affairs committees. These committees were highly influenced by the Veterans Administration and by veterans' organizations such as the American Legion and VFW, all of which openly opposed the WASP bill. If the militarization of the WASPs was to occur, it would have to be endorsed by veterans, as well as active members of the armed forces.

The Stars and Stripes Gives Official Voice to the WASPs

The WASP Military Committee received a tremendous boost in September 1977, when *The Stars and Stripes,* "The Only National Veterans' Newspaper," allowed the WASPs a weekly column to publicize their attempts at receiving militarization. The endorsement of the veterans' newspaper quickly resulted in other veterans' organizations offering public support to the WASPs. Local chapters of the American Legion and VFW also issued statements in support of the bills, which were contrary to those issued by their national offices.

The Stars and Stripes first offered substantial coverage of the WASP bill on June 2, 1977, with several pages of excerpts from the testimony before the Senate Committee on Veterans' Affairs on May 25. The testimony of former WASP Dora Dougherty Strother was featured on the front page, and subsequent pages continued her testimony and included statements of support from several members of Congress, including Senator Goldwater, sponsor of the bill, and statements of opposition from the Veterans Administration, American Legion, and VFW. The June 16 issue of *The Stars and Stripes* featured a column from the National Association of Concerned Veterans, announcing its support of the WASP bill. In its statement of support, the association countered the arguments raised by the Veterans Administration that a dangerous precedent would be set:

> It is shameful that these women who served their country honorably in time of war have been denied veterans' benefits. It is shameful that they must still fight for these benefits after 30 years. And it is shameful that not only must they convince Congress of their right, but must also convince those with whom they served and who are now spokesmen for the veterans' organizations.
>
> There are certain facts which must be kept in mind. These women were assigned flight activities that were not assigned to other civilian pilots. They conformed to military discipline and military courtesy. They participated in physical training required at duty bases, were required to learn infantry drill, and they carried weapons.
>
> Under current law a male reservist who serves on active duty for only two weeks and is injured while on active duty is eligible to apply for VA benefits. A woman who served her country in time of war, functioned in combat zones and served in essential areas when there existed a "manpower" shortage, is not eligible to apply for VA benefits.
>
> The argument that granting WASPs veterans' benefits would set a dangerous precedent is an untenable position. There have been many civilian groups asking Congress for veterans' benefits. But, it is unfair to consider all these groups solely under the heading "civilian." Let each group be considered separately and on its own merit.[50]

The Combat Pilots Association also endorsed the WASP bill and extended its membership to former WASPs, stating: "While they didn't necessarily engage in aerial combat, they did provide for the added and needed deployment of male pilots."[51] By September, *The Stars and Stripes* was running a weekly column by former WASP Patricia Collins Hughes about the WASP bill. Hughes also directly confronted the claims that the WASPs were simply another civilian group requesting benefits.

> Still other surface opposition to WASP recognition has been centered in the VA, strongly supported by the Headquarters of the American Legion and Veterans of Foreign Wars, which have voiced fears that recognition of the legendary lady fliers will denigrate the meaning of the term "veteran" while opening the floodgates for literally dozens of groups such as the Civil Air Patrol, Merchant Marine, American War Correspondents, etc., all of whom performed service with or for the armed forces since the Civil War.[52]

Hughes carefully deconstructed this argument by listing eleven ways that the WASPs markedly differed from other civilian groups, which included their being trained to be part of the military "when proven operationally ef-

fective," decorating their members "by military orders in military ceremonies," and being officially sponsored by the AAF and the War Department
to receive militarization. Because the current debate in Congress was also influenced by what was published in the 1944 *Congressional Record*, Hughes's
column frequently dealt with topics more than thirty years old by publishing
reports and memorandums from World War II. One of the more interesting
declassified pieces printed in Hughes's column was an order directing a flight
of armed B-17 bombers that included three WASPs on "an emergency combat
war mission" to Cuba and Puerto Rico.[53] In that mission, the WASP pilots
maintained civilian status, while the male flight crews received combat pay
and credit. The mission ended up being a routine flight over areas considered
to be occupied by the enemy; however, the planes were armed and the crews
were on alert.

An important issue to Congress in 1977 was whether the AAF truly had intended for the WASP program to be militarized. The WASP debate centered
on a Catch-22 argument: The Veterans Administration and veterans' service
groups were willing to support WASPs' requests for benefits if they were veterans or former members of a formal military branch; while the reason WASPs
were fighting for veterans' standing and subsequent benefits was that the
branch of which they were members had not been formally accepted into the
military. As Hughes wrote:

> The crux of the current argument against militarization apparently is that the
> WASPs do not meet the VA definition of veterans despite the fact that they
> were sworn in and served as part and parcel of the military, because a formal
> SOP discharge was never issued. They were disbanded, ergo, they were not cat-
> egorized as veterans and can not be considered as meeting the veteran defini-
> tion.
>
> Gentlemen and gentlewomen, that's what we've been saying for 33 years!
> That's why we are STILL petitioning! Your predecessors dumped us inglori-
> ously. We kept our commitment up to the letter of our sworn oath . . . they
> wrote us off as if we never existed. Give us a discharge based on the criteria used
> to qualify men for a discharge during the same war in the same MOS and the
> argument is settled.[54]

Besides providing details about the 1944 bid for militarization, congres-
sional hearings, and subsequent disbandment of the WASP program,
Hughes's columns also provided detailed updates about activities on Capitol
Hill. The WASPs were determined that this time the bill would not be lost in
debate within a secondary committee. In September, Hughes reported on the
Senate Veterans' Affairs Committee (and its Chair, Senator Alan Cranston),

which had deliberately delayed the WASP bill in committee since May;[55] announced that a Veterans Administration representative stated that President Carter had specifically ordered him to testify against the bill;[56] and publicized the statement by Representative Herbert Roberts of Texas, Chair of the House Committee on Veterans' Affairs, that "I will never let this bill come out of Committee."[57]

Hughes's column also served to organize former WASPs and gather important information. For example, when the Veterans Administration wrongly testified that civil service benefits had been paid to WASPs and their survivors, Hughes called for any WASPs who had been paid or who had information about such payments to come forward.[58] As a result of information received by the WASP Military Committee, those testifying on behalf of the WASPS were able to prove that the Veterans Administration was wrong.

Congressional Hearings Examine a Thirty-Year-Old Injustice

Following a persuasive and persistent introduction by Senator Goldwater (including the threat that he would attach the WASP amendment to all bills he introduced in Congress if the Senate Committee on Veterans' Affairs continued to deadlock the bill),[59] the WASP bill was finally under congressional consideration in 1977. The WASP Military Committee was sophisticated and organized, and its members had studied the 1944 congressional documents to ensure that the mistakes made then would not be repeated. In 1944, military secrecy and the AAF's fear that the women pilots would fail kept Congress and the American public from knowing about the missions the WASPs had performed. Individual WASPs did not testify before Congress or submit letters or telegrams in support of the program—indeed, they were strictly forbidden from doing so. Because the War Department's official public relations' policy on the WASPs prohibited media contact,[60] the WASPs and the AAF did not counter spurious information that arose in media accounts, which had been fostered by the male civilian pilots' lobby. In Congress, sponsors of the WASP bill did not submit emotional appeals on behalf of the WASPs, even to counter such appeals submitted by the male pilots' lobby. In 1944, the sponsors of the WASP bill had quietly underplayed the bill, expecting that simple documentation and the War Department's endorsement would pass the bill. Indeed, all other women's auxiliaries had met with congressional approval, and the resistance against them on Capitol Hill had been among members of Congress who doubted that women could successfully serve in the military.

With the WASPs, the AAF had documentation about their performance. However, the AAF and the sponsors of the WASP militarization bill had underestimated the powerful role that gender would play in the debate. The 1944 congressional debate over WASP militarization was not logical or factual; indeed, it was not even about the WASPs. The 1944 debate was about whether women should be allowed to perform military missions that men wanted to perform, and it was about privileges certain civilian men expected—such as avoiding the draft and receiving flight pay. Key to the debate was the worth of women, but sponsors of the bill had made the mistake of attempting to address the bill specifically on its merits, in a factual and understated manner, without emotional tactics and without media attention.

In 1977, the WASPs were not going to allow the same mistakes to occur. Beginning in 1976, the WASPs generated constant and supportive media attention. With classified documents now released and no sanctions in place preventing the former WASPs from speaking publicly about their missions, the WASPs were able to provide detailed accounts of their missions, the risks they took, and the losses they incurred. Individual WASPs could now discuss their experience, as well as the impact a lack of militarization or even public recognition had on their lives. Those who were in need of Veterans Administration medical benefits also came forward. It helped that the media had changed enough in the thirty-three years that had passed to be willing to publish balanced and even positive stories about women pilots of military planes. For this congressional battle, the WASPs were not silent. They told their stories, revealed their faces and raised their voices.

In 1944, members of Congress opposed to WASP militarization regularly introduced negative newspaper editorials into the *Congressional Record* in the weeks before the introduction of the WASP bill. This had a profound impact on Congress; debate often focused on fictional issues that had been created in these opinion pieces. In 1977, WASP bill sponsors used this tactic to benefit the WASPs. In September, when the WASPs were testifying before a select subcommittee of the House Veterans' Affairs Committee (the same committee that had deliberately delayed the bill since May), both Senator Goldwater and Representative Margaret Heckler of Massachusetts submitted newspaper pieces supporting the WASPs to the Senate and House floors.

Goldwater submitted an article written by Paul Dean, a columnist distributed throughout Arizona, who had interviewed four former WASPs and wrote about their experiences as well as the proposed legislation. Said Goldwater: "Mr. Dean describes the numerous instances in which the women pilots were identical to male military pilots—identical in all but one important technicality, that is. For the women were barred by law from being commissioned as flight officers and had to remain civilians."[61] Dean's "Big War's Flying Females Stifle Yawns over New Crop" contrasted the 10 women pilot recruits with the 1,074 WASPs, including the 38 who died. The piece concluded:

> The ten who graduate from Williams AFB are eligible, as they have been since signature at a recruiting office, for college on the GI bill, disability benefits, lifetime pensions and space—available air travel anywhere in the world once retired and full fringes from free treatment at veterans' hospitals to the macabre moment of subsidized burial with a free flag on the casket.
>
> But the WASPs of World War II?
>
> They received nothing beyond backpats when their service was disbanded in 1945. They have been given no benefits since. They are not considered veterans.
>
> They don't have the authority to buy a BX [Base Exchange] aspirin to cure headaches earned at their occasional reunions at military airfields.
>
> Bills to bring veteran's benefits to the WASPs have been aborted by Congress since 1944. A new, stronger, unified, tighter organized drive, with Sen. Barry Goldwater, R-Ariz., as pilot-in-command, continues to be jostled by Senate and House and their committees.
>
> So the Mmes. Nyman, Kindig, Blake and Tamblin [the WASPs Dean interviewed] do not downgrade the efforts, proficiency, dedication and deserved status of the flying ladies of Williams.
>
> Nor are they seeking retroactive liberation.
>
> But they would like equity with today's military women.[62]

Heckler submitted a piece that had been distributed in newspapers throughout the country. The piece, entitled "To Right a 33-Year-Old Wrong," had the byline of William Randolph Hearst, Jr., whom Heckler referred to as "one of the most outspoken and respected journalists of our time."[63] Heckler said:

> Mr. Hearst calls upon Americans everywhere to urge Congress to approve full veterans' benefits for the World War II Women's Airforce Service Pilots, universally known as the WASP's.
>
> I would like to publish this excellent article in the Record in its entirety. Additionally, I would like to quote one brief passage which eloquently summarizes the WASP cause:
>
> "These courageous ladies piloted fighter craft and bombers to all parts of the world. Their role was to relieve male pilots for combat duty because there was a pressing shortage of combat-ready pilots in the war's early days, and they— the women—performed their jobs with courage, dispatch and efficiency. So dedicated were they that 38 of them lost their lives."

Mr. Speaker, as a member of the Committee on Veterans' Affairs and as the sponsor of H.R. 5087—a bill which would grant veterans' benefits to the WASP's—I commend Mr. Hearst for his support of these deserving women.

In addition to Mr. Hearst, the number of distinguished Americans supporting the WASP cause is large and impressive.[64]

Goldwater followed in the Senate, submitting a lengthy article entitled "WASP's: The Forgotten 'Warriors'," which began:

It's a sign of the times.

Some military pilots now wear lipstick instead of mustaches, just as some 18 women are now flying for 10 major U.S. airlines.

They aren't the first women to enter the world of professional aviation: only the first to be recognized for it.

During the black years of 1942-1944 women pilots were the forgotten warriors. This unique group of aviators was known as the WASP's, which stood for Women's Airforce Service Pilots. They were not actual members of the service, but contract employees—a status they fought then and are still fighting today. The 850 surviving WASP's want recognition and full veteran's rights for their wartime exploits.

There were 1,074 WASP's performing the often dull and mundane—and sometimes dangerous—flying missions at home. Although they wore military flying gear while piloting the latest aircraft of the Army Air Forces and logged some 60 million air miles ferrying a myriad of aircraft types to and from ports of embarkation, the law at that time prohibited women from being commissioned as pilots. They had a choice of being commissioned in the WAC's and limited to desk jobs or of becoming WASP contract employees in order to fly for their country.[65]

Goldwater noted that the WASPs were receiving a great deal of support in Congress, among voters, and in newspapers. By demonstrating that the WASPs had been refused military standing solely because of their gender, he also skillfully countered the argument that approval of veterans' status for the WASPs would set a dangerous precedent. In the 1970s claims of sex discrimination were being taken seriously by the federal government, and by focusing on the ruling of the AAF that had allowed male Ferrying Squadron pilots to receive commissions but prohibited the same allowance for the women pilots, Goldwater transformed the WASP issue from one of historical import to a pertinent, political, and public contemporary issue:

Mr. President, the WASP's have attracted an unusual amount of interest in the news media, which is natural when one considers the extreme unfairness of treatment these ladies have received under our laws compared with their great achievements and de facto military status during wartime.

Prominent newspapers in at least 40 States have printed numerous articles about the contributions of the WASP's and their struggle for recognition as veterans. Several magazines have joined in heralding in the women pilots and proving that their performance as aviators was every bit as competent as that of male pilots.

The myth that the designation of these ladies as veterans would set a precedent for other civilian groups to claim veterans' rights has been exposed time and again. The girl pilots were denied commissions as military officer for one reason alone—their sex.

A law which the Air Corps wanted to use to bring women pilots into the service as regular officers was ruled by the Comptroller General as not applying to women.

Horror of horrors, the interpretation of the law needed to authorize the commissioning of women would have required considering them to be "persons," since the law permitted the Army Air Corps to grant temporary commissions to "qualified persons."

The Comptroller General's ruling stated that is would be "revolutionary" to include women as "persons" and so the female pilots had to remain civilians.

Now, if there was any other group who was up against a unique and discriminatory law like this one, I would like to hear about it. I doubt if there are any, which pretty well demonstrates the fact that correction of this past injustice, whereby women could not even be considered as "persons" in the eyes of the law, would not open the gates to a flood of similar claims.[66]

In the fall of 1977, support for WASP militarization was so high that no fewer than fourteen House resolutions were proposed,[67] and Senate Bill 247 was cosponsored by twenty-nine Senators.[68]

Testimony before the Senate Committee on Veterans' Affairs

Both the House and Senate veterans' affairs committees were major sources of opposition to the bill that would grant veterans' status to the WASPs. The Senate committee had deliberately delayed the WASP bill for more than four months,[69] and Representative Roberts had told the WASPs who were testifying before his committee that he would "never let this bill come out of Committee."[70] If the WASP bill failed to make it out of either committee, the WASP Military Committee was considering following in the footsteps of members of the Russian Railway Service Corps of 1917 and 1918, who, after years of legislative failure, sued the Army in 1971 and received basic benefits.[71] The railway workers were not, however, recognized as veterans, which was a significant goal of the WASPs. The WASPs would take this approach only if all legislative attempts failed.

Very similar testimony was heard at the hearings of the Senate committee, which began May 25, 1977, and those of the House committee, which began September 20, 1977. Testifying on behalf of the WASPs were several former WASPs; Colonel William Bruce Arnold, retired, U.S. Air Force, the son of AAF Commanding General H. H. Arnold; and various members of Congress. Testifying against the bill were the Veterans Administration, American Legion, and VFW. First to testify at the Senate committee hearings was former WASP Dora Dougherty Strother, who at that time was a lieutenant colonel in the Air Force Reserve and chief of the Human Factors Engineering and Cockpit Arrangement Group at Bell Helicopter. Strother began:

> We come before you today to speak on behalf of the Women Airforce Service Pilots, the WASPs of World War II. We are here to urge your support of S. 247 sponsored by Senator Barry Goldwater. This bill will recognize the WASP as having been de facto Army Air Forces officers and aviators.
>
> Many of the women who served their country as Women Airforce Pilots are in the witness room today. Each of them could tell you essentially the same militarization story of our Army Air Forces experience, what we were told and promised, what we expected, and how the Army Air Forces in fact "militarized" us in every respect of our training and operational duties.
>
> This is the first time the rank and file members of the WASP have had a chance to tell their story. We have waited many years to tell our story.[72]

Former WASPs Strother, Margaret Kerr Boylan, Doris Bricker Tanner, and Bernice Falk Haydu provided heavily documented testimony about training, daily regiments, required uniforms, missions, and commendations and discharges that were handled in accordance with military procedures and practice. All provided documentation and testified about expectations toward militarization, and all gave accounts of missions at air bases alongside male Air Forces officers, in which commanding officers believed the WASPs to be regular AAF troops.[73] Particular attention was given by the WASPs and Colonel Arnold in their testimony toward the specific differences between WASPs and members of civilian groups, such as the Civil Air Patrol. From twenty-four-hour duty missions to military drilling and uniforms, from service alongside male Air Forces officers to top secret missions, the WASPs outlined important differences. Senators and congressional representatives who testified backed up these claims and further explained the loss of benefits that arose from the WASPs' lack of status as military or civil service. The WASPs received no hospitalization or death benefits during or after the war.

Those who opposed WASP militarization argued that the WASPs had received civil service benefits, and that they had not distinguished their service markedly enough from civilians to deserve veterans' status. Leading the opposition was the Veterans Administration, for which Dorothy Starbuck, chief benefits director, testified:

> Whatever similarities to military service the employment of these civilians bore, fundamental distinctions remained. As civil servants they were eligible for Federal Employees Compensation for job-related injuries, and in the event of death their surviving spouses and children became eligible for death benefits under this same program.[74]

This was untrue. Because the original intention of the Army Air Forces was to militarize the WASPs, the program was never given civil service standing. The WASPs gathered documentation of this, which they later submitted to Congress.[75] Starbuck further testified:

> It is by definition the Veterans Administration's mission to administer benefits programs for which entitlement arises by reason of the service of "veterans." The term veteran is defined as "a person who served in the active military, naval or air service and who was discharged or released under conditions other than dishonorable. . . . Entitlement to Veterans Administration benefits is, under current law, dependent upon service in the armed forces proper. . . .
>
> During the wars in which the United States has been engaged, many civilians were subject to hazards and dangers while rendering worthwhile services on behalf of this Nation. . . .
>
> We are fully aware of the commendable service performed and the skill exhibited by the Women Airforce Service Pilots, as well as the esteem in which they were held by military members of the Army Air Forces. Nevertheless, singling out WASP participants for veterans' status would clearly discriminate against those countless other civilians who have likewise contributed greatly in times of grave national need. . . .
>
> It remains that, as civil servants, these individuals performed employment under conditions which differed from that of members of the armed forces proper. It is a substantial rather than formal difference that these civilians could resign at any time, and that their wartime disciplinary infractions subjected them to no more than civil service penalties. . . .
>
> In summary, we believe benefits under laws administered by the Veterans Administration should be limited to persons who rendered active service in the

armed forces and to their dependents. Accordingly, and in view of discriminatory and precedential aspects of S. 247, the Veterans Administration opposes its
enactment.[76]

The VFW also sent a representative to the committee hearings to voice its
opposition to the WASP bill. Donald Schwab, director of National Legislative
Service for the organization, argued on the same principle as did the Veterans
Administration—that because the WASPs had never truly been called soldiers, they could not now be called veterans. Like the others, Schwab first
noted the WASP record of accomplishment before giving the reasons for their
opposition:

> There is no question the flying performed by these young ladies was both a def-
> inite asset to our national war effort and patriotic. . . . Notwithstanding the
> meritorious contribution to the war effort made by these ladies, the fact re-
> mains that they were civil servants with war service appointments subject to the
> national retirements acts and civil service leave regulations. They were super-
> vised by the Civil Service establishment officers, with the right to resign at any
> time and they were not subject to any form of military discipline. To deviate
> from the established criteria of veterans' status, as enunciated in Title 38, USC
> [United States Code], and grant such to these ladies would open a Pandora's box
> and make it extremely difficult for the Congress of the United States to deny
> these benefits to many, many other groups. Such action would eventually de-
> stroy the special status of veterans and do irreparable damage to veterans' ben-
> efits.[77]

The American Legion representative approached the hearings with the
same strategy but took his argument further. Robert Lyngh, deputy director
of the American Legion's National Veterans Affairs and Rehabilitation Commission, emphasized the honor of the American veteran, whom Lynch always
referred to as a "he":

> The American Legion cannot support this bill. Its enactment would, in our
> judgment, jeopardize the entire concept upon which the program of veterans'
> benefits have been constructed. . . .
> We have read the record of how the [1944] bill failed of passage on the floor
> of the House, and perhaps the House should have, in fact, passed the bill at that
> time, possibly resulting in the militarization of the WASPS, and thus making
> this subject, now before the Committee, moot.
> But the bill was not passed. The WASPS were not militarized, and the com-
> plete record of their service establishes that they functioned in a civilian capacity.
> The question, then, that must now be answered is whether as civilians, in
> the service of the Army for performance of a specific and limited task, admit-

tedly involving appreciable risk to life and limb, the former members of the WASPs should be accorded the same rights and benefits that appertain to honorable service in the Armed forces during World War II. The American Legion firmly believes that this should not be done.

The point is not whether the WASPs performed important and valuable service. The point is the retention of the concept of veterans and veterans' benefits, as this concept has been developed and maintained throughout the history of the Republic. . . .

In the history of our Nation, the veteran has, from the time of the Revolution, occupied a special place in relationship to the American people. In the main, our wars have been fought and won by the citizen-soldier who, in responding to the nation's call, is fulfilling a basic obligation of citizenship. The citizen-soldier takes the soldier's oath. He is enrolled for the duration of the war. He is subject to military control and discipline. He is required to bear arms, and to engage in combat according to the orders of the officers appointed over him. Upon honorable completion of the prescribed term of service, he is honorably discharged and he becomes a veteran. And at that point in time he becomes entitled to the honors an benefits that have been bestowed on veterans by a grateful nation.

The role of the veteran in America is a very special one. . . . How does one precisely define the term "veteran"? The American Legion will stand with the definition provided by section 101 of title 38 of the United States Code. Paragraph (2) of section 101 reads: The term "veteran" means a person who served in the active military, naval, or air service, and who was discharged or released therefrom under conditions other than dishonorable.

On the basis of that definition, the former members of the WASPs are not veterans. And if that is true, the question that then presents itself is whether, notwithstanding the fact that WASPs performed in a civilian capacity, they should nevertheless be accorded the rights, privileges and benefits that are accorded to veterans. We of the American Legion say not.

Of all the points that can be made against them, the overriding one, in our judgment, is that to legislate such a grant of benefits would denigrate the term "veteran" so that it will never again have the value that presently attaches to it. For, once the precise definition of the term is breached, it will no longer be possible to defend it.[78]

The opposition the WASPs faced in 1977 was decidedly different from that of 1944. This time, the WASPs had organized and powerful allies in Congress and in the media. With the declassification of most World War II records, they finally had documentation about the dangerous, varied, and valuable missions they had performed. In 1944, Congress did not have access to information regarding the missions many WASPs were involved with; in fact, during the

WASP militarization hearing of that year, Representative William Miller had voiced his support for the WASP program and expressed frustration over the limited facts to which other members of Congress had access.[79] In 1977, these facts were available in great abundance, and the argument shifted to one of semantics. The WASPs had successfully proven their worth, and in this congressional battle they were not being slandered. However, the WASPs and their supporters had not come to Washington to receive compliments; the WASPs wanted nothing less than full veterans' recognition and the benefits that went with it.

The question at hand was what defined a veteran. All of those voicing opposition to the WASP bill turned to the United States Code, which stated that a veteran was "a person who had served in the active military, naval, or air service, and who was discharged or released therefrom under conditions other than dishonorable."[80] Somehow the WASPs had to convince Congress that they too fit this definition.

Part of the WASP argument was correcting the assumption that they had been part of the civil service. If they could prove that they had never been designated as civil servants, they would be one step closer to proving that they had indeed served in the military. The other task was more difficult: Somehow the WASPs would have to convince Congress that they fit the definition of veterans. In the face of a 1944 congressional ruling that placed them outside the Army Air Forces, the WASPs had to show that the AAF not only had good intentions about militarizing the group, but that it had in some way made the WASPs part of the military.

Testimony before the House Committee on Veterans' Affairs

Four months passed before the WASP lobby was called before the House Committee on Veterans' Affairs in September. Rather than stressing their history and accomplishments as they did before the Senate Committee, this time the WASP supporters stressed the extent of the WASPs' military standing. They proved that WASPs did not have civil service standing, and they provided dozens of declassified documents that stressed the program's military regimentation, chain of command, use of military equipment, and issuance of military orders. Those testifying in opposition maintained the same strategy as before. This time, the Disabled American Veterans testified, also claiming that WASPs had come under the protection of civil service benefits. Their representative, William Gardiner, concluded:

In short, Mr. Chairman, the Disabled American Veterans is deeply sympathetic to the plight of these valiant ladies. They have earned our respect and admiration. We cannot, however, support the pending legislation, as we believe that its approval would be extremely detrimental to the existing programs of veterans benefits and services.

Enactment of the WASP bill (H.R. 3277) would violate this nation's historic principle of restricting VA benefits to veterans and their dependents only.[81]

In defense of the WASPs, Colonel Arnold focused on the solid intentions of his father to have the WASPs militarized and pointed out that the decision not to allow the WASPs into the military was a political decision influenced by a powerful male civilian pilots' lobby, rather than a decision emanating from the War Department. Arnold concluded his remarks by specifically taking on the arguments put forth by the Veterans Administration and its accompanying service groups:

On each side of the door of the Veterans Administration in large letters are the words, "to care for him who shall have borne in battle . . ." And, in theory, these words of Abraham Lincoln are fitting for the Bureau. We know that wars create many battles; bloody battles in foreign lands where the finest men of our country are killed and wounded. There were also battles in the United States borne by finance clerks, chauffeurs, staff personnel: fate seems to determine the battles we as individuals are asked to fight.

We realize that your committee jealously guards the term "veteran" in order to protect it from misuse—and we heartily agree. Only the veteran should be cared for as it is he that has borne the battle.

But, tell me, sir, who is more deserving, a young girl, flying on written official military orders who is shot down and killed by our own anti-aircraft artillery while carrying out those orders, or a young finance clerk with an eight to five job in a Denver finance office? And, is not a WASP, flying co-pilot in a B-25 crew just as deserving of a military funeral and other veterans' benefits as the male pilot and other members of the crew, when that plane crashed and killed them all?

From the Veterans Administration point of view, neither of these women should have any veterans' benefits whatsoever, but the men in both cases should have all benefits.

We hope that this committee will remember that the WASP too have borne the battle, a battle that left 79 of them killed or injured. Not to care for them also makes a mockery of the motto of the Veterans Administration as well as the whole Veterans Administration system in our country.[82]

Assembled for the WASP hearings were 114 pages of copies of orders, forms, discharges, and other official documents. Entitled "Evidence Supporting Military Service by Women Airforce Service Pilots of World War II," the thick presentation, written and assembled by Byrd Howell Granger, former commanding officer of a WASP Squadron in Palm Springs, California, provided ample support that the role of WASPs was recognized by the AAF as having been military service during World War II. From passing the Cadet Qualifying Examination[83] and entering official cadet training,[84] up through the receipt of World War II service ribbons after disbandment,[85] to the granting of permission for WASPs who later joined the Air Force to display their WASP wings on their uniform,[86] the collection provided ample documentation and numerous firsthand accounts of the military service of a nonmilitarized organization.

Granger's presentation refuted many of the charges elicited by the opposition to the bill. The assumption that WASPs were free to come and go as they pleased was negated by orders of transfer,[87] identification cards, and Army Instrument Pilot Certificates[88] that WASPs were required to have in their possession while on flight duty. In addition, WASP testimonials revealed that WASPs were on twenty-four-hour call rather than working civilian hours.[89] Court-martial sentences of WASPs disproved the supposition that they were not subject to military discipline,[90] while duty assignments revealed that WASPs participated in top secret military missions.[91] In another section, WASPs recounted firearms training and the requirements for WASPs to carry and draw arms while guarding top secret planes and equipment,[92] which were backed by Ordinance records.[93]

One document that was not part of Granger's "Evidence," but which would have profound impact on the Committee on Veterans' Affairs, was the Army Honorable Discharge certificate of WASP Helen Porter.[94] A solid component of the United States Code defining a veteran was receipt of an honorable discharge from an active military service.[95] Before the WASPs disbanded in December 1944, Commanding General Henry H. Arnold had issued orders to all commanding officers of bases at which WASPs served that the women pilots be issued a certificate similar to an honorable discharge.[96] Arnold did not issue any specifications on what the certificate should look like, and as a result, several commanding officers simply issued the WASPs who had served at their bases certificates of Honorable Discharge from the Army. Helen Porter, who had been the only WASP stationed at Strother Field in Kansas at the time of disbandment, was one of these WASPs. She passed her certificate to the WASP Military Committee, who provided copies of it to the House Committee on Veterans' Affairs. It was the final piece of documentation the committee needed to make its decision.

On October 19, 1977, the Senate unanimously voted to add an amendment calling for WASP veterans' recognition to the GI Improvement Act.[97] Then, on November 3, 1977, the House voted for passage of WASP veterans' status.[98] The following day, the Senate passed the GI Improvement Act, which included provisions for the WASPs to "have their service recognized as active military service by the Secretary of Defense"[99] and to receive honorable discharges and full veterans' benefits.[100]

President Carter signed the bill into law on November 23, 1977, one day before Thanksgiving, "officially declaring the Women's Airforce Service Pilots as having served on active duty in the Armed Forces of the United States for purposes of laws administered by the Veterans Administration."[101] The WASPs were now recognized as veterans of the Army Air Forces. "We were finally recognized for what we had done thirty years before," said Nadine Nagle.[102] The successful passage of the bill brought out WASPs who had found their treatment at the end of World War II so painful that they tried to forget the entire experience. "When it was finally passed, then I finally went to a reunion," said Kaddy Steele.[103]

On March 8, 1979, Air Force Assistant Secretary Antonia Chayes signed the Department of Defense document that authorized official discharges for the WASPs.[104] This was the final document needed. Soon afterwards, WASPs individually applied for and received certificates of Honorable Discharge, became eligible for veterans' benefits, and those no longer living could have a flag placed on their coffins—the final recognition that they had served their country. In 1979, the war was officially over for the WASPs, and this time they were victorious.

8

Recognizing the Gendered Warrior

History and Theory Intersect with the Fate of the WASPs

The Women Airforce Service Pilots of World War II were disbanded before the war's end, and before the women who had served in the program received the militarization promised them, simply because the culture in which they existed was not prepared for women to succeed in roles that were associated with and desired by men. Events and situations surrounding the group's disbandment in 1944 and the struggle of members to obtain militarization most clearly illuminate the consequences of the construction of the gendered warrior. The preceding chapters have noted the intersections between the WASPs and the multiple cultural forces that inhabited their terrain, such as the Army Air Forces, the male civilian pilots' lobby, the media, and Congress. This chapter introduces theories of feminist history, cultural studies, and women's military involvement and notes the way these theories intersect with the facts surrounding WASP disbandment.

A clear confrontation between the WASPs and cultural values in support of male dominance occurred when the positions occupied by the WASPs became desired by men. Here, the threat of the WASPs became palpable. They were flying the newest and best planes that the military had developed, and they were flying in the relative safety of the continental United States. Male pilot trainees whose services were not needed domestically were being released for infantry duty. Despite strong evidence that the male pilot trainees were not qualified to perform the missions of the WASPs, the male civilian pilots publicly expressed their resentment of the WASP program and successfully launched a media and public opinion campaign against the program, which resulted in its disbandment. As demonstrated by the media accounts quoted in this study, the existence of the WASPs as a military unit populated entirely by women pilots ran counter to popular assumptions about the capabilities and limitations of women. Because of this, substantial opposition arose to the efforts made by the AAF to militarize these women.

Constructions of Cultural Power

The notion of hegemony is useful in understanding how cultural forces clashed with the WASPs. According to social theorist Antonio Gramsci, hegemony is a relation of domination not through force, but through consent that occurs by means of political and ideological control.[1] In other words, hegemony is a system of control that occurs through the consent of individuals whose behaviors are modified by ideologies that are disseminated throughout their culture. With hegemony, individuals are not forced into certain behaviors, but instead are forced to believe that the behaviors are ideal. Struggles over hegemonic power occur when there are shifts in the distribution of power, control, and ideological understanding. In America during World War II, a number of these shifts were occurring. The activities of women, racial minorities, and lower-class individuals were more visible than during peacetime, and their contributions to the war effort were publicly recognized as valuable. Women in particular were participating in specific military units as well as in war factories and other domestic support positions that not only challenged existing assumptions about the abilities and limitations of women as a cultural group, but also provided women with greater mobility, freedom, education, and income than they had previously enjoyed.[2] As the status and power of women in America began to shift, attempts were made by the dominant male power structure to conserve and defend the previously existing system, a construction of national identity that had already been weakened by the experiences of the Great Depression. As the likelihood of victory for the United States and its Allies increased, so too did attacks against female participants in the war effort. The work of women in factories and in the military was criticized, and women were let go from their jobs to make room for returning male servicemen.

The WASPs became an important target in the effort to maintain hegemonic control over the sexes. Because they overlook this hegemonic enforcement, many historians who only examined military documents and personal accounts have not been able to explain why the WASPs were disbanded eight months before the war's end, despite efforts by AAF leaders to maintain and even expand the program, or why the WASPs were the only women's military auxiliary during World War II that did not receive the militarization requested by the War Department. The answers to these questions lie not with the WASPs specifically but in the larger American cultural landscape, of which the WASPs were but a singular component. Within the cultural terrain that the WASPs inhabited, the points of intersection and conflict between the WASP program and dominant cultural constituents are uncovered. These points of intersection not only provide the reasons for which the program was disbanded, but also help us understand the cultural construction of gender during this historical period specifically and in other periods generally.

The Performance of Gender

Although most people understand the categories of "man" and "woman" to be tied to assumptions about biological sex, gender is not fixed historically or biologically. Gender is defined by the meanings that a given culture assigns to individuals with specific biological bodies[3] and is a "historically specific knowledge about sexual difference."[4] It therefore changes over time and can vary among different nations and cultures. Once women and men are placed in cultural categories, their behaviors, expectations, occupations, and thoughts are shaped by the meanings their culture has established about what constitutes being of a specific gender.

There is thus an instability to gender. Dominant cultural forces attempt to deny this instability by assigning rigid rules that determine acceptable actions for individuals depending on their gender. Threats to gender assumptions are taken very seriously when they occur, and extreme consequences face the individuals or groups who put forth these challenges. Such challenges generally occur during cultural crises, moments when the definitional barriers between the genders are removed to accommodate some larger threat, such as that which occurs in nations during war.

Significantly, relationships between the genders are heavily influenced by power. Because the dominant power controls the generally accepted systems of belief within a given culture, these constructions are such that the dominant category—in this case men—is established as the norm. According to Gerda Lerner, such constructions form the basis for the historical development of patriarchy. Within the system of patriarchy, the "metaphors of gender" are constructed so that the male is normative, "whole and powerful," while the female is deviant, mutilated, and dependent.[5] Women and men are constructed as diametrically opposed to each other, and categorical differences are heightened and invoked as "proof" that natural differences exist between the genders. Because the definitional system that supports the constructions of gender is based on this oppositional categorization, women cannot be allowed to perform in men's spaces, because their performances risk revealing that gender and therefore power are artificial constructions. Thus, the entire existence of this system of power is supported by the denial of the artificial construction of gender; instead, the consequences of gender performances are interpreted as natural differences.

Contingent also to this diametric construction of gender is the notion of the couple. This notion, which provides the most basic organizational construction in Western thought, is sexed; organizational couples (like strong and weak, active and passive, and war and peace) have concealed beneath their oppositional arrangement gender constructions in which the dominant gender is always privileged.

Such constructions enforce a culturally developed notion that men are superior to women, an assumption that is maintained by the control of any findings that may raise questions about this purportedly natural arrangement. For example, findings about biological differences between genders have overlooked the documented presence of women in categories deemed unsuitable for them and have denied that individual differences within gender groups are larger than the average differences between groups.[6] Arguments about sexual difference developed by dominant groups serve to conceal both the cultural constructions of the powers held by members of the dominant group and the artificial constructions of the body by claiming that the differences these arguments acknowledge are "natural" in their formation. In examining the construction of gendered work in nonindustrial cultures, noted anthropologist Margaret Mead found that when women began to do what had previously been labeled "men's work," the men would shift to an area of labor that was not yet labeled according to gender, would designate this area as being exclusively "men's work," and would subsequently redefine it as being the work that makes men different from women, effectively constructing an area of work that "proves" that they are indeed men.[7] In addition, Mead found that the space occupied by men and the activities they performed were assigned greater cultural significance and value than the spaces and activities of women.

Gender categories remain fiercely defended and place roles and limitations on individuals based entirely upon the category they occupy. Judith Butler has explained this phenomenon in part by revealing the normative function that gender performs for the culture, and by the regulatory processes that produce the bodies it governs. Butler defines gender as a construction determined and sustained by performances influenced by a culture's assumptions about itself.[8] The category of "woman" thus becomes not a living body, but a boundary that varies according to outside regulation. In other words, the body of woman is determined by cultural rules and expectations. The transitory construction of gender is in danger of being revealed at those points where challenges to such cultural rules and expectations are raised. If, as Butler asserts, gender is a performance, a ritual reenactment of socially established learning in which the act of repetition conceals its origins,[9] then a challenge that interrupts this repetition can disrupt the entire performance and its assumptions by drawing attention to the instability and fiction of the performance. If this occurs, the culture that constructed these gendered boundaries will have to enforce a return to the repetitive performances and either deny that any rupture occurred or punish those individuals who shifted the culture's prescribed performance of gender by naming their actions as unnatural transgressions.

Intersections of Feminist Historical Inquiry

During World War II, military strategists used three-dimensional terrain maps to plan the movements of troops and material. Intelligence groups supplied information that detailed the maps, such as enemy placements, civilian groupings, and weather, thus enabling strategists to envision fully the terrain and texture of the intended battlefield. The same strategy has been used in this study of an important facet of World War II history. To thoroughly understand the history of a subject, we must not only examine the subject, but also invoke and envision the relationships, experiences, and cultural landscape inhabited by that subject.

The process of feminist historical inquiry not only offers insight into the specific people or events being (re)discovered, but also uncovers valuable information about the processes through which the identities and expectations of the separate genders have been and are being developed. Feminist historian Joan Scott has argued that the purpose served by feminist explorations into history is to explicate the occurrences of gender constructions.[10] Historical accounts frequently have served to support dominant assumptions about constructions of gender (as well as race, class, nationality, etc.) by normalizing the concepts of dual and opposing genders as stable and real, rather than as constructions perpetually in flux. Through feminist history, this normative positioning of gender can be represented and contested.

Feminist historical inquiry not only improves our understanding of events that women have participated in, but also uncovers constructions of gender that better develop the body of knowledge through which feminist theorists approach their subjects. According to feminist theorist Teresa de Laurentis, the "essential difference" of feminism is found not in the category of women, but in feminism's "historic specificity" in understanding the ways that women live (and have lived) differently from men and from each other.

Feminist history is not the "history of women." Because of the multiplicity of factors that constitute individuals, there can be no history particular to women. When women are assessed individually, however, certain patterns do arise that can be applied categorically. A significant pattern that has arisen in feminist historical inquiry is that of flux. The categories that establish"men" and "women" (essentially, constructions of masculinity and femininity that are culturally accepted as normative behavior) change over time and vary throughout and even within different cultures. There exists no stable group identity, and the definitions of both categories are developed in relation to each other so that any changes in one gender category impact definitions of the other. Through applications of feminist historical technique to specific entities during particular times, patterns of change become visible.

Feminist historical inquiry has been integral in understanding notions of hegemony and cultural constructions by illustrating some of the mechanisms operating within cultures that exert powerful control over the thoughts and behaviors of individuals. The relations of power and consent that constitute hegemonic control are revealed through the study of the historically specific. Furthermore, feminist historical inquiry helps change the assumptions guiding historical studies by focusing its scholarship on critical examinations of documents. Such scholarship recognizes that written records and their preservation reflect the values of a given culture about what is important more so than they exist as evidence of what has previously occurred within that culture.

Certainly, questions of the subjectivity of historical accounts have been debated within many schools of history. However, attempts at rediscovering the history of women had considerable impact on the understanding of historical subjectivity, because accounts of women's history frequently pointed to the hegemonic process by which events are given historical importance more than they focused on the history of women. As a result, not only did the historian begin to question whether she was writing a reflection of her time, but she began to question her understanding of larger, hegemonic structures of culture and their impact on the shaping of the subject. Therefore, the telling of history through feminist analyses not only reflects the dynamics of contemporary times, but also becomes the story of larger cultural constructions rather than of individual subjects. It is not enough to simply examine the specific subject of inquiry, for doing so risks categorizing and restricting the subject. As Joan Scott has noted, examinations of the experiences of hidden lives only reproduce the system that produced the silence.[11]

Within the techniques of feminist history, the value of examining the historical subject comes not from telling the specific story of the subject (which is presumed to be impossible to recover fully), but from mapping out the cultural landscape in which a particular historical subject was situated and then examining the relationships of that subject with others who populate this landscape, thus tracing the movements and transitions of the subject within and throughout the given space. It is not enough to tell a specific story—the position of the subject within that story must also be accounted for. For example, by positioning individuals identified as women in the cultural landscape from which they came, there is less likelihood of falling into a trap of universalizing the category of women into a normative and thus exclusionary category. Those we now call women in contemporary American culture are not members of a unified and cohesive group within this historical period, let alone throughout history.

Historical periods in which gender crises existed (such as times of war) can be used as points of entry to examine the transitional aspect of sex roles and identity. Women have been agents not only in changing their presumed gender roles, but also in the larger events that comprise history. This change has not always been positive, and women have not always had a positive impact on events; nevertheless, the various roles that women have played and continue to play in historical and current events should not be overlooked in explorations of women's history. Yet even if we see women as powerful and active entities, inequities still exist that prevent them from full agency in many cultural situations.

Legal and societal restraints often impose barriers on the roles allowed women. During times of national crises, however, these barriers are frequently dissolved, resulting in increased participation by women in historically significant events. This participation causes another crisis—in the representations of masculinity and femininity—because any redefinition of gender roles immediately has significant impact upon both sexes due to the binary construction of sex identity and roles. Therefore, an expansion of the rights and roles of women almost immediately results in a crisis of masculinity. Feminist theorist Elaine Showalter has explained that there exists a thin "sexual borderline" between the masculine and the feminine, and when definitions of women's roles and identities change, the borderline becomes a "vanishing point of sexual difference."[12] Therefore, changes in assumptions about who women are and what roles they can perform in any given culture not only immediately impact masculine identity and assumptions of male roles, but also threaten the entire construction of difference between men and women.

One such period in which cultural assumptions about men and women were contested and changed was during World War II. Many historians, anthropologists, and cultural critics have written about the impact World War II had not only upon altering constructions of gender, but also constructions of race, class, sexuality, and nationalism. Because World War II was a "total war,"[13] efforts of all citizens had to be focused on the war. In the United States, total war resulted in the recruitment of women and even teenagers to work in manufacturing plants and the incorporation of women into all branches of the military, participating in nearly all military actions except for combat.

The introduction of women into what had previously been established as a proving ground for masculinity subsequently resulted in a crisis of representation regarding gender. Because gender is a cultural construction, we can presume that the greater the threat to gender identity, the greater the backlash against those individuals who constituted that threat.

A Man Is Not Born a Soldier

The military has tremendous impact upon the gender performances of both men and women in contemporary American culture. For the purposes of this study, the military is defined as a stable, governmentally sponsored, and societally recognized institution that is responsible for the maintenance of a nation's worldwide standing through the exercise of force, typically expressed as wars or other actions involving combat. Revolutionary forces, guerrilla forces, and so-called terrorist organizations are excepted from this definition. The defining differences are governmental sponsorship, societal recognition, and stability.

Warfare and gender are "intimately connected."[14] Constructions of gender formed within the military establishment have a wide reach because military metaphors are often used both within and outside the military to define and defend gender roles. Combat narratives are specifically invoked to distinguish men from women, especially because of the impact combat has in the symbolic process of becoming a man. Thus, recognizing women within combat narratives disrupts expectations of gender and confuses male identity. Works by feminist military theorists Cynthia Enloe and Jean Bethke Elshtain examine the development and enhancement of soldiers' masculinity, both through highly feminized and sometimes degrading portrayals of women who serve the military in support roles, and by the elimination of accounts of female soldiers from military narratives. Enloe argues that the military system controls soldiers' wives as thoroughly as it does soldiers, and she documents how military structures prevent wives (most notably wives of officers) from obtaining jobs deemed as not being feminine. For example, the military provides wives with jobs as cashiers at the USO, or encourages their involvement in charity work, but prevents them from taking factory jobs.[15] Enloe also traces the historical roots of what she calls the feminization of military nurses,[16] in which nurses are stereotyped as nurturers and are exempted from traditional personnel classifications to deny their importance and numbers.[17]

Masculinity—"the set of images, values, interests, and activities held important to a successful achievement of male adulthood in American culture"—is intrinsically linked with military involvement through a range of popular culture products.[18] Several things occur within the space in which combat-as-masculinity is performed that benefit the institution that fosters these constructions and also enforce culturally constructed normative standards of gender. For example, military recruitment benefits from the establishment of unspoken rules of male conduct that include a proverbial conditioning under fire. Because these rules are unspoken, it is difficult for members of our culture to articulate a resistance toward them.

Ron Kovic is one of many Vietnam veterans who have written convincingly about confusing combat service with becoming a man. He places the responsibility for his disabling war injury not with the Vietnamese, but with a national consciousness that articulated that a boy must fight in a war in order to become a man. While notions similar to Kovic's proliferate in Vietnam accounts (perhaps because the loss of the war prevented American servicemen from symbolically achieving manhood through combat victory), they also occur in personal narratives from all wars. Highly decorated World War II hero and 1950's movie actor Audie Murphy wrote about the connections he saw between being a soldier and becoming a man in his 1949 autobiography *To Hell and Back*, which was later transformed into a Hollywood movie starring Murphy. He wrote: "When the Japanese hit Pearl Harbor, I was half-wild with frustration. Here was war itself; and I was too young to enlist. I was sure it would all be over in a few months and I would be robbed of the great adventure that had haunted my imagination."[19] Murphy tried to enlist in the Marines, which he described as being "the toughest of the lot,"[20] but was rejected by them and later by the Army paratroopers because of his small and boyish stature. He joined the Army infantry, where he fought being assigned as a cook, which was for him "humiliation,"[21] and subsequently became a rifleman stationed in Europe. Murphy's autobiography is an account of one soldier's coming of age (becoming a man) in the American wartime military. Despite his subsequent horror toward the war, which is developed throughout the account, Murphy never doubted that for him becoming a war hero and becoming a man were linked.

Wartime accounts such as these provide tangible examples of the tenuous and lethal place of gender performances in the military. In this, the male soldier assumes a variation of Simone de Beauvoir's maxim "one is not born a woman, one becomes a woman," in which one is not born a man, but one becomes a man. The man is created and performed within a culturally prescribed construction, in which men are willing to risk danger, dismemberment, and death to prove their masculinity. Combat is not the only dangerous and frequently deadly proving ground for men—other arenas include the running of the bulls in Spain, football, and boxing. However, combat remains the ultimate site within which one proves manhood, for either one is successful or one dies.

A cultural focus upon the performances of masculinity within the military benefits the institution itself by helping to keep secret the true means by which it works. Contemporary military systems rely more on technologies and political activities than on individual brute force to win battles; therefore, if war is presented as stories of individual combat soldiers fighting, the range and depth of wartime activities can be easily concealed. Examples of this can be found in dominant media coverage of American military involvement in the Gulf War. The Gulf War was technologically based, with results determined by the complexity of weapons systems rather than by individual soldiers or the field battles in which they participated. Despite encouragement by the Pentagon to publicize the technological aspect of the war (such as video shots of the purportedly "smart" bombs' tracking devices), the American media still attempted to fit the war into stories in which the individual soldier assumed importance. Focusing on individual soldiers enabled the U.S.-led coalition forces to conduct battles in controlled secrecy while a wealth of stories generated by the media gave some a perception of seamless coverage of the war and its battles.[22] A focus on individual soldiers diverts attention from the important agendas, goals, and political weights of battles, and creates a myopic space in which the audiences believe they are receiving a complete account of wartime occurrences, when instead they have only been given a minimum of information.

The creation of the American soldier in narratives does more than avoid the larger or more significant accounts of real wars; it also serves to silence many truths of war. Battle accounts, as they appear in dominant media sources, do not demonstrate the realities encountered by real people in wars as much as they continue and substantiate commonly held and culturally constructed beliefs about men and women, the cultures within which they live, and the cultures to which theirs is opposed. War narratives are frequently concocted by the military itself to increase the morale of both the soldiers directly involved in war and the civilians they represent. Paul Fussell documents how accounts of military failures and individual acts of cowardice are transformed by military institutions into battle narratives of courage and strength, which become more frequent and reach greater mythical proportions the further a nation is from obtaining victory.[23] Important to these narratives are constructions of the masculine soldier, which become internalized by the soldiers themselves and are incorporated into their own narratives, regardless of the facts. For example, Fussell points to soldiers who idealized their own masculinity in battle stories, while at the same time surveys revealed "fears so deep they often vomited, urinated, or lost control of their bowels."[24] Reality need not enter the battlefield narrative.

Among the realities lost in the cultural constructions of war are the contributions, involvements, and experiences of women. Because the military has been the place where masculinity is "tested and confirmed" in boys and men, the "presence of women contributes to the erasure of this symbolic feature."[25] In addition to constructed masculinity, another gendered component is integral to the battlefield narrative—the absence of femininity, that is, the controlled absence of women and their combat stories. Women cannot be allowed to exist within these narratives if combat is to continue to be a proving ground for masculinity. If war is ideologically the place of men, it follows the boundaries of binary opposition upon which gender is constructed that war is therefore not the place of women. Men are made in combat, according to this rationale, because it is a place where women cannot survive and therefore cannot exist. The symbolic absence of women is key to understanding how the military develops gender.

By looking at how real participants—namely, women—have been eliminated from military performance narratives, it becomes evident that this is a space in which artificial gendering and its subsequent performances can be seen clearly. The metaphorical significance of the military (and more specifically of combat) has frequently been linked with masculinity primarily because women have been excluded from popular accounts, institutionally sanctioned narratives, and widely accepted notions. Metaphorically, men fight in the space of war, while women occupy another space and activity—maintaining the home front. The distinct images that result from these gendered assumptions were used successfully during World War II to recruit both women and men into various war efforts.[26]

The absence of women from military performance narratives is significant to the development and understanding of assumptions about the female gender. Not only is the military important as a proving ground for men, but it also serves an integral role as a proving ground for women. The symbolic absence of women from military narratives has meanings key to assumptions of who women are, what they are capable of, and what cultural reactions they should have. If, in war narratives, military involvement demonstratively proves men's strength and courage (and, because of their symbolic absence, proves the physical and emotional weakness of women), then to understand the realities of gender constructions we must explore both the realities and the perceptions of women's and men's involvement in the military.

If gender differences are biologically determined, then the performance of men and women in the military, particularly during times of crisis, would differ decidedly and consistently. However, if gender is an artificial construction, then the differences between men's and women's behaviors and abilities would be fluid or even nonexistent. In other words, if a solid, biological difference existed between the sexes in the arena of soldiering, all wars would be fought solely by men, military engagement would be something all men would aspire to do, and all women would be absent from all wars. There would exist for both genders stable and secure places for them and between them—places that would not have to be artificially created or maintained. Because the military is a significant performance place for gender, there exists substantial distance between the historically demonstrated involvement of women and the idealized beliefs or developed narratives about the absences of women. The culture has invested considerable energy in maintaining its notions of gender, despite documented evidence that invalidates these beliefs. Indeed, because differences exist between realities and ideologies of gender, we can assess the importance of any given performance in determining gender roles by measuring the efforts taken to disguise its realities and write new performances. In doing so, we can isolate moments of performance that are integral to maintaining gender constructions.

Women have served many roles in the military (and, more specifically, in combat), but they are not part of war narratives because their presence would disrupt the military's role as a masculine proving ground. Therefore, women are not allowed to experience symbolically the presence on the battlefield that they have experienced historically. Combat is a place where attributes generally equated with masculinity—such as domination, self-control, violence, physical expression, and conquest—are rewarded in men, while accounts of women expressing the same attributes are denied. Military's basic training asserts that being a man means not being a woman, thus drill instructors humiliate male cadets by calling them women or girls. The very existence of women on the battlefield throws into question culturally created assumptions of gender division and gender roles; in order to deal with this confusion, the military separates men and women into artificially designated positions that are, through regulatory decree, occupied solely by men. The primary position of exclusively male occupation within the military is combat. While in the contemporary American military certain combat positions, such as fighter pilots, are only recently being minimally occupied by women, the definitions are shifting to define more strictly what constitutes combat, such as hand-to-hand fighting, and thus to exclude women.

If combat and military metaphors of masculinity extend into and highlight larger cultural assumptions about gender, accounts of women in battle situations would unsettle status quo expectations. To prevent this, artificial boundaries are clearly laid down on the stage of battle. Women have long participated in front-line situations (most frequently as nurses, drivers, and supply officers), but their positions have been designated as noncombat, regardless of whether they experienced combat conditions. These boundaries often are quite ridiculous. In World War II, British anti-aircraft guns were run by crews consisting of both men and women. Women were prohibited from actually firing the guns but were involved with all other aspects of using the weapons, such as aiming, loading, and unloading. Yet the women on those crews were designated as noncombat personnel, the men as combat personnel.[27] The topic of this book, the WASPs of World War II, often served as pilots in bombers in which all other crew members were male; on at least one mission, the male crew members were designated as combat personnel, while the WASPs were civilians. Indeed, the ultimate result of combat—killing the enemy—does not always define what constitutes combat. In the contemporary U.S. Air Force, women serve as missile officers, and as such, their mission is to fire missiles (some of which are capable of killing millions), yet they are designated as noncombat personnel.

Proximity to the front is another component used by the military to define combat, but the concept of the front has changed radically as weapons have become more sophisticated. With the appearance of long-range artillery in World War I and of bombers and missiles in World War II, the concept of the front became ambiguous. In World War I, 5 percent of casualties were civilians; by World War II, civilian casualties had risen to 50 percent, and the casualty rates in contemporary wars average 80 percent civilian.[28] The majority of wartime casualties occur at great distance from what is designated as the front. Definitions of combat based on proximity to the front and the use of a weapon are arbitrarily determined, supporting Enloe's contention that an "elastic definition" of combat is used to exclude women from specific classifications.[29] It is of note that within the military, combat positions, which are denied women, result in swifter promotions among career military personnel.

The act of women fighting in war is labeled unnatural not because it constitutes a constructed crime against nature, but because it negates culturally anticipated narratives. In these situations, women become problematic when they knowingly act in ways that contradict the status quo of gender constructions. Accounts of women who disguised themselves as men to join the military offer interesting glimpses into the dynamics formed by the complex arrangements of gender codes and the confusion generated by encouraging patriotism in women while placing limitations upon their behavior. Feminist author Julie Wheelwright argues that women who disguised themselves as men and became soldiers had no desires to be men, but instead wanted male privileges and experiences, one of which was military participation.[30] Once their true genders were discovered, cultural reactions to these women have been multiple and complex. On the one hand, these women were sometimes rewarded for their service, often to encourage recruitment of men into the military. On the other hand, the same women were punished if they attempted to continue to demand any privileges gained by their masquerade. The presence of women in war itself is not a challenge to military structures. Indeed, military institutions have long run campaigns specifically to recruit women. In World War II, all branches of the military except the Army Air Forces ran recruitment campaigns for women. This effort ranged from media articles in newspapers and magazines promoting the need for women to serve as nurses[31] to the Women's Army Auxiliary Corps placing recruitment advertisements in popular publications.[32] However, the participation of women in the military, though encouraged during times of war, does challenge cultural expectations of gender roles. Acknowledging the presence of women in an institution that is significant in the development of masculinity questions assumptions of biologically determined sex roles, pointing instead to the fluidity of gender roles and revealing that the notion of gender is nothing more than a cultural construction. Thus the battleground becomes a proving ground not for masculinity but for enforcing the artificial construction of gender performances.

The Constructed Absence of Women from War

In the space that exists between the military's need for women and the culture's need to deny their role, an interesting phenomenon arises in which real women who served their militaries during wars or other national crises are effectively erased from war narratives. Thus, in the consciousness of their cultures, they cease to exist. Several components arise from this metaphorical disappearance. Because the "ideological construction of soldiering is so securely linked with soldiering, stories have been constructed in which women happened to be on the front, because of a singular accident."[33] This "singular accident" construction occurs in fictionalized narratives about real women warriors. For example, the Amazons have long been delegated to a position of myth, despite accounts of their historical existence, and the narratives about Amazons have been fictionalized to add sexualized components, extreme (or unnatural) displays of aggression, and self-hatred. The myth of Amazons severing their breasts to become archers is one example. This myth is offered as proof of women's inability to be combatants unless they are unnaturally altered to become more like men. In this, the Amazons deplete their femininity and begin to replicate the male, taking on not only the "male" guise of soldier, but also the guise of the male body.

Feminist military theorist Mady Wechsler Segal has developed a model to portray the various forces that influence the degrees to which women will participate in the military. The elements with the greatest impact in this model are not the military and threats to national security, but social structures and cultural influences. According to Segal, a given culture's values and social constructions about gender are most likely to affect the roles of women in the military.[34] Needs of the labor force and national security conform to these cultural influences. In cultures where women are not valued as equal participants, a pattern emerges in which women are called into the military when a need exists and released when the crisis is past. Furthermore, when the military needs women, "their prior military history is recalled to demonstrate that they can perform effectively in various positions. There is, however, a process of cultural amnesia of the contributions women made during emergency situations. In the aftermath of war, women's military activities are constructed as minor."[35]

The real deployment and subsequent disbandment of military women during times of war occur within symbolic constructions in which women are absent from cultural representations of the military. Gender constructions are allowed malleability only when it benefits dominant interests; therefore, women are deployed in wartime situations when they are needed, but only for the duration of the war. The use of large groups of women in a war effort is justified by the supposition that war is an unnatural time for a culture. This both explains women's wartime functions in nonthreatening ways and justifies their subsequent removal from the military during peacetime. It also portrays the involvement of women as something unnatural to the social order and potentially damaging to the culture if allowed (like killing) to continue into peacetime. The continued presence of women in the peacetime military threatens gender constructions and negates the authority of male superiority and strength (as "proven" by military involvement). After a war, national institutions put substantial effort into returning their culture to prewar normality. War is portrayed as an abnormality that arises and must be dealt with, while peace is portrayed as normal and separate from war. Many things that occur in wars, such as mass killings, are thus not perceived as normal, but as necessary within the boundaries of combat. The function of women in roles previously defined as exclusively male receives much the same treatment as killing—that is, something that occurs in abnormal times, out of necessity, but is itself never normal.

The deployment of women in the military, particularly during peacetime, also alters the way the women themselves are perceived. To explain their continued involvement in military institutions during times of peace, the culture constructs these women as being unnatural in their desires to remain. In keeping with the dichotomized separations of gendered behaviors, female behavior is sexualized; hence, the abnormality of female soldiers in a peacetime military is explained in sexualized terms. The female soldier is constructed as either being excessively sexual or excessively nonsexual (in a heterosexual cultural reality), for which she is tagged as either "whore" or "lesbian." This sexualized naming maintains the repetition of gendered performance within the military by explaining the peacetime participation of women as an unnatural phenomenon. Normal women have returned to the home; therefore, women who remain are not normal and either want to be men or want to have sex with men outside of culturally sanctioned norms.

In the United States, with the advent of the all volunteer force, women have constituted a greater percentage of the military than ever before. Women represent about 10 percent of military personnel in the United States.[36] In 1990, 223,000 women were on active duty.[37] And with the attention accorded to women who participated in the Gulf War, the image of the soldier as a masculine entity has changed. This has resulted in a gender crises within the very institution through which concepts of masculinity are shaped.

Technology and science have also impacted the model of women's involvement in the military by lessening the need for soldiers to fight by brute force.[38] A result of the increase in technology and the increase of women in the military has been to redefine the image of the soldier as a professional. The media portrayal of American soldiers in the Gulf War invoked this construction,[39] claiming that the contemporary soldier relied on technology rather than physical strength, in an effort to preserve an icon of the masculine combat soldier.

Segal notes that because the military serves such a critical role in society with regards to the development and maintenance of ideals about masculinity, "For women to participate, either the military has to be perceived (by policy makers and the populace) as transformed to make it more compatible with how women are (or perceived to be) or women have to be perceived as changing in ways that make them more seemingly suited to military service."[40]

The importance of women's involvement in military service extends beyond the basic economic, educational, and other opportunities accorded to the individual soldier. In the United States, military service and full citizenship rights are inextricably linked. Historically, these links have been consistently maintained, and consequently "enfranchisement and civil service rights drives have been more successful after wars."[41] The question of women's roles in the military is not simply about the career choices of individuals, but rather about "whether they should share, as a matter of citizenship, the same rights and obligations as men for their nation's defense; and if not, what the legitimate parameters for their participation should be."[42]

Theories and Realities Intersect with the WASPs

This study of the disbandment of the Women Airforce Service Pilots analyzes the reactions that several dominant components of the American cultural terrain had toward one small group of women who assumed, in World War II, one of the most desired military roles among men, one that was at the time strongly associated with the development of masculinity and male sexual prowess—that of piloting military planes. The focus of this study has been on the WASP program's disbandment, which was not caused by military request or necessity, but was instead a reflection of larger cultural fears during a period when gender roles were being contested in America.

The WASPs were not simply participants in a world war. They were engaged in a critical cultural battle over the identity and representation of the categories of men and women and the boundaries that exist between them. An examination of the events leading to the disbandment of this particular group of women furthers our knowledge of the larger history of representation reflecting the instability of gender categories and the continuing contestation of gender norms.

The reasons behind the disbandment of the WASPs are important not only because they provide a greater awareness of the program, these particular service women, and the time in which they served, but also because they reveal many of the weaknesses in arguments currently being used against the full participation of women in the U.S. military, and because they uncover the frightening implications of the power members of Congress have in voting upon issues about which they know little or nothing. The story of the disbandment of the WASPs is one in which ignorance and fear dominated decision-making, and in which cultural assumptions about gender had more influence than the facts surrounding women's actual involvement in wartime efforts. Examining the circumstances involved in the disbandment of the WASPs provides us now with a precise model of how discrimination and assumptions overcame patriotism and documented success, and resulted in the termination of a successful and groundbreaking World War II military operation.

The historical evidence on the WASPs presented in this study intersects with theories of feminist history to reveal a pattern in which cultural gender constructions were forcefully maintained because of erosions that were occurring as women substantially increased their roles in the work force and the military. Examination of this evidence uncovers connections that further our understanding of the construction and enforcement of gender norms. Normative expectations of gender are usually maintained through cultural control, but in times of gender crisis the controlling mechanisms become more visible. In tracing the history of the WASPs, we discovered two institutional mechanisms within the WASPs' cultural terrain that maintained and prescribed normative behaviors for these women pilots: the media and Congress.

The weekly magazine *Life* featured women who supported the war effort from within stratified gender roles—that is, as volunteers or in support roles to men, such as wives and mothers—more often than it featured women in factory work or the military. *Life's* coverage of women in the war effort carefully maintained existing expectations of the roles and behaviors of women, and depictions of women soldiers were more likely to focus on their uniforms than on the duties they performed. As the war shifted in the Allies' favor, the media became more critical of women's involvement in the military and began encouraging women to return to the home and prewar standards of existence.

It was during this time that the issue of WASP militarization was raised in the media. The attacks on the WASPs were strong and consistent. In pieces like "Army Passes Up Jobless Pilots to Train Wasps: Prefers Women to Older, Experienced Flyers," the media called for the WASP program to be ended so that "experienced men pilots [be] given the ferrying jobs."[43]

The main critique raised against the WASPs in the media was that they were women. Reporters were incredulous that women would be in the positions men wanted, and because of ideological blinding, they overlooked the motives of the majority of these men, which was to avoid being drafted into the Army's ground forces. Instead, the media sharply criticized the WASPs for overstepping the boundaries allowed to women, and subsequently portrayed them not as patriotic, but as hindrances not only to the male pilots, but also to the war effort.

Similarly, Congress imposed cultural values about gender roles on the WASPs when it refused to grant them militarization as requested by the Army Air Forces and the War Department. Again, the WASPs' missions and their success in fulfilling them was not the issue. What was being contested was the notion and reality of women serving in roles that cultural standards had deemed beyond what was normative and allowable for women. The Ramspeck Committee, which conducted a very biased congressional subcommittee investigation of the WASPs program, began its report: "The implication contained in the proposal, that it is now either necessary or desirable to recruit stenographers, clerks, school teachers, housewives, factory workers, and other inexperienced personnel for training at great outlay of public funds as pilots for the military planes of the Government, particularly when there already exists a surplus of personnel to perform these identical duties, is as startling as it is invalid."[44] The issue was very clearly not about the WASPs as pilots, but about women who were going beyond culturally constructed normative boundaries of how women were expected to behave, and who were serving in what were constructed to be male roles.

Issues of maintaining gender order dominated Congress's debate on the WASP bill. Debate moved from the bill itself to issues of whether men or women should serve in the domestic pilot positions. With the maintenance of gender roles being the issue raised in the congressional debate during a time when gender constructions were being contested in American culture, there was no chance for the WASP bill to be successful. Objection to the bill was swift and adamant. Said Representative Edouard Izac of California when offering a motion to strike out the enacting clause of the bill: "My object here is to kill this bill because we do not need such a bill. It is the most unjustified piece of legislation that could be brought before the House."[45]

The struggle for WASP militarization reflected struggles for changes in ideological constructions of women's behaviors, and it thus constituted a threat to constructions of masculine identity. The WASPs would not succeed in obtaining militarization for more than thirty years because it was necessary for the United States to change its ideological understanding and the distribution of cultural power before an act that so solidly reflected gendered assumptions could be allowed. By the 1970s, assumptions about gender had changed dramatically, and the media and Congress were at a very different level of understanding regarding the issue of WASP militarization than they had been in 1944.

This study has followed the methods of feminist historical inquiry by working to understand the notions of hegemony and cultural control implicit in the involvement of women pilots of World War II. By studying the historically specific (in this case, a unit of 1,074 women), some of the relations of power and consent that constitute hegemonic control could be revealed. Furthermore, this study supports feminist historical inquiry's critical stance toward the historical document by evaluating a subject that has largely been "lost" in most traditional historical accounts of World War II and the U.S. Air Force. Written records and their preservation reflect the values of a given culture about what is important, and as a result, valuable documents about the WASPs no longer exist. Indeed, the amount of information on the WASPs that does exist is remarkable and is largely attributable to the collection and storage efforts of WASP veterans themselves.

Throughout this inquiry, the experiences surrounding the disbandment of the WASPs have been examined as representing discursive points of departure from the constructions articulated and imposed by World War II era American culture upon gendered subjects. Rather than accepting the designation of "women" as a cultural given, the enforcement of this gender construction has been analyzed as an element of the power relations occurring within cultural systems. The issues surrounding the disbandment debate in the media and in Congress reveal the pervasive positioning of gender as a symbol denoting systems of control and elements of representation. The WASPs were women in that they were entities whose histories were determined by societal pressures, expectations, and conditioning specific to that gender.

The WASPs' successes in their missions provided a tangible threat to overall contructions of masculinity to those men who had failed to pass the rigid requirements of the Ferrying Squadron, which the women pilots had successfully done. The male pilots were able to invoke cultural fears about the usurpation of men to "prove" that the WASPs could not have passed the same requirements that these men had failed. In other words, it was a cross-cultural crisis of masculinity that brought the male-dominated media and Congress to support the cause of the male pilots despite the facts that supported the WASPs. Congress and the media were not advocating for the male civilian pilots as much as they were for an enforcement of prewar gender roles and a suppression of a state of gender crisis.

As stated previously, changes in assumptions about who women are and what roles they can perform within any given culture threaten the entire construction of defined difference between men and women. The greater the threat to division of gender identity, the greater the backlash against those who constitute the threat. Since piloting military planes was one of the most desired roles among men during World War II, it follows that the WASPs would pose a greater threat to gender constructions than women who served in other military branches. Certainly, the WASPs suffered the greatest backlash among service women: They were refused militarization, disbanded before the war's end, and refused veterans' status after the war.

The constrictions placed upon the WASPs and the rigid enforcement of gender roles they incurred as the result of requesting militarization strongly attest to a pattern of gender crisis in the United States during World War II. Documentation of the enforced gendering of the WASPs is thus a valuable addition to the larger body of feminist historical knowledge about gender constructions across various times and cultures. Such data allow us to confront the traditional assumptions about the consistency and stability of sex roles and positions.

When theories of women and war are applied specifically to the WASPs and their disbandment, the artificial boundaries created to develop assumptions of military might and male superiority are revealed. This study has approached the military institution as a fixed variable, placing no valuations on the military, the Army Air Forces, or World War II; instead, the U.S. military, particularly the Army Air Forces, and World War II are presented and assessed as factors that affected a specific group of women and consequently the development of gender constructions during World War II. Furthermore, no essential constitution for women is assumed; gender is disclosed as an artificial and regulated construction. Indeed, one of the stated purposes of this study is to uncover the stabilizing cultural role that encouraged the construction of distinct gender roles in the American military during World War II.

As noted, one of the leading feminist theories of women and the military involves the symbolic absence of women from war, and particularly from combat narratives. The WASPs of World War II represent one unit of female participants in war whose narratives were eliminated from wartime accounts.

This exclusion began during the war years, when media accounts of the program were negligible. To further distance the experiences of the WASPs from wartime narratives, those few accounts that did appear on the women pilots were constructed in ways that negated their contribution to the wartime effort and instead portrayed them as adventurous women at play. By the end of the war, the WASPs had already been disbanded and were thus excluded from accounts of the Allied victory. In the two decades following World War II, the WASPs made several attempts to receive recognition for their service and involvement and to be included as full participants in the newly formed Air Force. But these attempts failed because American culture did not accept that women should be involved with the military outside of national crises and as heroes. It was not until the 1970s, when many attempts were being made to recover the lost history and recognize the significant achievements of women, that the WASPs were finally able to get their story covered by the media. Even today, there are only a handful of historical accounts of the WASPs, and these are typically positioned as women's history or as individualized stories rather than as true representations of military history, thus continuing the marginalization of an important component within the American military experience.

The elimination of real participants from military experience creates a space in which the construction of gender and its subsequent performances can be studied. The effort to eliminate female military narratives demonstrates the attempts by a given culture to restructure historical events to fit normative constructions of the behaviors, roles, and experiences of women. The WASPs were removed from World War II narratives before the war had ended because they constituted a serious threat to constructed gender identities at a historical point at which their culture was trying to reduce the existing gender crisis by imposing prewar gender identities and roles. Unfortunately for the WASPs, their roles did not fit within the enforced limits for behaviors culturally permitted women at that time; therefore, they were eliminated.

When war makes necessary the inclusion of women in the military, artificially designated positions, such as "combat," are constructed to separate the genders. In terms of the participation of women in World War II, the WASPs placed the most pressure on this parameter, and they were subsequently refused militarization because of the threat that they imposed. In chapters 3 and 5, examinations of the congressional debate over militarization bills for the Women's Army Corps and the WASPs during World War II reveal the strict boundaries imposed by Congress upon the levels of participation allowed to women's auxiliaries and the gendered rhetoric that Congress invoked in its arguments. Members of Congress strictly imposed limits on women, prohibiting any activities that might be construed as combat. Indeed, Congress was very clear that specific divisions between men and women be maintained within the military branches. The WASPs were problematic with regard to this prohibition because they were solidly integrated with male pilots on missions, and because their missions, while not strictly defined as combat, did fit an ideological definition of combat. During World War II, piloting military planes was perceived as dangerous and adventurous, and just as the military institution rewarded combat duty with increased pay, male military pilots were rewarded for their dangerous roles by the receipt of additional flight pay. Indeed, certain flight duties that were performed by WASPs, such as test piloting and engineering flights, were recognized within the Air Forces as being akin to combat with regard to the level of risk, and at least one mission flown by WASPs was considered to be a combat mission for the participating male crew members, because it extended over waters designated as enemy territory. However, receipt of military recognition, let alone combat status, was not to be allowed the WASPs. The development of the Women's Army Corps and the WASP program reveals a careful structuring on the part of Congress and the military to maintain separate classifications for women. The WAC was first designated as a voluntary auxiliary because, at the beginning of World War II, officially involving women in military branches would have extended their participation beyond the space constructed for women. As the war's expansion increased the need for women in the military, this separation proved unwieldy and was thus eliminated. However, the women were still maintained in separate military units, which were prohibited from becoming integrated with the "true" military branch and whose members were refused any rank over men.

One incident in the history of the WASP program that unveils the artificial separation between the genders is when the AAF sought to directly commission WASPs in the Ferrying Division, just as it had the men they served alongside. Despite any specific exclusion by sex in the rules governing direct commissioning of pilots in the AAF, military leaders determined that the term *persons* in the law that privileged direct commissioning of pilots was not intended to include women. In other words, women were so far removed from war narratives that they could not legally be considered as persons within the Army Air Forces.

Another contention developed by feminist military theorists is that the military participation of women is limited to the duration of a war or other necessity, and that women who desire to continue in such roles are considered unnatural. Chapter 4 traces the change in media depictions of women in the war effort from encouragement to discouragement as America turned from underdog to victor. By 1944, when the United States was certain it would be victorious, articles reflected a concern for the postwar economy and encouraged a return to prewar values, which placed women in the home rather than in factories and the military. Articles on women in the military became sharply critical as the war reached its end. No longer celebrated as patriotic symbols, these women were seen as threats to men returning from overseas and as a liability to the postwar economy. Unfortunately for the WASPs, it was in this climate that they attempted to acquire militarization. Given this cultural climate, it is not surprising that the WASPs were not only refused militarization, but were strongly attacked. The culture was focused on a return to prewar gender constructions, which had no place for women as pilots of military planes, particularly when the men vying for their jobs included returning servicemen who desired to supplement their military pay with flight pay. Public sympathies were most decidedly with the servicemen. The WASPs were shaped by the media as women with unnatural demands who were not serving any valuable roles for their country, but instead were threatening the positions of male pilots and taking money that could be better used to improve the postwar economy. For the WASPs, involvement past a necessary duration was constructed as unnatural and selfish. Despite the Air Forces' assertions to the contrary, in the public's eye the need for pilots was over. American culture, as represented by Congress and the media, had determined that the war was over and was working to return the country to a peacetime structure. In this ideological construction, there was no place for the WASPs because their continued existence would have symbolized a war that was not yet won, a shift in the roles allowed to women, or both.

In feminist theories of women and war, the culmination of all the factors involved results in one singular fact—that women soldiers cease to exist. This was the fate of the WASPs. Because they were not granted militarization and the resulting veterans' status, the Women Airforce Service Pilots of World War II were erased from the narratives of the war they had served in and even died in. Their history did not fit into normative constructions of American women. Even as the narratives of women war workers and women who served in other military branches became known, the stories of the WASPs remained hidden simply because they did not comfortably fit into these other structures, and also because the story of their disbandment led directly to the space in which the warrior becomes gendered. The missions of the WASPs were too oriented toward combat and too specific to masculine military constructions to settle into more comfortable notions of women's experiences in World War II. Just as the majority of accounts of women soldiers are denied or restructured to fit cultural expectations of women and war, so too were the narratives of the Women Airforce Service Pilots effectively erased from cultural consciousness.

9

Coda

    The story of the Women Airforce Service Pilots is far from being over. The majority of the more than eight hundred WASPs living today regularly attend the national biennial reunions and numerous regional reunions. The vitality of the national organization of WASP veterans is considerable. "It is probably the strongest support group I have other than my own family. We are a very cohesive group. We seem to generate our own energy once we get together for a few hours," said Ethel Finley.[1]

    Through the 1970s, the WASP organization focused on obtaining retroactive militarization. Now it campaigns on behalf of other women pilots of military planes and continues in its efforts to preserve and engage the history of the WASPs. "We were all proud of what we did, but I was proud of it in 1945, too; the only trouble was nobody was proud of me then. Now they're all proud of me, so I might as well be proud too," said Katherine (Kaddy) Landry Steele.[2]

    At WASP reunions, the link between the WASPs and contemporary women military pilots is unmistakable. Women pilots from the Air Force, Army, Navy, Marines, and Coast Guard regularly attend reunions to meet their heroes, thank their flying ancestors, and share stories. "We set a presence of women in aviation. The women [pilots] today, they say, 'We look up to you; you started things and you stuck through it; and men had to accept you. If it hadn't been for you we wouldn't be flying today,'" said Betty Stagg Turner.[3]

    Former WASPs continue to make outstanding contributions—nationally, in their communities, and within their families. Many WASP veterans remain active pilots. "My identity will always be as a woman who flew or flies, and that cannot change," said Madge Rutherford Minton.[4]

    Perhaps the most valuable contribution the WASPs have made occurred long after World War II had ended. What makes the WASPs heroes is not their flying records, their war records, or their acts of heroism during the war; instead, they are heroes because when their culture turned against them, when everyone refused to acknowledge their efforts and achievements, they continued to fight for recognition, for benefits that were rightfully theirs, and for the place they had earned in history to be publicly acknowledged. The WASPs are heroes because they would not give up. With great reserve and even greater dignity, they worked diligently and quietly for more than thirty years, until they received their rightful places as veterans and the next flock of women military pilots was able to take their place in the skies.

As Thelma K. (Hench) Miller said: "Women can do it—that's the whole thing. And that's what helps these gals today. There's no question about it. You still have people fighting that, so you have to keep fighting back. Every inch of the way, you have to keep telling them, you have to keep telling them."[5]

Notes

NOTES TO CHAPTER I

1. Muir, Kate, *Arms and the Woman*, 1992.
2. Mitchell, Brian, *Weak Link: The Feminization of the American Military*, 1989, 14.
3. Treadwell, Mattie, *The Women's Army Corps*, 1954.
4. Army Air Forces, *History of the Women Airforce Service Pilots*, 1945. Captain Marx gave this as a primary reason for WASP disbandment, and book accounts by Byrd Howell Granger (*On Final Approach: The Women Airforce Service Pilots of W.W. II*, 1991) and Jean Hascall Cole (*Women Pilots of World War II*, 1992) make similar allusions.

NOTES TO CHAPTER 2

1. *Women Who Flew*, unedited interview tapes, 1994.
2. Ibid.
3. Ibid.
4. Cochran, Jacqueline, *Final Report, Women Pilot Program*, February 1945, 45.
5. War Department News Release, *Memorandum for the Press*, 10 September 1942.
6. Granger, Byrd Howell, *On Final Approach: The Women Airforce Service Pilots of W.W. II*, 1991, 5-6.
7. Central Flying Training Command, Army Air Forces, *History of the WASP Program*, 20 January 1945, 8.
8. Ibid.
9. War Department News Release, *Jacquelyn [sic] Cochran Designated Director of Women Pilots for AAF*, 5 July 1943.
10. A number of variations on the WASP acronym were used during and after World War II, including "Women Air Service Pilots" and "Women's Auxiliary Service Pilots." There are two acceptable names for the WASPs: "Women's Air Force Service Pilots" and "Women Airforce Service Pilots." The first was the title given the program by AAF Memorandum 20-8 on August 5, 1943, and was the official title used by the War Department's Press Division. In 1944, AAF Regulation 40-8, Utilization of Women Pilots, used the name "Women Airforce Service Pilots." This was the name officially used by the AAF until the end of the war, and it is the designation used by WASP veterans to this day. Because of this, "Women Airforce Service Pilots" is the version I use throughout this study.

11. Central Flying Training Command, *History of the WASP Program*, 179.

12. Cochran, *Final Report*, 28.

13. Perret, Geoffrey, *Winged Victory: The Army Air Forces in World War II*, 1993, 376.

14. Ibid.

15. Ibid., 1.

16. Tunner, Lt. Gen. William, *Over the Hump*, 1964, 39.

17. Ibid., 28.

18. Army Air Forces, *Women Pilots in the Air Transport Command*, January 1945, 161.

19. Cochran, *Final Report*, 33.

20. *Women Who Flew*, unedited interview tapes.

21. Perret, *Winged Victory*, 5.

22. McFarland, Stephen Lee, and Newton, Wesley Phillips, *To Command the Sky: The Battle for Air Superiority over Germany, 1942-1944*, 1991, 21.

23. Arnold, Henry H., *Global Mission*, 1947, 165.

24. Perret, *Winged Victory*, 57.

25. McFarland and Newton, *To Command the Sky*, 73.

26. Rubel, David, *Webster's 21st Century Concise Chronology of World History*, 1993, 206.

27. Arnold, *Global Mission*, 179.

28. Perret, *Winged Victory*, 34, 57.

29. Arnold, *Global Mission*, 267.

30. Perret, *Winged Victory*, 140.

31. Tunner, *Over the Hump*, 11, 18.

32. Arnold, *Global Mission*, 294.

33. Tunner, *Over the Hump*, 23.

34. Ibid., 12.

35. Cochran, *Final Report*, 28.

36. Ibid., 39.

37. Granger, *On Final Approach*, A-103.

38. Hartmann, Susan, *The Home Front and Beyond: American Women in the 1940s*, 1982, 15.

39. Central Flying Training Command, *History of the WASP Program*, 178.

40. Holden, Henry, and Griffith, Lori, *Ladybirds: The Untold Story of Women Pilots in America*, 1992.

41. Army Air Forces, *Women Pilots*, 161.

42. Ibid., 8.

43. Arnold, Gen. H. H., Remarks, Final WASP Graduation, December 1944.

44. Cochran, Jacqueline, Memorandum to Col. Robert Olds, 21 July 1941.

45. War Department News Release, 5 July 1943.

46. Perret, *Winged Victory*, 376.

47. Army Air Forces, *Women Pilots*, 13.

48. Ibid., 12.

49. Arnold, *Global Mission*, 294.

50. Ibid.

51. Army Air Forces, *Women Pilots*, 131.

52. Ibid., 15.

53. Ibid., 13.

54. Cochran, *Final Report*, 4.

55. Tunner, *Over the Hump*, 23.

56. Cochran, Memorandum to Col. Robert Olds.

57. Cochran, *Final Report*, 2.

58. War Department News Release, 10 September 1942.

59. *Women Who Flew*, unedited interview tapes.

60. Cochran, *Final Report*, 1.

61. Ibid., 4.

62. *Women Who Flew*, unedited interview tapes.

63. Ibid.

64. "Congressmen Clip Wings of 9 Wasps: Detroit Girl Fliers Downed in Texas," *Detroit Free Press*, 2 June 1944.

65. Central Flying Training Command, *History of the WASP Program*, 4.

66. Ibid., 9.

67. *Women Who Flew*, 1994.

68. *Women Who Flew*, unedited interview tapes.

69. Bergemann, Clarice, telephone interview with author, March 1994.

70. Wyall, Marty, telephone interview with author, March 1994.

71. Nagle, Nadine, telephone interview with author, March 1994.

72. Central Flying Training Command, *History of the WASP Program*, 9.

73. Ibid., 126.

74. Poole, Barbara, "Requiem for the WASP," *Flying Magazine*, December 1944, 56.

75. Cochran, *Final Report*, 4.

76. Granger, *On Final Approach*, Appendix D.

77. Cochran, Jacqueline, and Odlum, Floyd, *The Stars at Noon*, 1954, 127-128.

78. Osur, Alan, *Blacks in the Army Air Forces during World War II*, 1980.

79. Pentagon, *Fact Sheet: Tuskegee Airmen*, 1995.

80. Ibid.

81. Osur, *Blacks in the Army Air Forces*.

82. Cochran, *Final Report*, 8.

83. Ibid., 9.

84. Perret, *Winged Victory*, 59.

85. Arnold, *Global Mission*, 181.

86. Central Flying Training Command, *History of the WASP Program*, 9.

87. Ibid., 22.

88. Central Flying Training Command, *History of the WASP Program*, 23.

89. Ibid., 26.

90. Ibid.
91. Ibid., 27.
92. Ibid.
93. Ibid., 46.
94. Ibid., 47.
95. Ibid., 48.
96. Nagle, Nadine, telephone interview with author, March 1994.
97. Central Flying Training Command, *History of the WASP Program*, 52.
98. Ibid., 54.
99. Ibid., 55.
100. Ibid., 56.
101. Ibid., 62.
102. Ibid., 65.
103. Ibid., 62.
104. Ibid., 64.
105. Ibid., 65, 72.
106. Stagg, Betty, Postcard to Mr. Donald Stagg, 15 May 1944.
107. Ibid.
108. Stagg, Betty, Postcard to Mr. and Mrs. Donald Stagg, 20 June 1944.
109. Knight, Charlotte, "Service Pilots," *Skyways*, 1944, 50.
110. Central Flying Training Command, *History of the WASP Program*, 49.
111. Ibid., 78.
112. *Life*, 19 July 1943, 75.
113. *Women Who Flew*, unedited interview tapes.
114. Nagle, Nadine, telephone interview with author, March 1994.
115. Central Flying Training Command, *History of the WASP Program*, 119.
116. Eastern Flying Training Command, Army Air Forces, *History of the Women Airforce Service Pilots, Eastern Flying Training Command*, January 1945, 4.
117. Army Air Forces, *History of the Women Airforce Service Pilots, Gardner Field*, January 1945, 3.
118. Eastern Flying Training Command, *History of the Women Airforce Service Pilots*, 4.
119. Knight, "Service Pilots," 74.
120. *Women Who Flew*, unedited interview tapes.
121. Eastern Flying Training Command, *History of the Women Airforce Service Pilots*, 10.
122. Wyall, Marty, telephone interview with author, March 1994.
123. Army Air Forces, *History of the WASP Detachment at Blytheville Army Air Field*, January 1945, 8.
124. Army Air Forces, *Army Air Forces Historical Studies*, January 1945, 144.
125. Army Air Forces, *History of the WASPs at Buckingham Army Air Field*, January 1945, 61.
126. Army Air Forces, *Army Air Forces Historical Studies*, 144.

127. Knight, "Service Pilots," 70.

128. Army Air Forces, *Army Air Forces Historical Studies*, 145.

129. *Women Who Flew.*

130. Cochran, *Final Report*, 28.

131. Tunner, *Over the Hump*, 23.

132. Ibid., 39.

133. Cochran, *Final Report*, 28.

134. Army Air Forces, *Women Pilots in the Air Transport Command*, 168.

135. *Women Who Flew*, unedited interview tapes.

136. Granger, Byrd Howell, *Evidence Supporting Military Service by Women Airforce Service Pilots, World War II*, 1977, 74.

137. *Women Who Flew*, unedited interview tapes.

138. Cochran, *Final Report*, 28.

139. Granger, *Evidence*, 48.

140. Ibid., 1-2, 48.

141. Arnold, *Global Mission*, 358.

142. Nagle, Nadine, telephone interview with author, March 1994.

143. Arnold, *Global Mission*, 358.

144. *Women Who Flew*, unedited interview tapes.

145. Cochran, *Final Report*, 28.

146. *Women Who Flew*, unedited interview tapes.

147. Bergemann, Clarice, telephone interview with author, March 1994.

148. Wells, Mary Retick, "An Open Letter to Rep. Olin E. Teague Re. WASP," *Stars and Stripes*, 8 September 1977.

149. Granger, *Evidence*, 1.

150. "Sugar and Spice! B-26 Gentle as Lamb in Hands of WASPS," *Martin City Star*, February 1944.

151. Poole, "Requiem for the WASP," 148.

152. Cochran, *Final Report*, 32.

153. Ibid., 32, 1.

154. *Women Who Flew*, unedited interview tapes.

155. Army Air Forces, *Army Air Forces Historical Studies*, 211.

156. Army Air Force, *Medical Considerations of the WASPs*, 21August 1945, 9.

157. Strother, Lt. Col. Dora Dougherty, *The WASP Program: An Historical Synopsis*, September 1971, 31.

158. Army Air Forces, *Army Air Forces Historical Studies*, 179.

159. Arnold, Gen. H. H., Letter to Each Member of the WASP, 1 October 1944.

160. "WASPS End Wartime Flying Contribution," *New York Times*, 19 December 1944.

161. Army Air Forces, *Army Air Forces Historical Studies*, 6.

162. Cochran, Memorandum to Col. Robert Olds, 21 July 1942, and Memorandum to General Arnold, October 1942.

163. Bergemann, Clarice; Nagle, Nadine; and Wyall, Marty, telephone interviews with author, March 1994.
164. Granger, *Evidence*, 118.
165. Ibid.
166. Central Flying Training Command, *History of the WASP Program*, 159.
167. Ibid., 130.

NOTES TO CHAPTER 3

1. Odom, Col. T. C., *Report to Commanding General of the Army Air Forces*, 5 August 1943.
2. Cochran, Jacqueline, Memorandum to Col. Robert Olds, 21 July 1941.
3. Ibid., 3.
4. Central Flying Training Command, Army Air Forces, *History of the WASP Program*, 20 January 1945, 8.
4. Cochran, Jacqueline, Memorandum to Col. McNaughton, 15 December 1942.
6. Kraus, Brig. Gen. Walter F., Memorandum to Gen. Arnold, 19 December 1942.
7. Tunner, Col. William, Memorandum to Gen. Arnold, 30 November 1942.
8. Ibid.
9. Committee on Military Affairs, *Hearings before the Committee on Military Affairs*, 20 January 1942, 22.
10. Ibid.
11. Ibid., 5.
12. Tunner, Memorandum to Gen. Arnold.
13. Granger, Byrd Howell, *Evidence Supporting Military Service by Women Airforce Service Pilots, W.W. II*, 1977, 38.
14. Wyall, Marty, telephone interview with author, March 1994.
15. Bergemann, Clarice, telephone interview with author, March 1994.
16. Nagle, Nadine, telephone interview with author, March 1994.
17. Central Flying Training Command, Army Air Forces, *History of the WASP Program*, 10 January 1945, 130.
18. Ibid., 159.
19. Ibid., 166.
20. Granger, *Evidence*, 1-2.
21. Central Flying Training Command, *History of the WASP Program*, 166.
22. Ibid., 5.
23. Ibid., 7.
24. Ibid.
25. Committee on Military Affairs, *Hearings before the Committee on Military Affairs*, 1 May 1942, 4.
26. Ibid., 36.
27. *Congressional Record*, 12 May 1942, 4086.

28. Committee on Military Affairs, *Hearings*, 1 May 1942, 30.
29. Ibid., 5.
30. *Congressional Record*, 12 May 1942, 4087.
31. Ibid., 4088.
32. Ibid., 4087.
33. Ibid., 4088.
34. Committee on Military Affairs, *Hearings*, 1 May 1942, 41.
35. Ibid., 10.
36. *Congressional Record*, 12 May 1942, 4088.
37. Committee on Military Affairs, *Hearings*, 20 January 1942, 5.
38. Ibid., 18.
39. Ibid., 9.
40. Ibid, 20, 16.
41. Committee on Military Affairs, *Hearings*, 1 May 1942, 7.
42. Ibid.
43. Ibid., 22.
44. Ibid., 34.
45. Ibid., 22.
46. Ibid.
47. Ibid.
48. Ibid., 7.
49. Ibid., 15.
50. *Congressional Record*, 12 May 1942, 4092.
51. Ibid., 4090.
52. *Congressional Record*, 14 January 1943, 193.
53. *Congressional Record*, 1 May 1943, 4993.
54. *Congressional Record*, 15 February 1943, 938.
55. Whitney, Col. Courtney, Memorandum to Brig. Gen. Luther Smith, 20 June 1943.
56. Treadwell, Mattie, *The Women's Army Corps*, 1954.
57. *Congressional Record*, 15 February 1943, 938.
58. Treadwell, *Women's Army Corps*.
59. Stratemeyer, Major Gen. George E., Memorandum to Brig. Gen. Luther S. Smith, 24 November 1942.
60. Arnold, Gen. H. H., Memorandum to Gen. Marshall, 14 June 1943.
61. Tunner, Memorandum to Gen. Arnold, 1.
62. Cochran, Memorandum to Col. McNaughton.
63. Arnold, Memorandum to Gen. Marshall.
64. Tunner, Memorandum to Gen. Arnold, 2.
65. Whitney, Memorandum to Brig. Gen. Luther Smith, 20 June 1943.
66. Cochran, Memorandum to Col. McNaughton.
67. Ibid.

68. Arnold, Memorandum to Gen. Marshall.
69. Ibid.
70. Ibid.
71. Ibid.
72. Tunner, Memorandum to Gen. Arnold.
73. Ibid.
74. Arnold, Memorandum to Gen. Marshall.
75. Whitney, Memorandum to Brig. Gen. Luther Smith.
76. Odom, Report to Commanding General of the Army Air Forces, 6.
77. Whitney, Memorandum to Brig. Gen. Luther Smith.

NOTES TO CHAPTER 4

1. War Department, Bureau of Public Relations, *Public Relations Policy for WASP*, 3 December 1943.
2. Central Flying Training Command, Army Air Forces, *History of the WASP Program*, 20 January 1945, 134.
3. *Life*, 14 September 1942, 121.
4. *Life*, 23 March 1942.
5. *Life*, 5 January 1942, cover and 65.
6. *Life*, 19 January 1942, 58.
7. *Life*, 26 October 1942, 29.
8. Ibid., 35.
9. *Life*, 6 July 1942, 41.
10. *Life*, 8 March 1943, 21.
11. *Life*, 1 February 1943, 65.
12. *Life*, 9 August 1943, cover.
13. Ibid., 75.
14. *Life*, 2 February 1942, 50.
15. *Life*, 20 April 1942.
16. *Life*, 11 May 1942, 4.
17. *Life*, 9 March 1942, 12.
18. *Life*, 11 May 1942, 4.
19. *Life*, 22 June 1942, cover.
20. *Life*, 29 June 1944, cover.
21. *Life*, 15 June 1942, 73.
22. *Life*, 12 October 1942, 56.
23. *Life*, 2 November 1942, back cover.
24. *Life*, 23 February 1942, back cover.
25. *Life*, 4 October 1943, back cover.
26. *Life*, 31 May 1943, 29.
27. *Life*, 9 November 1942, 28.

28. *Life*, 16 November 1942, 137.
29. *Life*, 25 October 1943, 118.
30. *Life*, 25 January 1943, 74; 5 April 1943, 82.
31. *Life*, 23 February 1942.
32. *Life*, 8 June 1942, 26.
33. *Life*, 7 September 1942, 74.
34. *Life*, 26 July 1943, 55-57.
35. *Life*, 16 February 1942, 2.
36. *Life*, 27 April 1942, 39.
37. Ibid., 63.
38. *Life*, 15 March 1943, 72.
39. Ibid., 73.
40. *Life*, 19 April 1943, 31.
41. *Life*, 31 May 1943, 26-27.
42. *Life*, 1 November 1943, 36-37.
43. *Life*, 10 August 1942, 20.
44. *Life*, 5 October 1942, 126.
45. *Life*, 19 April 1943, 41.
46. *Life*, 2 February 1942, 38.
47. *Life*, 6 April 1942, cover.
48. Ibid., 62.
49. *Life*, 4 May 1942, cover.
50. *Life*, 11 May 1942, 50.
51. *Life*, 18 May 1942, cover and 73.
52. *Life*, 13 July 1942, cover and 43.
53. *Life*, 28 September 1942, 92.
54. *Life*, 30 November 1942, 75.
55. *Life*, 28 September 1942, 32.
56. Ibid., 40.
57. *Life*, 19 July 1943, cover.
58. Ibid, 73-80.
59. *Life*, 9 August 1943, 2.
60. *Life*, 17 January 1944, 26.
61. *Life*, 13 March 1944, 26.
62. *Life*, 27 March 1944, 129.
63. *Life*, 28 August 1944, cover.
64. *Life*, 4 September 1944, 28.
65. *Life*, 11 September 1944, 75.
66. Ibid., 117.
67. *Life*, 9 October 1944, inside cover.
68. *Life*, 18 September 1944, 98.
69. *Life*, 25 September 1944, cover.

70. Ibid., 36.

71. Ibid., 111-119.

72. *Life*, 26 March 1945, 110.

73. *Life*, 15 December 1941, 12.

74. Central Flying Training Command, *History of the WASP Program*, 179.

75. Granger, Byrd Howell, *On Final Approach*, 1991, 124.

76. War Department News Release, *Memorandum for the Press*, 10 September 1942.

77. Schisgall, Oscar, "The Girls Deliver the Goods."

78. Ibid.

79. Ibid.

80. Ibid.

81. War Department, Bureau of Public Relations, *Public Relations Policy for WASP*.

82. "Seek Women Pilots to Ferry Planes," 3 December 1942.

83. Mendelson, Frances, "Women Pilots Towing Targets for Army Anti-Aircraft Practice: Originally Restricted to Ferrying Planes from Factories, They Are Achieving Success in Highly Specialized Jobs at Camp Davis," *Washington Herald Tribune*, 25 October 1943.

84. "Nation's First Class of Women Air Ferry Pilots Awarded Wings," *Houston Chronicle*, 25 April 1943.

85. Ibid.

86. War Department, Bureau of Public Relations, *Public Relations Policy for WASP*.

87. Habas, Ralph, "Women Pilots Here Anxious to Join WAFS," *Chicago Sunday Times*, 13 September 1942.

88. "Women Ferry Pilots Start Operating out of Wichita," *The Wichita Beacon*, 25 April 1943.

89. "Biggs Field Male Personnel Perks Up When Expert Wasps Arrive on Scene," *El Paso Times*, 1943.

90. "Cobras Have a 'Lady Pilot,'" *The Bellringer*, 1943.

91. Ibid.

92. "Women Train in West Texas for Army Ferry Flying: Their Duty Will Be to Fly Planes from Factory to Field and from Field to Field within U.S," *Christian Science Monitor*, 8 May 1943.

93. Cahoon, Yvonne, "WASP Head Believes Women Pilots Face Duty on War Fronts," *Evening Star*, 25 October 1943.

94. Mendelson, "Women Pilots Towing Targets."

95. Ibid.

96. Stevick, Ann, "WASPS Who Tow Air Targets May Soon Be Real U.S. Soldiers," October 1943.

97. Eads, Jane, "Girl Fliers on Varied Tasks in Complicated Games High up in the Air, Towing Targets Is One of Hazardous Duties on Which They Train," Cincinnati, 25 October 1943.

98. Ibid.

99. Williams, Dorothy, "Gal Fliers Help Perfect Aim," *New York Daily News*, 25 October 1943.

100. Kidney, Daniel M., "Women Air Service Pilots Do Satisfactory Job," *Washington Daily News*, 25 October 1943.

101. Stephenson, Malinna, "WASPS—Unsung Heroines of Our Air War," *King Features Syndicate*, 19 March 1944.

102. "Army Passes Up Jobless Pilots to Train Wasps: Prefers Women to Older, Experienced Pilots," *Chicago Tribune Press Service*, 11 February 1944.

103. Ibid.

104. "Men Pilots Jobless, House Unit Considers Investigating WASP," *Washington Evening Star*, 14 March 1944.

105. Sarles, Ruth, "Lay That Airplane Down, Babe, Cry Grounded He-Man Pilots," *Washington Daily News*, 31 March 1944.

106. "House to Probe Need of Women as Fliers," Associated Press, 4 March 1944.

107. O'Donnell, John, "Capitol Stuff," *Washington Times Herald*, 31 March 1944.

108. "End of Recruiting Untrained WASPS Urged by House Unit," *Washington Star*, 5 June 1944.

109. Sarles, Ruth, "50 Army Planes Speed Signatures of CAA Fliers to Head Off Bill," *Washington Daily News*, 26 April 1944.

110. *Women Who Flew*, unedited interview tapes, 1994.

111. Lombard, Helen, "Flying Women Guarded from Wrong Publicity," *Times* (Roanoke, Va.), 24 April 1944.

112. "Air Force Accused of Waste on WASPS," *World Telegram*, 31 May 1944.

113. "He-Pilots Get Some Support in Bid for Gals' Ferry Jobs," *Washington Daily News*, 13 April 1944.

114. "Commission Urged for Women Pilots: Gen. Arnold Hopes to Send Every Male Flier Overseas," United Press, 22 March 1944.

115. "WASPS to Be Part of Army under War Department Plan," Associated Press, 4 May 1944.

116. "Secretary Stimson Denies WASP Training Will Affect Training of Male Air Pilots," *The Service Woman*, 12 May 1944.

117. "WASPS Vs CAA: Fight to Give Men Flying Instructors Equality with Girls," *Doylestown (Pa.) Intelligence*, 20 May 1944.

118. "Clipping WASPS' Wings," *Washington D.C. News*, 13 July 1944.

119. "Glamorous Fliers," *Anderson (N.C.) Independent-Tribune*, 23 June 1944.

120. "WASPS to Get Snappy Outfits Costing $505," *Washington D.C. Star*, 10 June 1944.

121. "WASP Training Plans Assailed in House," Associated Press, June 1944.

122. "Explaining the Wasps: To the Editor," *St. Louis Globe-Democrat*, 10 May 1944.

123. "Arnold Faces Congressional Uproar over WASPS; Lady Fliers Now Replace Instead of Release Men," 5 August 1944.

124. "That WASP Bill," 22 July 1944.

125. "First Lady's Hand Is Seen," *Worcester (Mass.) Gazette*, 7 June 1944.

126. "CAA Men 'Tossed to the Wolves,' Air Staff Officer Informed."

127. "WASP Bill Hinges on Rights for Men," *Independent News Service*, 20 May 1944.

128. "Wasps May Oust 5,000 Instructors," *Washington Times Herald*, 21 May 1944.

129. "Aviators Stung by WASPS: Fliers Resented Proposed Corps," *Scripps-Howard*, 13 July 1944.

130. "Pilots Seek to Continue Instructing: Denied Jobs Women Pilots Now Receiving Training For," *Cuero (Tex.) Record*, 8 May 1944.

131. "Air Force Accused of Waste on WASPS."

132. "Glamorous Fliers."

133. "House Fight on WASP Bill Hinted by Sparkman Motion," *Washington D.C. News*, 16 May 1944.

134. Ibid.

135. "Male Fliers May Switch Tactics and Sponsor Their Own Bill," *Washington D.C. News*, 9 May 1944.

136. "WASPS Would Quit Army, Is Report," *Washington D.C. News*, 12 June 1944.

137. Ibid.

138. Kelley, Andrew R., "Points and Pointers on the Amusement Market: 'Ladies Courageous' Arrive at a Time When Congress Is Debating WASP Measure," 1944.

139. Mortimer, Lee, "The Movies: 'Ladies Courageous' Glorified WAFS," 1944.

140. "The Washington Merry-Go-Round: Arnold Faces Uproar over His Continued Use of WASPS," 5 August 1944.

141. "Shortage or Conscience?" *Idaho Statesman*, 4 June 1944.

NOTES TO CHAPTER 5

1. Costello, Rep. John, *H.R. 3358, A bill to provide for the appointment of female pilots in the Air Forces of the Army*, 30 September 1943.

2. Costello, Rep. John, Letter to Jacqueline Cochran, 4 October 1943.

3. Committee on Military Affairs, *Hearings before the Committee on Military Affairs on HR 4219*, 22 March 1944, 1-2.

4. Ibid., 3.

5. Cottrell, Ann, "Pilot Trainees Being Sent to Infantry Units: Arnold Says 36,000 Will Be Shifted; Assets Women May Replace Ferry Flyers," *New York Herald Tribune*, 23 March 1944.

6. Committee on Military Affairs, *Hearings*, 22 March 1944, 2.

7. Ibid.

8. "Arnold Visions All-Woman U.S. Air Transport," *Washington Evening Star*, 22 March 1944.

9. Committee on Military Affairs, *Hearings*, 22 March 1944, 6.

10. Ibid., 3.

11. Ibid., 4-5.

12. Ibid., 5.

13. Ibid., 6.

14. Ibid., 8.

15. Ibid.

16. Ibid., 9.

17. Stimson, Henry L., Letter to Andrew J. May, Chairman of the Committee on Military Affairs, 16 February 1944.

18. Committee on Military Affairs, *Report No. 1277: Providing for the Appointment of Female Pilots and Aviation Cadets of the Army Air Forces*, 22 March 1944, 1-2.

19. Ibid., 2.

20. Ibid.

21. "WASPS," *Washington Post*, 25 June 1944.

22. *Women Who Flew*, unedited interview tapes, 1994.

23. Committee on the Civil Service, *Interim Report No. 1600: Concerning Inquiries Made of Certain Proposals for the Expansion and Change in Civil Service Status of the WASP*, 5 June 1944, 1.

24. Ibid.

25. Cochran, Jacqueline, Letter to Robert Ramspeck, 5 April 1944.

26. Love, Nancy Harkness, "Résumé of Conversation between Mrs. Love and Col. McCormick of Ramspeck Committee," 17 April 1944, 1.

27. Committee on the Civil Service, *Interim Report No. 1600*, 1.

28. Ibid.

29. Ibid., 3.

30. Ibid., 2.

31. Ibid., 11.

32. Ibid., 4.

33. Ibid., 5.

34. Ibid.

35. Ibid.

36. Ibid., 6-7.

37. Ibid., 7.

38. Ibid., 8.

39. Ibid., 9.

40. Ibid.

41. Ibid., 13.

42. Ibid., 5.

43. Ibid., 13.

44. Ibid., 14.

45. Committee on Appropriations, *Report No. 1606, Military Establishment Appropriation Bill, 1945*, 7 June 1944, 9.

46. Ibid.
47. Ibid., 10.
48. Ibid.
49. Ibid., 4.
50. *Congressional Record—Appendix*, 16 June 1944, A3305.
51. Ibid.
52. *Congressional Record—Appendix*, 10 June 1944, A3171.
53. Ibid.
54. Ibid., A3172.
55. *Congressional Record—Appendix*, 17 June 1944, A3342-3343.
56. *Congressional Record—Appendix*, 7 June 1944, A3287-3288.
57. Ibid., A3288.
58. *Congressional Record—Appendix*, 8 June 1944, A3095.
59. Ibid., A3096.
60. *Congressional Record—Appendix*, 17 June 1944, A3344.
61. Ibid.
62. *Congressional Record—Appendix*, 10 August 1944, A3857.
63. *Congressional Record—Appendix*, 8 June 1944, A3096.
64. *Congressional Record*, 20 June 1944, 6412.
65. Ibid., 6409-6411.
66. Ibid., 6398, 6400, 6409, 6411, 6412.
67. *Congressional Record*, 21 June 1944, 6398.
68. *Women Who Flew*, 1994.
69. Nagle, Nadine, telephone interview with author, March 1994.
70. *Congressional Record*, 21 June 1944, 6398.
71. Ibid.
72. Ibid.
73. Ibid.
74. Ibid., 6399.
75. Ibid., 6403.
76. Ibid., 6404.
77. Ibid.
78. Ibid.
79. Ibid., 6046.
80. Ibid., 6045.
81. Ibid., 6406.
82. Ibid.
83. Ibid., 6407.
84. Ibid.
85. Ibid., 6408.
86. Ibid., 6409.
87. Ibid., 6410.

88. Ibid.

89. Ibid., 6412.

90. *Congressional Record—Appendix*, 17 June 1944, A3344.

91. *Congressional Record*, 21 June 1944, 6412.

92. Ibid.

93. Ibid., 6413.

94. Ibid., 6411.

95. Ibid.

96. Ibid., 6413.

97. Ibid.

98. Ibid.

99. Ibid., 6414.

100. Ibid.

101. Ibid.

102. Ibid., 6415.

103. Sarles, Ruth, "CAA Bill Introduced after WASPS Rejected," *Washington D.C. News*, 22 June 1944.

104. *Women Who Flew.*

105. Sarles, "CAA Bill Introduced."

106. *Congressional Record*, 21 June 1944, 6415-6416.

107. Ibid.

108. Ibid.

109. "WASPS," *Washington Post*, 25 June 1944.

NOTES TO CHAPTER 6

1. "WASP Training Courses to End," Associated Press, 26 June 1944.

2. "WASP Training Ends in December, Arnold Announces," United Press, 27 June 1944.

3. Ponder, Ed, Letter to R. Earl McKaughan, 25 July 1944.

4. McKaughan, R. E., Letter to Commanding General, Training Command, 14 July 1944.

5. Arnold, Gen., *Telegram to Eleanor Watterud*, 26 June 1944.

6. Ibid.

7. "Dozen Would-Be Wasps, Stranded, Fight Back," *Detroit Times*, 6 July 1944.

8. *Women Who Flew*, unedited interview tapes, 1994.

9. Wadlow, Mrs. Thomas, Record of Telephone Conversation to Miss Jacqueline Cochran, 27 June 1944.

10. Scull, Elaine, Record of Telephone Conversation to Miss Jacqueline Cochran, 27 June 1944.

11. Ibid.

12. Bogart, Miss, Record of Telephone Conversation to Miss Edwards, 27 June 1944.

13. Scull, Record of Conversation with Miss Cochran.

14. Fluke, Emmy Lou, Record of Telephone Conversation to Miss Jacqueline Cochran, 27 June 1944.

15. "Congressmen Clip Wings of 9 Wasps: Detroit Girl Fliers Downed in Texas," *Detroit Free Press*, 2 June 1944.

16. "114 Stranded WASPS Get a Free Trip to Cool Off," *Detroit Free Press*, 4 July 1944.

17. Wyall Marty, telephone interview with author, March 1994.

18. "Dozen Would-Be Wasps, Stranded, Fight Back."

19. "Detroit Would-Be Wasps Find Hollywood Exciting," *Detroit Free Press*, 12 July 1944.

20. "Dozen Would-Be Wasps, Stranded, Fight Back."

21. "Bills Face Congress for Wasps' Travel: Girls Who Paid Way to Texas for Training Ask Refund," *New York Times*, 7 July 1944.

22. "Man Power and the WASP," *National Aeronautics*, June 1944.

23. "WASPS 'Burn' as Congress Cracks Up Program: Congress Halts Training Despite Gen. Arnold's Plea," *The Service Woman*, 14 July 1944.

24. "End of Recruiting Untrained WASPS Urged by House Unit," *Washington Star*, 5 June 1944.

25. Steely, H. H., "Fight against WASP Gaining As Idle Airmen's Ranks Grow," *Oklahoman*, 26 June 1944.

26. Ibid.

27. Ibid.

28. "WASPs May Disband Soon, Says Magazine," *Washington Daily News*, 31 July 1944.

29. Ibid.

30. "The Washington Merry-Go-Round: Arnold Faces Uproar over His Continued Use of WASPS," 5 August 1944.

31. Ibid.

32. "Deny Report WASPs to Become Air WACs," *Aviation News*, 7 August 1944.

33. "The WASP Row," *Minneapolis Star-Journal*, 10 August 1944.

34. "Are They Needed?" *Washington D.C. Star*, 10 August 1944.

35. "WASPS May Disband Soon, Says Magazine."

36. Cochran, Jacqueline, *WASP Report, to Commanding General, Army Air Forces*, 1 August 1944, 1.

37. Ibid., 2.

38. Ibid., 7.

39. Ibid., 6.

40. Ibid., 8.

41. Ibid., 11.

42. Ibid., 8-9.

43. Ibid., 10.

44. Ibid., 11.

45. "WASP Director Demands Army Status for Group," *Shelby Daily Globe*, 8 August 1944.

46. "WASPS Ask General Arnold for Bars or Discharge," *Washington Daily News*, 8 August 1944.

47. "Miss Cochran Would Commission Wasps or Junk Organization," *Washington Post*, 8 August 1944.

48. "The WASP Row."

49. "A Fair Proposal," *Fort Worth Star Telegram*, 16 August 1944.

50. Ibid.

51. "WASPs Deserve Army Status," *Muncie (Ind.) Star*, 13 August 1944.

52. Elliott, Major Richard G., Memorandum to Office of the Commanding General, 24 August 1944, 1.

53. Ibid.

54. Ibid., 2.

55. Ibid.

56. Ibid., 3.

57. "WASPs Begin New Pressure Drive to Make Congress Reverse Vote," *Washington Daily News*, 6 September 1944.

58. "Inside Washington: Wasps May Still Get into Army," *Central Press*, 15 August 1944.

59. Craig, Major General M. A., Memorandum for Chief of Air Staff, 12 September 1944.

60. Arnold, Commanding Gen. H. H., Memorandum to Director of Women Pilots, 1 October 1944.

61. Ibid.

62. Cochran, Jacqueline, Memorandum to Commanding General, Army Air Forces, 1 October 1944.

63. Arnold, Gen. H. H., Letter to Each Member of the WASP, 1 October 1944.

64. Cochran, Jacqueline, Letter to All WASP, 2 October 1944.

65. Cochran, Jacqueline, Letter to the WASPs at Avenger Field, 3 October 1944.

66. *Women Who Flew*, unedited interview tapes.

67. War Department News Release, *AAF to Inactivate WASP on December 20*, 3 October 1944.

68. Ibid.

69. "WASPs to Lose Wings Dec. 20, Arnold Rules," *Washington Daily News*, 4 October 1944.

70. "Men Take Over: Army to Drop Women Fliers Next Dec. 20," *Washington Post*, 4 October 1944.

71. "'Let Us Fly,' Plea of WASPS: Grounding of 1,000 Girls Brings Many Heartaches," *New York Journal*, 22 October 1944.

72. Pasley, Virginia, "Women Pilots Have No Future, Says WASP Head," *Washington Times Herald*, 29 March 1944.

73. "Bob Hope's Communiqué," *Washington Post*, 11 November 1944.

74. "Wasps Want to Keep Flying as Civil Pilots," *Herald Tribune*, 2 December 1944.

75. Ibid.

76. Winchell, Walter, "Man about Town," *Daily Mirror*, 4 December 1944.

77. "No Place for WASPS," *Boston Post*, 5 December 1944.

78. Wilson, Gill Robb, "Wasps to Be Demobilized Dec. 20: Of Nine Hundred of Them, Two Hundred Are Experts, Needed in War Work," *New York Herald Tribune*, 13 December 1944.

79. Ibid.

80. "We Can't Spare Them," *New York Herald Tribune*, 13 December 1944.

81. "Army Refuses Women Fliers' Work Offer," *Detroit Free Press*, 21 December 1944.

82. "Wasps Want to Serve, Other Women Not So Anxious," *Los Angeles Times*, 22 December 1944.

83. "Willing But Grounded," *Sacramento Bee*, 26 December 1944.

84. "Army Refuses Women Fliers' Work Offer."

85. Pentagon, *Fact Sheet: Women's Airforce Service Pilots*, 1995.

86. Nowland, Brig. Gen. Bob E., Secret Memorandum to Commanding General, Air Transport Command, 1 November 1944.

87. Bevans, Major J. M., Assistant Chief of Air Staff, Secret Memorandum to Commanding General, Air Transport Command, 22 November 1944.

88. Committee on Appropriations, *Report No. 1606, Military Establishment Appropriation Bill, 1945*, 7 June 1944, 10.

89. Cochran, Jacqueline, Letter to All Members of the WASP, 3 November 1944.

90. Military Poll Committee, Letter to WASP, n.d.

91. Cochran, Jacqueline, Letter to All Former WASP, 22 February 1945.

92. "Passing of WASP Mourned by Ardent Few Who Created This Un-Needed Service," *St. Petersburg Times*, 22 October 1944.

93. Central Flying Training Command, Army Air Forces, *History of the WASP Program*, 20 January 1945, 174.

94. Granger, Byrd Howell, *On Final Approach: The Women Airforce Service Pilots of W.W. II*, 1991, A-89.

95. Central Flying Training Command, *History of the WASP Program*, 171-182.

96. Ibid., 172.

97. Ibid.

98. Ibid., 174.

99. Ibid., 176-177.

100. Ibid., 178.

101. Ibid.

102. Ibid., 151.

103. Wyall, Marty, telephone interview with author, March 1994.

104. Giles, Lt. Gen. Barney, Deputy Commander, Army Air Forces and Chief of Air Staff, AAF Ltr 40-34 to Commanding Generals, All Air Forces and All Independent and Subordinate AAF Commands; Director, AAF Technical Service Command; and Commanding Officers of All AAF Bases (in continental United States), 1 November 1944, 2.

105. Wyall, Marty, telephone interview with author, March 1994.

106. *Women Who Flew,* unedited interview tapes.

107. Bergemann, Clarice, telephone interview with author, March 1994.

108. Wyall, Marty, Telephone interview with author, March 1994.

109. *Women Who Flew,* unedited interview tapes.

110. Kinch, Sam, "Arnold Praises WASPS at Valedictory Ceremony," *Fort Worth Star Telegram,* 8 December 1944.

111. "Wasps Go into Retirement after Valiant War Service," *Christian Science Monitor,* 20 December 1944.

112. Boyden, Sarah Brown, "Prospect of Holidays Soothes Jobless WASPS," *Chicago Sun,* 14 December 1944.

113. "Hail to the Wasp," *Indianapolis Star,* 19 December 1944.

114. "Women Pilots out of Work as Wasp Quits," *Washington Times-Herald,* 21 December 1944.

115. Lindsay, Malvina, "The Gentler Sex: Women Unafraid," *Washington Post,* 19 December 1944.

116. "WASPS Shorn of Wings: Women War Fliers Gripe on Inactivity," *Philadelphia Inquirer,* 1 April 1945.

117. Perret, Geoffrey, *Winged Victory: The Army Air Forces in World War II,* 1993, 376.

118. Central Flying Training Command, *History of the WASP Program,* 177.

119. *Women Who Flew,* unedited interview tapes.

NOTES TO CHAPTER 7

1. *Women Who Flew,* unedited interview tapes, 1994.

2. Granger, Byrd Howell, *On Final Approach: The Women Airforce Service Pilots of W.W. II,* 1991, 467.

3. Williams, Betty Jane, President, Order of Fifinella, Letter to Helen Luts, 3 June 1947, 1.

4. Ibid., 2.

5. *Congressional Record—House,* 21 April 1948, 4806.

6. Ibid., 4809.

7. Ibid., 4810.

8. Ibid., 4807.

9. Ibid., 4809.

10. Ibid., 4830.

11. Ibid., 4809.

12. Ibid., 4814.

13. Ibid., 4820.

14. Ibid., 4808.

15. Ibid., 4830.

16. Ibid.

17. Ibid., 4831.

18. Ibid., 4832.

19. Ibid., 4806.

20. Ibid., 4821.

21. Ibid., 4811.

22. Ibid.

23. Ibid.

24. Edwards, Lt. Gen. I. H., Air Force Deputy Chief of Staff, Memorandum to Secretary of the Air Force, 17 June 1948.

25. Ibid.

26. Ibid.

27. Verges, Marianne, *On Silver Wings: The Women Airforce Service Pilots of World War II, 1942-1944*, 1991, 231.

28. Edwards, Lt. Gen. I. H., Air Force Deputy Chief of Staff, Memorandum to Secretary of the Air Force, 17 June 1948.

29. Wyall, Marty, telephone interview with the author, March 1994.

30. Crew, Nancy B., President of the Order of Fifinella, Memorandum to All WASPs, 15 June 1973.

31. Wyall, Marty, telephone interview with the author.

32. WASP Military Committee, *Brief History on WASP Struggle for Militarization*, 1976.

33. Crew, Memorandum to All WASPs.

34. Ibid.

35. *Women Who Flew*, unedited interview tapes.

36. WASP Military Committee, *Brief History on WASP Struggle for Militarization*, 1976.

37. Ibid.

38. "WASP's: The Forgotten `Warriors,'" *Air Line Pilot Magazine*, October 1977.

39. "To Right a 33-Year-Old Wrong," *Hearst Publications*, 26 September 1977.

40. "Glamorous Fliers," *Anderson (N.C.) Independent-Tribune*, 23 June 1944.

41. *Women Who Flew*, unedited interview tapes.

42. Ibid.

43. "The WASPS: Maybe They'll Get More, But All They Want Is Recognition," *Dayton Daily News*, 15 May 1977.

44. "World War II's Women Pilots Feel Forgotten, Their Benefits Ignored," *Baltimore Evening Sun*, 14 October 1976.

45. Ibid.

46. "Real Live Nieces of Our Uncle Sam Born With a Yearning to Fly," *Panorama,* 9 July 1978.

47. WASP Military Committee, *Brief History on WASP Struggle.*

48. "Woman Opposes WASP Push for Vet Benefits," *Tennessean,* 26 May 1977.

49. Ibid.

50. Moore, Kathleen, National Secretary, National Association of Concerned Veterans, "NACV Supports WASP Bill," *Stars and Stripes,* 16 June 1977.

51. "CPA Extends Membership to WASPs," *Stars and Stripes,* 29 September 1977, 3.

52. Hughes, Patricia Collins, "WASPs Stalemate Nears End," *Stars and Stripes,* 15 September 1977, 3.

53. Hughes, Patricia Collins, "Were WASPs First Combat Women?" *Stars and Stripes,* 20 October 1977, 3.

54. Hughes, Patricia Collins, "11 Bills Pending for Veterans Status," *Stars and Stripes,* 1 September 1977, 3.

55. Hughes, "WASPs Stalemate Nears End."

56. Ibid.

57. Hughes, Patricia Collins, "Roberts Vows to Keep WASP Bill Tied Up in Committee," *Stars and Stripes,* 22 September 1977, 3.

58. Hughes, Patricia Collins, "Were WASPs Paid Benefits?" *Stars and Stripes,* 13 October 1977, 3.

59. Hughes, "Roberts Vows to Keep WASP Bill Tied Up."

60. War Department, Bureau of Public Relations, *Public Relations Policy for WASP,* 3 December 1943.

61. *Congressional Record—Senate,* 22 September 1977, S15379.

62. Ibid.

63. *Congressional Record—House,* 28 September 1977, H10302.

64. Ibid.

65. *Congressional Record—Senate,* 6 October 1977, S16572.

66. Ibid.

67. Hughes, "Were WASPs First Combat Women?"

68. *Congressional Record—Senate,* 6 October 1977, S16572.

69. Hughes, "WASPs Stalemate Nears End."

70. Hughes, "Roberts Vows to Keep WASP Bill Tied Up."

71. WASP Public Affairs Office, News Release, September 1977.

72. Strother, Dora Dougherty, "Dora Dougherty Strother Testifies for WASPs Veterans' Status," *Stars and Stripes,* 2 June 1977, 1.

73. Ibid.

74. "Administration Opposes WASPs Bill," *Stars and Stripes,* 2 June 1977.

75. Hughes, "Were WASPs Paid Benefits?"

76. "Administration Opposes WASPs Bill," 9.

77. "V.F.W. Opposes WASP Bill," *Stars and Stripes*, 2 June 1977.

78. "American Legion Opposes WASPs Bill," *Stars and Stripes*, 2 June 1977, 15.

79. *Congressional Record*, 21 June 1944, 6410.

80. "American Legion Opposes WASPs Bill."

81. Gardiner, William B., Statement of William B. Gardiner, National Director of Legislation, Disabled American Veterans, Before the Select Subcommittee on the WASPs of the House Committee on Veterans' Affairs, 20 September 1977, 4-5.

82. Arnold, William Bruce, Arnold's Copy, Statement by William Bruce Arnold, Colonel, U.S. Air Force (Retired), Before the U.S. House of Representatives Committee on Veterans' Affairs, 20 September 1977.

83. Granger, Byrd Howell, *Evidence Supporting Military Service by Women Airforce Service Pilots of World War II*, 1977, 3.

84. Ibid., 4.

85. Ibid., 113.

86. Ibid.

87. Ibid., 13.

88. Ibid., 41.

89. Ibid., 98-99.

90. Ibid., 79.

91. Ibid., 90.

92. Ibid., 74.

93. Ibid., 74a.

94. Porter, Helen, *Certificate of Honorable Discharge from the Army*, 20 December 1944.

95. "American Legion Opposes WASPs Bill," 15.

96. Cochran, Jacqueline, Memorandum to Commanding General, Army Air Forces, 1 October 1944; Cochran, Jacqueline, Letter to All WASP, 2 October 1944.

97. "Senate Votes 91-0 for WASP Status!" *Stars and Stripes*, 27 October 1977, 3.

98. *Congressional Record—Senate*, 4 November 1977, S18812.

99. Ibid., S18813.

100. Ibid., S18819.

101. "Real Live Nieces of Our Uncle Sam," 15.

102. Nagle, Nadine, telephone interview with author, March 1994.

103. *Women Who Flew*, unedited interview tapes.

104. Roberts, Lillian Conner, Memorandum to All WASP, Trainees, and Survivors of WASP, March 1979.

NOTES TO CHAPTER 8

1. Simon, Roger, *Gramsci's Political Thought: An Introduction*, 1991, 22.

2. Hartmann, Susan, *The Home Front and Beyond: American Women in the 1940s*, 1982, 79.

3. Scott, Joan Wallach, *Gender and the Politics of History*, 1988, 32.

4. Lerner, Gerda, *The Creation of Patriarchy*, 1986, 9.

5. Ibid., 3.

6. Birke, Lynda, *Women, Feminism and Biology: The Feminist Challenge*, 1986.

7. Mead, Margaret, *Male and Female: A Study of the Sexes in a Changing World*, 1967.

8. Butler, Judith, *Bodies That Matter: On the Discursive Limits of "Sex,"* 1993, 1.

9. Butler, Judith, *Gender Trouble: Feminism and the Subversion of Identity*, 1990.

10. Scott, Joan Wallach, "Experience," 1992.

11. Ibid., 25.

12. Showalter, Elaine, *Sexual Anarchy: Gender and Culture at the Fin de Siècle*, 1990, 8.

13. Luce, Henry R., editorial comment, *Life*, 15 December 1941, 12.

14. Stiehm, Judith Hicks, "Bananas, Beaches, and Bases: Making Feminist Sense of the International Politics by Cynthia Enloe," 1992.

15. Enloe, Cynthia, *Does Khaki Become You? The Militarisation of Women's Lives*, 1983, 53-55.

16. Ibid., 100.

17. Ibid., 106.

18. Jeffords, Susan, *The Remasculinization of America: Gender and the Vietnam War*, 1989, xii.

19. Murphy, Audie, *To Hell and Back*, 1949, 7.

20. Ibid.

21. Ibid., 8.

22. Jeffords, Susan, and Rabinovitz, Lauren, eds., *Seeing through the Media: The Persian Gulf War*, 1994.

23. Fussel, Paul, *Wartime: Understanding and Behavior in The Second World War*, 1989.

24. Ibid., 277.

25. Addis, Elisabetta, Russo, Valeria E., Sebesta, Lorenza, Eds., *Women Soldiers: Images and Realities*, 1994, xii.

26. Rupp, Leila, *Mobilizing Women for War: German and American Propaganda, 1939-1945*, 1978.

27. Enloe, *Does Khaki Become You?* 123.

29. Vickers, Jeanne, *Women and War*, 1993, 36.

30. Enloe, *Does Khaki Become You?* 157.

31. *Life*, 5 January 1942, 65.

32. *Life*, 5 April 1943, 82.

33. Enloe, *Does Khaki Become You?* 122.

34. Segal, Mady Wechsler, "Women's Military Roles Cross-Nationally: Past, Present, and Future," 1995, 759.

35. Ibid., 761.

36. Korb, Lawrence. "The Pentagon's Perspective," 1989, 24.

37. Holms, Maj. Gen. Jeanne, Ret., *Women in the Military: An Unfinished Revolution*, 1992, 397.

38. Goldman, Nancy Loring, eds., *Combatants or NonCombatants? Historical and Contemporary Perspectives*, 1982, 4.

39. Wheelwright, "The Media's Use of the Feminine in the Gulf War," 131.

40. Segal, "Women's Military Roles Cross-Nationally," 758.

41. Wilcox, Clyde, "Race, Gender, and Support for Women in the Military," 1992, 310.

42. Holms, *Women in the Military*, xv.

43. "Army Passes Up Jobless Pilots to Train Wasps: Prefers Women to Older, Experienced Flyers," *Chicago Tribune Press Service*, 11 February 1944.

44. Committee on the Civil Service, *Interim Report No. 1600: Concerning Inquiries Made of Certain Proposals for the Expansion and Change in Civil Service Status of the WASP*, 5 June 1944, 2.

45. *Congressional Record*, 21 June 1944, 6414.

NOTES TO CHAPTER 9

1. *Women Who Flew*, unedited interview tapes, 1994.

2. *Women Who Flew*, 1994.

3. *Women Who Flew*, unedited interview tapes.

4. Ibid.

5. Ibid.

Bibliography

ARTICLES

"Administration Opposes WASPs Bill." *Stars and Stripes*, 2 June 1977. The WASP Collection. Texas Women's University Archives. Denton, Texas.

"Air Force Accused of Waste on WASPS." *World Telegram*, 31 May 1944. The Jacqueline Cochran Collection. The Eisenhower Center Archives. Abilene, Kansas.

"American Legion Opposes WASPs Bill." *Stars and Stripes*, 2 June 1977. The WASP Collection. Texas Women's University Archives. Denton, Texas.

"Are They Needed?" *Washington D.C. Star*. 10 August 1944. The Jacqueline Cochran Collection. The Eisenhower Center Archives. Abilene, Kansas.

"Army Passes Up Jobless Pilots to Train Wasps: Prefers Women to Older, Experienced Flyers." *Chicago Tribune Press Service*, 11 February 1944. The WASP Collection. Texas Women's University Archives. Denton, Texas.

"Army Refuses Women Fliers' Work Offer." *Detroit Free Press*, 21 December 1944. The Jacqueline Cochran Collection. The Eisenhower Center Archives. Abilene, Kansas.

"Arnold Faces Congressional Uproar over WASPS; Lady Fliers Now Replace Instead of Release Men." 5 August 1944. The Jacqueline Cochran Collection. The Eisenhower Center Archives. Abilene, Kansas.

"Arnold Visions All-Woman U.S. Air Transport." *Washington Evening Star*, 22 March 1944. The Jacqueline Cochran Collection. The Eisenhower Center Archives. Abilene, Kansas.

"Aviators Stung by WASPS: Fliers Resented Proposed Corps." *Scripps-Howard*, 13 July 1944. The Jacqueline Cochran Collection. The Eisenhower Center Archives. Abilene, Kansas.

"Biggs Field Male Personnel Perks Up When Expert Wasps Arrive on Scene," *El Paso Times*, 1943. The WASP Collection. Texas Women's University Archives. Denton, Texas.

"Bills Face Congress for Wasps' Travel: Girls Who Paid Way to Texas for Training Ask Refund." *New York Times*, 7 July 1944. The Jacqueline Cochran Collection. The Eisenhower Center Archives. Abilene, Kansas.

"Bob Hope's Communiqué." *Washington Post*, 11 November 1944. The Jacqueline Cochran Collection. The Eisenhower Center Archives. Abilene, Kansas.

Boyden, Sarah Brown. "Prospect of Holidays Soothes Jobless WASPS." *Chicago Sun*,

14 December 1944. The WASP Collection. Texas Women's University Archives. Denton, Texas.

"CAA Men 'Tossed to the Wolves,' Air Staff Officer Informed." No date. The Jacqueline Cochran Collection. The Eisenhower Center Archives. Abilene, Kansas.

Cahoon, Yvonne. "WASP Head Believes Women Pilots Face Duty on War Fronts." *Evening Star*, 25 October 1943. The Jacqueline Cochran Collection. The Eisenhower Center Archives. Abilene, Kansas.

"Clipping WASPS' Wings." *Washington D.C. News*, 13 July 1944. The Jacqueline Cochran Collection. The Eisenhower Center Archives. Abilene, Kansas.

"Cobras Have a 'Lady Pilot.'" *The Bellringer*. 1943. The WASP Collection. Texas Women's University Archives. Denton, Texas.

"Commission Urged for Women Pilots: Gen. Arnold Hopes to Send Every Male Flier Overseas." United Press, 22 March 1944. The Jacqueline Cochran Collection. The Eisenhower Center Archives. Abilene, Kansas.

"Congressmen Clip Wings of 9 Wasps: Detroit Girl Fliers Downed in Texas." *Detroit Free Press*, 2 June 1944. The WASP Collection. Texas Women's University Archives. Denton, Texas.

Cottrell, Ann. "Pilot Trainees Being Sent to Infantry Units: Arnold Says 36,000 Will Be Shifted; Assets Women May Replace Ferry Flyers." *New York Herald Tribune*, 23 March 1944. The Jacqueline Cochran Collection. The Eisenhower Center Archives. Abilene, Kansas.

"CPA Extends Membership to WASPs." *Stars and Stripes*, 29 September 1977. The WASP Collection. Texas Women's University Archives. Denton, Texas.

"Deny Report WASPs to Become Air WACs." *Aviation News*, 7 August 1944. The Jacqueline Cochran Collection. The Eisenhower Center Archives. Abilene, Kansas.

"Detroit Would-Be Wasps Find Hollywood Exciting." *Detroit Free Press*, 12 July 1944. The WASP Collection. Texas Women's University Archives. Denton, Texas.

"Dozen Would-Be Wasps, Stranded, Fight Back." *Detroit Times*, 6 July 1944. The Jacqueline Cochran Collection. The Eisenhower Center Archives. Abilene, Kansas.

"Drew Pearson's Merry-Go-Round: Protest Women Fliers." *Grand Forks Herald*, 6 August 1944. The Jacqueline Cochran Collection. The Eisenhower Center Archives. Abilene, Kansas.

Eads, Jane. "Girl Fliers on Varied Tasks in Complicated Games High up in the Air, Towing Targets Is One of Hazardous Duties on Which They Train." Cincinnati, 25 October 1943. The Jacqueline Cochran Collection. The Eisenhower Center Archives. Abilene, Kansas.

"End of Recruiting Untrained WASPS Urged by House Unit." *Washington Star*, 5 June 1944. The Jacqueline Cochran Collection. The Eisenhower Center Archives. Abilene, Kansas.

"Explaining the Wasps: To the Editor." *St. Louis Globe-Democrat*, 10 May 1944. The Jacqueline Cochran Collection. The Eisenhower Center Archives. Abilene, Kansas.

"A Fair Proposal." *Fort Worth Star Telegram*, 16 August 1944. The Jacqueline Cochran Collection. The Eisenhower Center Archives. Abilene, Kansas.

"First Lady's Hand Is Seen." *Worcester (Mass.) Gazette*, 7 June 1944. The Jacqueline Cochran Collection. The Eisenhower Center Archives. Abilene, Kansas.

"Glamorous Fliers." *Anderson (N.C.) Independent-Tribune*, 23 June 1944. The Jacqueline Cochran Collection. The Eisenhower Center Archives. Abilene, Kansas.

Habas, Ralph. "Women Pilots Here Anxious to Join WAFS." *Chicago Sunday Times*, 13 September 1942. The Jacqueline Cochran Collection. The Eisenhower Center Archives. Abilene, Kansas.

"Hail to the Wasp." *Indianapolis Star*, 19 December 1944. The Jacqueline Cochran Collection. The Eisenhower Center Archives. Abilene, Kansas.

"He-Pilots Get Some Support in Bid for Gals' Ferry Jobs." *Washington Daily News*, 13 April 1944. The Jacqueline Cochran Collection. The Eisenhower Center Archives. Abilene, Kansas.

"House Fight on WASP Bill Hinted by Sparkman Motion." *Washington D.C. News*, 16 May 1944. The Jacqueline Cochran Collection. The Eisenhower Center Archives. Abilene, Kansas.

"House to Probe Need of Women as Fliers." Associated Press, 14 March 1944. The WASP Collection. Texas Women's University Archives. Denton, Texas.

Hughes, Patricia Collins. "11 Bills Pending for Veterans Status." *Stars and Stripes*, 1 September 1977. The WASP Collection. Texas Women's University Archives. Denton, Texas.

———. "Roberts Vows to Keep WASP Bill Tied Up in Committee." *Stars and Stripes*, 22 September 1977. The WASP Collection. Texas Women's University Archives. Denton, Texas.

———. "WASPs Stalemate Nears End." *Stars and Stripes*, 15 September 1977. The WASP Collection. Texas Women's University Archives. Denton, Texas.

———. "Were WASPs First Combat Women?" *Stars and Stripes*, 20 October 1977. The WASP Collection. Texas Women's University Archives. Denton, Texas.

———. "Were WASPs Paid Benefits?" *Stars and Stripes*, 13 October 1977. The WASP Collection. Texas Women's University Archives. Denton, Texas.

"Inside Washington: Wasps May Still Get into Army." *Central Press*, 15 August 1944. The Jacqueline Cochran Collection. The Eisenhower Center Archives. Abilene, Kansas.

Kelley, Andrew R. "Points and Pointers on the Amusement Market: 'Ladies Courageous' Arrive at a Time When Congress Is Debating WASP Measure." 1944. The Jacqueline Cochran Collection. The Eisenhower Center Archives. Abilene, Kansas.

Kidney, Daniel M. "Women Air Service Pilots Do Satisfactory Job." *Washington Daily News*, 25 October 1943. The Jacqueline Cochran Collection. The Eisenhower Center Archives. Abilene, Kansas.

Kinch, Sam. "Arnold Praises WASPS at Valedictory Ceremony." *Fort Worth Star*

Telegram, 8 December 1944. The WASP Collection. Texas Women's University Archives. Denton, Texas.

Knight, Charlotte. "Our Women Pilots." *Air Force: Official Journal of the U.S. Army Air Forces,* 1944. L2, Women Airforce Service Pilots. Air Force Museum Archives. Wright Patterson Air Force Base, Ohio.

————. "Service Pilots." *Skyways,* 1944. The WASP Collection. Texas Women's University Archives. Denton, Texas.

"'Let Us Fly,' Plea of WASPs: Grounding of 1,000 Girls Brings Many Heartaches." *New York Journal,* 22 October 1944. The Jacqueline Cochran Collection. The Eisenhower Center Archives, Abilene, Kansas.

Life Magazine, 1941-1945.

Lindsay, Malvina. "The Gentler Sex: Women Unafraid." *Washington Post,* 19 December 1944. The Jacqueline Cochran Collection. The Eisenhower Center Archives. Abilene, Kansas.

Lombard, Helen. "Flying Women Guarded from Wrong Publicity," *Times* (Roanoke, Va.), 24 April 1944. The Jacqueline Cochran Collection. The Eisenhower Center Archives. Abilene, Kansas.

"Male Fliers May Switch Tactics and Sponsor Their Own Bill." *Washington D.C. News,* 9 May 1944. The Jacqueline Cochran Collection. The Eisenhower Center Archives. Abilene, Kansas.

"Man Power and the WASP." *National Aeronautics,* June 1944. The Jacqueline Cochran Collection. The Eisenhower Center Archives. Abilene, Kansas.

Mendelson, Frances. "Women Pilots Towing Targets for Army Anti-Aircraft Practice: Originally Restricted to Ferrying Planes from Factories, They Are Achieving Success in Highly Specialized Jobs at Camp Davis." *Washington Herald Tribune,* 25 October 1943. The WASP Collection. Texas Women's University Archives. Denton, Texas.

"Men Pilots Jobless, House Unit Considers Investigating WASP." *Washington Evening Star,* 14 March 1944. The Jacqueline Cochran Collection. The Eisenhower Center Archives. Abilene, Kansas.

"Men Take Over: Army to Drop Women Fliers Next Dec. 20." *Washington Post,* 4 October 1944. The Jacqueline Cochran Collection. The Eisenhower Center Archives. Abilene, Kansas.

"Miss Cochran Would Commission Wasps or Junk Organization." *Washington Post,* 8 August 1944. The Jacqueline Cochran Collection. The Eisenhower Center Archives. Abilene, Kansas.

Moore, Kathleen, National Secretary, National Association of Concerned Veterans. "NACV Supports WASP Bill." *Stars and Stripes,* 16 June 1977. The WASP Collection. Texas Women's University Archives. Denton, Texas.

Mortimer, Lee. "The Movies: 'Ladies Courageous' Glorified WAFS." 1944. The Jacqueline Cochran Collection. The Eisenhower Center Archives. Abilene, Kansas.

"Nation's First Class of Women Air Ferry Pilots Awarded Wings." *Houston Chronicle,*

25 April 1943. The WASP Collection. Texas Women's University Archives. Denton, Texas.

Newsweek, 1941-1945.

"No Place for WASPS." *Boston Post*, 5 December 1944. The Jacqueline Cochran Collection. The Eisenhower Center Archives. Abilene, Kansas.

O'Donnell, John. "Capitol Stuff." *Washington Times Herald*, 31 March 1944. The Jacqueline Cochran Collection. The Eisenhower Center Archives. Abilene, Kansas.

"114 Stranded WASPS Get a Free Trip to Cool Off." *Detroit Free Press*, 4 July 1944. The WASP Collection. Texas Women's University Archives. Denton, Texas.

Pasley, Virginia. "Women Pilots Have No Future, Says WASP Head." *Washington Times Herald*, 29 March 1944. The Jacqueline Cochran Collection. The Eisenhower Center Archives. Abilene, Kansas.

"Passing of WASP Mourned by Ardent Few Who Created This Un-Needed Service." *St. Petersburg Times*, 22 October 1944. The Jacqueline Cochran Collection. The Eisenhower Center Archives. Abilene, Kansas.

"Pilots Seek to Continue Instructing: Denied Jobs Women Pilots Now Receiving Training For." *Cuero (Tex.) Record*, 8 May 1944. The Jacqueline Cochran Collection. The Eisenhower Center Archives. Abilene, Kansas.

Poole, Barbara. "Requiem for the WASP." *Flying Magazine*, December 1944. L2, Women Airforce Service Pilots. Air Force Museum Archives. Wright Patterson Air Force Base, Ohio.

"Real Live Nieces of Our Uncle Sam Born with a Yearning to Fly." *Panorama*, 9 July 1978. The WASP Collection. Texas Women's University Archives. Denton, Texas.

Sarles, Ruth. "CAA Bill Introduced after WASPS Rejected." *Washington D.C. News*, 22 June 1944. The Jacqueline Cochran Collection. The Eisenhower Center Archives. Abilene, Kansas.

———. "50 Army Planes Speed Signatures of CAA Fliers to Head Off Bill." *Washington Daily News*, 26 April 1944. The Jacqueline Cochran Collection. The Eisenhower Center Archives. Abilene, Kansas.

———. "Lay That Airplane Down, Babe, Cry Grounded He-Man Pilots." *Washington Daily News*, 31 March 1944. The Jacqueline Cochran Collection. The Eisenhower Center Archives. Abilene, Kansas.

Schisgall, Oscar. "The Girls Deliver the Goods." The WASP Collection. Texas Women's University Archives. Denton, Texas.

"Secretary Stimson Denies WASP Training Will Affect Training of Male Air Pilots." *The Service Woman*, 12 May 1944. The WASP Collection. Texas Women's University Archives. Denton, Texas.

"Seek Women Pilots to Ferry Planes." 3 December 1942. The WASP Collection. Texas Women's University Archives. Denton, Texas.

Segal, Mady Wechsler. "Women's Military Roles Cross-Nationally: Past, Present, and Future." *Signs*, 9, no.6, 1995, 757-775.

"Senate Votes 91-0 for WASP Status!" *Stars and Stripes*, 27 October 1977. The WASP Collection. Texas Women's University Archives. Denton, Texas.

"Shortage or Conscience?" *Idaho Statesman*, 4 June 1944. The Jacqueline Cochran Collection. The Eisenhower Center Archives. Abilene, Kansas.

Steely, H. H. "Fight against WASP Gaining As Idle Airmen's Ranks Grow." *Oklahoman*, 26 June 1944. The Jacqueline Cochran Collection. The Eisenhower Center Archives. Abilene, Kansas.

Stephenson, Malinna. "WASPS—Unsung Heroines of Our Air War." *King Features Syndicate*, 19 March 1944. The Jacqueline Cochran Collection. The Eisenhower Center Archives. Abilene, Kansas.

Stevick, Ann. "WASPS Who Tow Air Targets May Soon Be Real U.S. Soldiers." October 1943. The WASP Collection. Texas Women's University Archives. Denton, Texas.

Stiehm, Judith Hicks. "Bananas, Beaches, and Bases: Making Feminist Sense of the International Politics by Cynthia Enloe," *Signs*, 17, no. 4, 1992, 825-829.

Strother, Dora Dougherty. "Dora Dougherty Strother Testifies for WASPs Veterans' Status." *Stars and Stripes*, 2 June 1977. The WASP Collection. Texas Women's University Archives. Denton, Texas.

"Sugar and Spice! B-26 Gentle as Lamb in Hands of WASPS." *Martin City Star*, February 1944. L2, Women Airforce Service Pilots. Air Force Museum Archives. Wright Patterson Air Force Base, Ohio.

Tanner, Doris Brinker. "We Also Served." *American History Illustrated.* November 1985. WASP Collection. Archives. Women's International Air and Space Museum. Dayton, Ohio.

Taylor, Frank. "Our Women Warriors." *Liberty Magazine*, 29 January 1944. L2, Women Airforce Service Pilots. Air Force Museum Archives. Wright Patterson Air Force Base, Ohio.

"That WASP Bill." 22 July 1944. The Jacqueline Cochran Collection. The Eisenhower Center Archives. Abilene, Kansas.

Time, 1941-1945.

"To Right a 33-Year-Old Wrong." *Hearst Publications*, 26 September 1977. The WASP Collection. Texas Women's University Archives. Denton, Texas.

"V.F.W. Opposes WASP Bill." *Stars and Stripes*, 2 June 1977. The WASP Collection. Texas Women's University Archives. Denton, Texas.

"The Washington Merry-Go-Round: Arnold Faces Uproar over His Continued Use of WASPS." 5 August 1944. The Jacqueline Cochran Collection. The Eisenhower Center Archives. Abilene, Kansas.

"WASP Bill Hinges on Rights for Men." *Independent News Service,* 20 May 1944. The Jacqueline Cochran Collection. The Eisenhower Center Archives. Abilene, Kansas.

"WASP Director Demands Army Status for Group." *Shelby Daily Globe*, 8 August 1944. The Jacqueline Cochran Collection. The Eisenhower Center Archives. Abilene, Kansas.

"WASP Program Flayed in House." Associated Press, 19 June 1944. The Jacqueline Cochran Collection. The Eisenhower Center Archives. Abilene, Kansas.

"The WASP Row." *Minneapolis Star-Journal,* 10 August 1944. The Jacqueline Cochran Collection. The Eisenhower Center Archives. Abilene, Kansas.

"WASP Training Courses to End." Associated Press, 26 June 1944. The Jacqueline Cochran Collection. The Eisenhower Center Archives. Abilene, Kansas.

"WASP Training Ends in December, Arnold Announces." United Press, 27 June 1944. The Jacqueline Cochran Collection. The Eisenhower Center Archives. Abilene, Kansas.

"WASP Training Plans Assailed in House." Associated Press, June 1944. The Jacqueline Cochran Collection. The Eisenhower Center Archives. Abilene, Kansas.

"WASPS." *Washington Post,* 25 June 1944. The Jacqueline Cochran Collection. The Eisenhower Center Archives. Abilene, Kansas.

"WASPS Ask General Arnold for Bars or Discharge." *Washington Daily News,* 8 August 1944. The Jacqueline Cochran Collection. The Eisenhower Center Archives. Abilene, Kansas.

"WASPs Begin New Pressure Drive to Make Congress Reverse Vote." *Washington Daily News,* 6 September 1944. The Jacqueline Cochran Collection. The Eisenhower Center Archives. Abilene, Kansas.

"WASPS 'Burn' as Congress Cracks Up Program: Congress Halts Training Despite Gen. Arnold's Plea." *The Service Woman,* 14 July 1944. The Jacqueline Cochran Collection. The Eisenhower Center Archives. Abilene, Kansas.

"WASPs Deserve Army Status." *Muncie (Ind.) Star,* 13 August 1944. The Jacqueline Cochran Collection. The Eisenhower Center Archives. Abilene, Kansas.

"WASPS End Wartime Flying Contribution." *New York Times,* 19 December 1944. L2, Women Airforce Service Pilots. Air Force Museum Archives. Wright Patterson Air Force Base, Ohio.

"Wasps Go into Retirement after Valiant War Service." *Christian Science Monitor,* 20 December 1944. The Jacqueline Cochran Collection. The Eisenhower Center Archives. Abilene, Kansas.

"The WASPs: Maybe They'll Get More, But All They Want Is Recognition." *Dayton Daily News,* 15 May 1977. The WASP Collection. Texas Women's University Archives. Denton, Texas.

"WASPs May Disband Soon, Says Magazine." *Washington Daily News,* 31 July 1944. The Jacqueline Cochran Collection. The Eisenhower Center Archives. Abilene, Kansas.

"Wasps May Oust 5,000 Instructors." *Washington Times Herald,* 21 May 1944. The Jacqueline Cochran Collection. The Eisenhower Center Archives. Abilene, Kansas.

"WASPS Shorn of Wings: Women War Fliers Gripe on Inactivity." *Philadelphia Inquirer,* 1 April 1945. The Jacqueline Cochran Collection. The Eisenhower Center Archives. Abilene, Kansas.

"WASP's: The Forgotten 'Warriors.'" *Air Line Pilot Magazine,* October 1977. The WASP Collection. Texas Women's University Archives. Denton, Texas.

"WASPS to Be Part of Army under War Department Plan." Associated Press, 4 May 1944. The WASP Collection. Texas Women's University Archives. Denton, Texas.

"WASPS to Get Snappy Outfits Costing $505." *Washington D.C. Star*, 10 June 1944. The Jacqueline Cochran Collection. The Eisenhower Center Archives. Abilene, Kansas.

"WASPs to Lose Wings Dec. 20, Arnold Rules." *Washington Daily News*, 4 October 1944. The Jacqueline Cochran Collection. The Eisenhower Center Archives. Abilene, Kansas.

"WASPS Vs CAA: Fight to Give Men Flying Instructors Equality with Girls." *Doylestown (Pa.) Intelligence*, 20 May 1944. The Jacqueline Cochran Collection. The Eisenhower Center Archives. Abilene, Kansas.

"Wasps Want to Keep Flying as Civil Pilots." *Herald Tribune*, 2 December 1944. The Jacqueline Cochran Collection. The Eisenhower Center Archives. Abilene, Kansas.

"Wasps Want to Serve, Other Women Not So Anxious." *Los Angeles Times*, 22 December 1944. The Jacqueline Cochran Collection. The Eisenhower Center Archives. Abilene, Kansas.

"WASPS Would Quit Army, Is Report." *Washington D.C. News*, 12 June 1944. The Jacqueline Cochran Collection. The Eisenhower Center Archives. Abilene, Kansas.

"WASP Training Plans Assailed in House." Associated Press, June 1944. The Jacqueline Cochran Collection. The Eisenhower Center Archives. Abilene, Kansas.

"We Can't Spare Them." *New York Herald Tribune*, 13 December 1944. The WASP Collection. Texas Women's University Archives. Denton, Texas.

Wells, Mary Retick. "An Open Letter to Rep. Olin E. Teague Re. WASP." *Stars and Stripes*, 8 September 1977. The WASP Collection. Texas Women's University Archives. Denton, Texas.

Wilcox, Clyde. "Race, Gender, and Support for Women in the Military." *Social Science Quarterly*, 73, no. 2, 1992, 310-323.

Williams, Dorothy. "Gal Fliers Help Perfect Aim." *New York Daily News*, 25 October 1943. The Jacqueline Cochran Collection. The Eisenhower Center Archives. Abilene, Kansas.

"Willing But Grounded." *Sacramento Bee*, 26 December 1944. The Jacqueline Cochran Collection. The Eisenhower Center Archives. Abilene, Kansas.

Wilson, Gill Robb. "Wasps to Be Demobilized Dec. 20: Of Nine Hundred of Them, Two Hundred Are Experts, Needed in War Work." *New York Herald Tribune*, 13 December 1944. L2, Women Airforce Service Pilots. Air Force Museum Archives. Wright Patterson Air Force Base, Ohio.

Winchell, Walter. "Man about Town." *Daily Mirror*, 4 December 1944. The Jacqueline Cochran Collection. The Eisenhower Center Archives. Abilene, Kansas.

"Woman Opposes WASP Push for Vet Benefits." *Tennessean*, 26 May 1977. The WASP Collection. Texas Women's University Archives. Denton, Texas.

"Women Ferry Pilots Start Operating out of Wichita." *Wichita Beacon*, 25 April 1943. The WASP Collection. Texas Women's University Archives. Denton, Texas.

"Women Pilots out of Work as Wasp Quits." *Washington Times-Herald*, 21 December 1944. The Jacqueline Cochran Collection. The Eisenhower Center Archives. Abilene, Kansas.

"Women Train in West Texas for Army Ferry Flying: Their Duty Will Be to Fly Planes from Factory to Field and from Field to Field within U.S." *Christian Science Monitor*, 8 May 1943. The WASP Collection. Texas Women's University Archives. Denton, Texas.

"World War II's Women Pilots Feel Forgotten, Their Benefits Ignored." *Baltimore Evening Sun*, 14 October 1976. The WASP Collection. Texas Women's University Archives. Denton, Texas.

BOOKS

Addis, Elisabetta, Russo, Valeria E., and Sebesta, Lorenza, eds. *Women Soldiers: Images and Realities*. New York: St. Martin's Press, 1994.

Arnold, Henry H. *Global Mission*. New York: Harper & Brothers, 1947.

Ayling, Keith. *Calling All Women*. New York: Harper & Brothers, 1942.

Beauvoir, Simone de. *The Second Sex*. New York: Knopf, 1952.

Becraft, Carolyn. *Women in the U.S. Armed Services: The War in the Persian Gulf*. Washington, D.C.: Women's Research and Education Institute, 1991.

Birdwell, Russell. *Women in Battle Dress*. New York: Fine Editions Press, 1942.

Birke, Lynda. *Women, Feminism and Biology: The Feminist Challenge*. New York: Methuen Press, 1986.

Butler, Judith. *Bodies That Matter: On the Discursive Limits of "Sex."* New York: Routledge, 1993.

———. *Gender Trouble: Feminism and the Subversion of Identity*. New York: Routledge, 1990.

Butler, Judith, and Scott, Joan Wallach. *Feminists Theorize the Political*. New York: Routledge, 1992.

Churchill, Jan. *On Wings to War: Teresa James, Aviator*. Manhattan, Kans.: Sunflower University Press, 1992.

Cochran, Jacqueline, and Brinley, Maryann Bucknam. *Jackie Cochran: An Autobiography*. New York: Bantam Books, 1987.

Cochran, Jacqueline, and Odlum, Floyd. *The Stars at Noon*. Boston: Little, Brown, 1954.

Cole, Jean Hascall. *Women Pilots of World War II*. Salt Lake City: University of Utah Press, 1992.

Congressional Quarterly. *Congressional Quarterly's Guide to Congress*. 4th edition. Washington, D.C.: Congressional Quarterly, 1991.

Dailey, Janet. *Silver Wings, Santiago Blue*. New York: Poseidon Press, 1984.

Dorn, Edwin. "Statistical Trends." In *Who Defends America? Race, Sex, and Class in the*

Armed Forces, edited by Edwin Dorn. Washington, D.C.: Joint Center for Political Studies Press, 1989.

Douglas, Deborah. *United States Women in Aviation, 1940-1985*. Washington, D.C.: Smithsonian Institution, 1991.

Elshtain, Jean Bethke. *Women and War*. New York: Basic Books, 1987.

Enloe, Cynthia. *Does Khaki Become You? The Militarisation of Women's Lives*. London: South End Press, 1983.

Fraser, Antonia. *Boadicea's Chariot*. London: Weidenfield & Nicolson, 1988.

Fussel, Paul. *Wartime: Understanding and Behavior in the Second World War*. Oxford: Oxford University Press, 1989.

Goldman, Nancy Loring, ed. *Combatants or NonCombatants? Historical and Contemporary Perspectives*. Westport, Conn.: Greenwood Press, 1982.

Granger, Byrd Howell. *On Final Approach: The Women Airforce Service Pilots of W.W. II*. Scottsdale, Ariz.: Falconer Publishing Co., 1991.

Hartmann, Susan. *The Home Front and Beyond: American Women in the 1940s*. Boston: Twayne Publishers, 1982.

Holden, Henry, and Griffith, Lori. *Ladybirds: The Untold Story of Women Pilots in America*. Freedom, N.J.: Black Hawk Publishing Co., 1992.

———. *Ladybirds II: The Continuing Story of American Women in Aviation*. Freedom, N.J.: Black Hawk Publishing Co., 1993.

Holms, Maj. Gen. Jeanne, Retired. *Women in the Military: An Unfinished Revolution*. Novato, Calif.: Presidio Press, 1992.

Jeffords, Susan. *The Remasculinization of America: Gender and the Vietnam War*. Bloomington: Indiana University Press, 1989.

Jeffords, Susan, and Rabinovitz, Lauren, eds. *Seeing through the Media: The Persian Gulf War*. New Brunswick, N.J.: Rutgers University Press, 1994.

Keil, Sally Van Wagenen. *Those Wonderful Women in Their Flying Machines: The Unknown Heroines of World War II*. New York: Four Directions Press, 1990.

Korb, Lawrence. "The Pentagon's Perspective." In *Who Defends America? Race, Sex, and Class in the Armed Forces*, edited by Edward Dorn. Washington, D.C.: Joint Center for Political Studies Press, 1989.

Kovic, Ron. *Born on the Fourth of July*. New York: McGraw-Hill, 1976.

Laurentis, Teresa de. *Cultural Studies*. New York: Routledge, 1994.

Lerner, Gerda. *The Creation of Feminist Consciousness: From the Middle Ages to 1870*. New York: Oxford University Press, 1993.

———. *The Creation of Patriarchy*. New York: Oxford University Press, 1986.

Lynn, Vera. *Unsung Heroines: The Women Who Won the War*. London: Sidgwick & Jackson, 1990.

McFarland, Stephen Lee, and Newton, Wesley Phillips. *To Command the Sky: The Battle for Air Superiority over Germany, 1942-1944*. Washington, D.C.: Smithsonian Institution Press, 1991.

Mead, Margaret. *Male and Female: A Study of the Sexes in a Changing World.* New York: William Morrow, 1967.

Mitchell, Brian. *Weak Link: The Feminization of the American Military.* Washington, D.C.: Regnery Gateway, 1989.

Muir, Kate. *Arms and the Woman.* London: Sinclair-Stevenson Limited, 1992.

Murphy, Audie. *To Hell and Back.* New York: Holt, Rinehart and Winston, 1949.

Myles, Bruce. *Night Witches: The Untold Story of Soviet Women in Combat.* Novato, Calif.: Presidio Press, 1981.

Noggle, Ann. *For God, Country, and the Thrill of It: Women Airforce Service Pilots in World War II.* College Station: Texas A & M Press, 1990.

Osur, Alan. *Blacks in the Army Air Forces During World War II.* New York: Arno Press, 1980.

Pentagon: 50th Anniversary of World War II Commemoration Committee. *Fact Sheet: Tuskegee Airmen.* 1995.

————. *Fact Sheet: Women's Airforce Service Pilots.* 1995.

Perret, Geoffrey. *Winged Victory: The Army Air Forces in World War II.* New York: Random House, 1993.

Piercy, Marge. *Gone to Soldiers.* New York: Summit Books, 1987.

Rubel, David. *Webster's 21st Century Concise Chronology of World History.* Nashville, Tenn.: Thomas Nelson, 1993.

Rupp, Leila. *Mobilizing Women for War: German and American Propaganda, 1939-1945.* Princeton: Princeton University Press, 1978.

Rustad, Michael. *Women in Khaki: The American Enlisted Woman.* New York: Praeger Publishers, 1982.

Saywell, Shelley. *Women in War: From World War II to El Salvador.* Ontario: Penguin Books, 1985.

Scharr, Adela Riek. *Sisters in the Sky: Volume II—The WASP.* St. Louis: Patrice Press, 1988.

Scott, Joan Wallach. "Experience." In *Feminists Theorize the Political,* edited by Judith Butler and Joan Wallach Scott. New York: Routledge, 1992.

————. *Gender and the Politics of History.* New York: Columbia University Press, 1988.

Showalter, Elaine. *Sexual Anarchy: Gender and Culture at the Fin de Siècle.* New York: Viking, 1990.

Simon, Roger. *Gramsci's Political Thought: An Introduction.* London: Lawrence & Wishart, 1991.

Treadwell, Mattie. *The Women's Army Corps.* Washington, D.C.: Office of the Chief of Military History, Department of the Army, 1954.

Tunner, Lt. Gen. William. *Over the Hump.* New York: Duell, Sloan and Pearce, 1964.

Verges, Marianne. *On Silver Wings: The Women Airforce Service Pilots of World War II, 1942-1944.* New York: Ballantine, 1991.

Vickers, Jeanne. *Women and War.* London: Zed Books, 1993.

Wekesser, Carol, and Polesetsky, Matthew, eds. *Women in the Military.* San Diego: Grenhaven Press, 1991.

Wheelwright, Julie. *Amazons and Military Maids: Women Who Dressed As Men in the Pursuit of Life, Liberty and Happiness.* London: Pandora, 1989.

———. "The Media's Use of the Feminine in the Gulf War." In *Women Soldiers: Images and Realities,* edited by Elisabetta Addis, Valeria E. Russo, and Lorenza Sebesta. New York: St. Martin's Press, 1994.

Willenz, June. *Women Veterans: America's Forgotten Heroines.* New York: Continuum, 1983.

Williams, Vera. *WASPs: Women Airforce Service Pilots of World War II.* Osceola, Wis.: Motorbooks International, 1994.

Wood, Winifred. *We Were WASPs.* Coral Gables, Fla.: Glade House, 1945.

GOVERNMENTAL REPORTS AND DOCUMENTS

Army Air Forces. *Army Air Forces Historical Studies.* January 1945. The WASP Collection. Texas Women's University Archives. Denton, Texas.

———. *Army Air Forces Regulation 40-8, Utilization of Women Pilots.* 1944. L2, Women Airforce Service Pilots. Air Force Museum Archives. Wright Patterson Air Force Base, Ohio.

———. *The History of the WASPs at Buckingham Army Air Field.* January 1945. L2, Women Airforce Service Pilots. Air Force Museum Archives. Wright Patterson Air Force Base, Ohio.

———. *History of the Women Airforce Service Pilots, Gardner Field.* January 1945. L2, Women Airforce Service Pilots. Air Force Museum Archives. Wright Patterson Air Force Base, Ohio.

———. *The History of WASP Detachment at Blytheville Army Air Field.* January 1945. L2, Women Airforce Service Pilots. Air Force Museum Archives. Wright Patterson Air Force Base, Ohio.

———. *Medical Considerations of the WASPs.* 21 August 1945. The WASP Collection. Texas Women's University Archives. Denton, Texas.

———. *Women Pilots in the Air Transport Command.* January 1945. L2, Women Airforce Service Pilots. Air Force Museum Archives. Wright Patterson Air Force Base, Ohio.

Central Flying Training Command, Army Air Forces. *History of the WASP Program.* 20 January 1945. L2, Women Airforce Service Pilots. Air Force Museum Archives. Wright Patterson Air Force Base, Ohio.

Cochran, Jacqueline. *Final Report, Women Pilot Program.* February 1945. The WASP Collection. Texas Women's University Archives. Denton, Texas.

———. *WASP Report, to Commanding General, Army Air Forces,* 1 August 1944. The WASP Collection. Texas Women's University Archives. Denton, Texas.

Committee on Appropriations. *Report No. 1606, Military Establishment Appropriation Bill, 1945.* House of Representatives, 78th Congress, 2d Session, 7 June 1944. The Jacqueline Cochran Collection. The Eisenhower Center Archives. Abilene, Kansas.

Committee on Military Affairs. *Hearings before the Committee on Military Affairs.* 20 January 1942. The WASP Collection. Texas Women's University Archives. Denton, Texas.

———. *Hearings before the Committee on Military Affairs.* 1 May 1942. The WASP Collection. Texas Women's University Archives. Denton, Texas.

———. *Hearings before the Committee on Military Affairs on HR 4219.* 78th Congress, 2nd Session, 22 March 1944. The WASP Collection. Texas Women's University Archives. Denton, Texas.

———. *Report No. 1277: Providing for the Appointment of Female Pilots and Aviation Cadets of the Army Air Forces.* 78th Congress, 2nd Session, 22 March 1944. The Jacqueline Cochran Collection. The Eisenhower Center Archives. Abilene, Kansas.

Committee on the Civil Service. *Interim Report No. 1600: Concerning Inquiries Made of Certain Proposals for the Expansion and Change in Civil Service Status of the WASP.* 78th Congress, 2nd Session, 5 June 1944. The Jacqueline Cochran Collection. The Eisenhower Center Archives. Abilene, Kansas.

Congressional Record. 12 May 1942. The WASP Collection. Texas Women's University Archives. Denton, Texas.

Congressional Record. 14 January 1943. The WASP Collection. Texas Women's University Archives. Denton, Texas.

Congressional Record. 15 February 1943. The WASP Collection. Texas Women's University Archives. Denton, Texas.

Congressional Record. 1 May 1943. The WASP Collection. Texas Women's University Archives. Denton, Texas.

Congressional Record—Appendix. 7 June 1944. The WASP Collection. Texas Women's University Archives. Denton, Texas.

Congressional Record—Appendix. 8 June 1944. The WASP Collection. Texas Women's University Archives. Denton, Texas.

Congressional Record—Appendix. 10 June 1944. The WASP Collection. Texas Women's University Archives. Denton, Texas.

Congressional Record—Appendix. 16 June 1944. The WASP Collection. Texas Women's University Archives. Denton, Texas.

Congressional Record—Appendix. 17 June 1944. The WASP Collection. Texas Women's University Archives. Denton, Texas.

Congressional Record—Appendix. 10 August 1944. The WASP Collection. Texas Women's University Archives. Denton, Texas.

Congressional Record. 20 June 1944. The WASP Collection. Texas Women's University Archives. Denton, Texas.

Congressional Record. 21 June 1944. The WASP Collection. Texas Women's University Archives. Denton, Texas.

Congressional Record—House. 21 April 1948. The Jacqueline Cochran Collection. The Eisenhower Center Archives. Abilene, Kansas.

Congressional Record—House. 28 September 1977. The WASP Collection. Texas Women's University Archives. Denton, Texas.

Congressional Record—Senate. 22 September 1977. The WASP Collection. Texas Women's University Archives. Denton, Texas.

Congressional Record—Senate. 6 October 1977. The WASP Collection. Texas Women's University Archives. Denton, Texas.

Congressional Record—Senate. 4 November 1977. The WASP Collection. Texas Women's University Archives. Denton, Texas.

Costello, Rep. John. *H.R. 3358, A bill to provide for the appointment of female pilots in the Air Forces of the Army.* 30 September 1943, 78th Congress, 1st Session. The WASP Collection. Texas Women's University Archives. Denton, Texas.

Eastern Flying Training Command, Army Air Forces. *History of the Women Airforce Service Pilots, Eastern Flying Training Command.* January 1945. L2, Women Airforce Service Pilots. Air Force Museum Archives. Wright Patterson Air Force Base, Ohio.

Hearings before the Committee of Military Affairs. House of Representatives, 20 January 1942. The WASP Collection. Texas Women's University Archives. Denton, Texas.

Hearings before the Committee of Military Affairs. House of Representatives, 1 May 1942. The WASP Collection. Texas Women's University Archives. Denton, Texas.

Hearings before the Committee on Military Affairs. House of Representatives, 22 March 1944. The WASP Collection. Texas Women's University Archives. Denton, Texas.

Marx, Captain. *Women Pilots in the Air Transport Command.* January 1945. The WASP Collection. Texas Women's University Archives. Denton, Texas.

Odom, Col. T. C. *Report to Commanding General of the Army Air Forces.* 5 August 1943. The WASP Collection. Texas Women's University Archives. Denton, Texas.

Porter, Helen. *Certificate of Honorable Discharge from the Army.* 20 December 1944. The WASP Collection. Texas Women's University Archives. Denton, Texas.

Report of Investigation Regarding Proper Use of Women Pilots in the Army Air Forces. August 5, 1943. The WASP Collection. Texas Women's University Archives. Denton, Texas.

Strother, Lt. Col. Dora Dougherty. *The WASP Program: An Historical Synopsis.* Air Force Museum, Research Division, September 1971. L2, Women Airforce Service Pilots. Air Force Museum Archives. Wright Patterson Air Force Base, Ohio.

War Department, Bureau of Public Relations. *Public Relations Policy for WASP.* 3 December 1943. The Jacqueline Cochran Collection. The Eisenhower Center Archives. Abilene, Kansas.

NEWS RELEASES

War Department News Release. *Memorandum for the Press.* 10 September 1942. The Jacqueline Cochran Collection. The Eisenhower Center Archives. Abilene, Kansas.

War Department News Release. *Jacquelyn [sic] Cochran Designated Director of Women Pilots for AAF.* 5 July 1943. The Jacqueline Cochran Collection. The Eisenhower Center Archives. Abilene, Kansas.

War Department News Release. *AAF to Inactivate WASP on December 20.* 3 October 1944. The WASP Collection. Texas Women's University Archives. Denton, Texas.

WASP Public Affairs Office. News Release. September 1977. The WASP Collection. Texas Women's University Archives. Denton, Texas.

INTERVIEWS

Bergemann, Clarice. Telephone interview with author, March 1994.

Nagle, Nadine. Telephone interview with author, March 1994.

Wyall, Marty. Telephone interview with author, March 1994.

LETTERS, MEMORANDUMS, TELEGRAPHS AND
TELEPHONE TRANSCRIPTS

Army Air Forces Memorandum 20-8. 5 August 1943. The Jacqueline Cochran Collection. The Eisenhower Center Archives. Abilene, Kansas.

Army Air Forces Memorandum 40-8. 1944. The Jacqueline Cochran Collection. The Eisenhower Center Archives. Abilene, Kansas.

Arnold, Gen. H. H., Letter to Each Member of the WASP. 1 October 1944. L2, Women Airforce Service Pilots. Air Force Museum Archives. Wright Patterson Air Force Base, Ohio.

———. Memorandum to Director of Women Pilots. 1 October 1944. The Jacqueline Cochran Collection. The Eisenhower Center Archives. Abilene, Kansas.

———. Memorandum to General Marshall. 14 June 1943. The Jacqueline Cochran Collection. The Eisenhower Center Archives. Abilene, Kansas.

———. Telegram to Eleanor Watterud. 26 June 1944. The WASP Collection. Texas Women's University Archives. Denton, Texas.

Bevans, Major J. M., Assistant Chief of Air Staff. Secret Memorandum to Commanding General, Air Transport Command. 22 November 1944. The Jacqueline Cochran Collection. The Eisenhower Center Archives. Abilene, Kansas.

Bogart, Miss. Record of Telephone Conversation to Miss Edwards. 27 June 1944. The Jacqueline Cochran Collection. The Eisenhower Center Archives. Abilene, Kansas.

Cochran, Jacqueline. Letter to All Former WASP. 22 February 1945. L2, Women Airforce Service Pilots. Air Force Museum Archives. Wright Patterson Air Force Base, Ohio.

———. Letter to All Members of the WASP. 3 November 1944. L2, Women Airforce Service Pilots. Air Force Museum Archives. Wright Patterson Air Force Base, Ohio.

————. Letter to All WASP. 2 October 1944. L2, Women Airforce Service Pilots. Air Force Museum Archives. Wright Patterson Air Force Base, Ohio.

————. Letter to Robert Ramspeck. 5 April 1944. The Jacqueline Cochran Collection. The Eisenhower Center Archives. Abilene, Kansas.

————. Letter to the WASPs. 1 October 1944. The WASP Collection. Texas Women's University Archives. Denton, Texas.

————. Letter to the WASPs at Avenger Field. 3 October 1944. L2, Women Airforce Service Pilots. Air Force Museum Archives. Wright Patterson Air Force Base, Ohio.

————. Memorandum to General Arnold. October 1942. The Jacqueline Cochran Collection. The Eisenhower Center Archives. Abilene, Kansas.

————. Memorandum to Commanding General, Army Air Forces. 1 October 1944. The Jacqueline Cochran Collection. The Eisenhower Center Archives. Abilene, Kansas.

————. Memorandum to Col. McNaughton. 15 December 1942. The Jacqueline Cochran Collection. The Eisenhower Center Archives. Abilene, Kansas.

————. Memorandum to Col. Robert Olds. 21 July 1941. The Jacqueline Cochran Collection. The Eisenhower Center Archives. Abilene, Kansas.

————. Memorandum to Col. Robert Olds. July 1942. The Jacqueline Cochran Collection. The Eisenhower Center Archives. Abilene, Kansas.

Costello, Rep. John. Letter to Jacqueline Cochran. 4 October 1943. The Jacqueline Cochran Collection. The Eisenhower Center Archives. Abilene, Kansas.

Craig, Maj. Gen. M. A. Memorandum for Chief of Air Staff. 12 September 1944. The Jacqueline Cochran Collection. The Eisenhower Center Archives. Abilene, Kansas.

Crew, Nancy B., President of the Order of Fifinella. Memorandum to All WASPs. 15 June 1973. The WASP Collection. Texas Women's University Archives. Denton, Texas.

Edwards, Lt. Gen. I. H., Air Force Deputy Chief of Staff. Memorandum to Secretary of the Air Force. 17 June 1948. The Jacqueline Cochran Collection. The Eisenhower Center Archives. Abilene, Kansas.

Elliott, Maj. Richard G. Memorandum to Office of the Commanding General. 24 August 1944. The Jacqueline Cochran Collection. The Eisenhower Center Archives. Abilene, Kansas.

Fluke, Emmy Lou. Record of Telephone Conversation to Miss Jacqueline Cochran. 27 June 1944. The Jacqueline Cochran Collection. The Eisenhower Center Archives. Abilene, Kansas.

Giles, Lt. Gen. Barney, Deputy Commander, Army Air Forces and Chief of Air Staff. AAF Ltr 40-34 to Commanding Generals, All Air Forces and All Independent and Subordinate AAF Commands; Director, AAF Technical Service Command; and Commanding Officers of All AAF Bases (in continental United States). 1 November 1944. The WASP Collection. Texas Women's University Archives. Denton, Texas.

Kraus, Brig. Gen. Walter F. Memorandum to Gen. Arnold. 19 December 1942. The Jacqueline Cochran Collection. The Eisenhower Center Archives. Abilene, Kansas.

Love, Nancy Harkness. "Résumé of Conversation between Mrs. Love and Col. Mc-
Cormick of Ramspeck Committee." 17 April 1944. The WASP Collection. Texas
Women's University Archives. Denton, Texas.

McKaughan, R. E. Letter to Commanding General, Training Command. 14 July 1944.
The Jacqueline Cochran Collection. The Eisenhower Center Archives. Abilene,
Kansas.

Military Poll Committee. Letter to WASP. No date. L2, Women Airforce Service Pilots. Air Force Museum Archives. Wright Patterson Air Force Base, Ohio.

Nowland, Brig. Gen. Bob E. Secret Memorandum to Commanding General, Air
Transport Command. 1 November 1944. The WASP Collection. Texas Women's
University Archives. Denton, Texas.

Ponder, Ed. Letter to R. Earl McKaughan. 25 July 1944. The Jacqueline Cochran Collection. The Eisenhower Center Archives. Abilene, Kansas.

Roberts, Lillian Conner. Memorandum to All WASP, Trainees, and Survivors of
WASP. March 1979. The WASP Collection. Texas Women's University Archives.
Denton, Texas.

Scull, Elaine. Record of Telephone Conversation to Miss Jacqueline Cochran. 27 June
1944. The Jacqueline Cochran Collection. The Eisenhower Center Archives. Abilene, Kansas.

Stagg, Betty. Postcard to Mr. Donald Stagg, 15 May 1944. Photo File. Women Airforce Service Pilots. Air Force Museum Archives. Wright Patterson Air Force Base,
Ohio.

————. Postcard to Mr. and Mrs. Donald Stagg, 20 June 1944. Photo File. Women
Airforce Service Pilots. Air Force Museum Archives. Wright Patterson Air Force
Base, Ohio.

Stimson, Henry L. Letter to Andrew J. May, Chairman of the Committee on Military
Affairs. 16 February 1944. The WASP Collection. Texas Women's University
Archives. Denton, Texas.

Stratemeyer, Maj. Gen. George E. Memorandum to Brig. Gen. Luther S. Smith. 24
November 1942. The Jacqueline Cochran Collection. The Eisenhower Center
Archives. Abilene, Kansas.

Tunner, Col. William. Memorandum to Gen. Arnold, Through the Commanding
General of the Air Transport Command. 30 November 1942. The Jacqueline
Cochran Collection. The Eisenhower Center Archives. Abilene, Kansas.

Wadlow, Mrs. Thomas. Record of Telephone Conversation to Miss Jacqueline
Cochran. 27 June 1944. The Jacqueline Cochran Collection. The Eisenhower Center Archives. Abilene, Kansas.

Whitney, Col. Courtney. Memorandum to Brig. Gen. Luther Smith. 20 June 1943.
The Jacqueline Cochran Collection. The Eisenhower Center Archives. Abilene,
Kansas.

Williams, Betty Jane, President, Order of Fifinella. Letter to Helen Luts. 3 June 1947.
The WASP Collection. Texas Women's University Archives. Denton, Texas.

UNPUBLISHED SOURCES

Arnold, Gen. H. H. Remarks, Final WASP Graduation, December 1944.The WASP Collection. Texas Women's University Archives. Denton, Texas.

Arnold, William Bruce. Arnold's Copy, Statement by William Bruce Arnold, Colonel, U.S. Air Force (Retired), Before the U.S. House of Representatives Committee on Veterans' Affairs, 20 September 1977. The WASP Collection. Texas Women's University Archives. Denton, Texas.

Gardiner, William B. Statement of William B. Gardiner, National Director of Legislation, Disabled American Veterans, Before the Select Subcommittee on the WASPs of the House Committee on Veterans' Affairs, 20 September 1977. The WASP Collection. Texas Women's University Archives. Denton, Texas.

Granger, B. Howell. *Evidence Supporting Military Service by Women Airforce Service Pilots, World War II,* 1977. L2, Women Airforce Service Pilots. Air Force Museum Archives. Wright Patterson Air Force Base, Ohio.

WASP Military Committee. *Brief History on WASP Struggle for Militarization,* 1976. The WASP Collection. Texas Women's University Archives. Denton, Texas.

VIDEOS

Air Force News. Air Force News Videotape. June 1993. Audio/Visual Collection. Air Force Museum Archives. Wright Patterson Air Force Base, Ohio.

Forty-Eight Hours. CBS News. Eight-minute segment. July 1994. Author's collection.

Nagle, Nadine, WASP Veteran. Videotaped presentation. March 1992. Audio/Visual Collection. Air Force Museum Archives. Wright Patterson Air Force Base, Ohio.

Real People. NBC. Eleven-minute segment on the WASPs. 1980. Audio/Visual Collection. Air Force Museum Archives. Wright Patterson Air Force Base, Ohio.

Silver Wings and Santiago Blue. Sixty-minute documentary. 1981. The WASP Collection. Texas Women's University Archives. Denton, Texas.

We Were WASP. Twenty-three-minute documentary. 1990. The WASP Collection. Texas Women's University Archives. Denton, Texas.

Women of Courage of World War II. Sixty-minute documentary. 1993. The WASP Collection. Texas Women's University Archives. Denton, Texas.

Women Who Flew. Lipstik Productions. Eight-minute documentary. 1994. Author's collection.

Women Who Flew, unedited interview tapes. Lipstik Productions. 1994. Author's collection.

Index

About the Author

Molly Merryman is Director of the Women's Resource Center and an adjunct professor at Kent State University. A Ph.D. in American studies, she is a documentary filmmaker whose cooperatively made projects have received national and international screenings and awards, including three Emmys.